D1561652

REMEMBERING KARELIA

REMEMBERING KARELIA

꧁꧂

A Family's Story of Displacement during and after the
Finnish Wars

Karen Armstrong

First published in 2004 by **Berghahn Books**

www.BerghahnBooks.com

Library of Congress Cataloging-in-Publication Data

Armstrong, Karen
  Remembering Karelia : a family's story of displacement during and
after the Finnish wars / Karen Armstrong
      p.   cm.
  Includes bibliographical references and index.
  ISBN 1-57181-650-X (alk. paper)
    1. World War, 1939–1945—Russia (Federation)—Karelia. 2. World
War, 1939–1945—Deportation from the Soviet Union. 3. World War,
1939–1945—Personal narratives, Finnish. 4. Nationalism—Finland.
5. Karelia (Russia)—History—20th century. I. Title.

D764.7.K28A758 2003
940.53'092'39454104715—dc22   2003057832

British Library Cataloguing in Publication Data

A catalogue record for this book is available from the British Library

ISBN 1-57181-650-X hardback

CONTENTS

Contents

List of Illustrations

⚜

ACKNOWLEDGEMENTS

꧁❦꧂

My family and I were introduced to Finnish practices with an invitation from Maarit Alasuutari to join her family in a trip to the forest to pick mushrooms. Since that time, Maarit, her grandmother and great-grandmother, have opened the way for me to learn about Finnish society and, importantly, about Karelian society. During my research, I received kind and generous help from Rauno and Anja Pärssinen, from Kari and Eeva Pärssinen, and from all the other Pärssinens I met: Sanni, Ismo, Aarno, Sini, and Ilkka-Elias. Pirkko Linjama helpfully explained details about her grandmother, Helena Kuisma. I thank also two other family members with direct ties to Inkilä, whom I did not meet, but who contributed information for this work: Ilmari Kuisma and Esko Kuisma. This is not the book the family would write, but I hope they can somehow recognise themselves in it.

I owe much to my academic colleagues also, who know many details about Finnish culture and society, and therefore tried to keep me on the right path. I thank my colleagues at the University of Tampere, Matti Alestalo and Antti Eskola, and the teaching staff, researchers and students in the anthropology department at the University of Helsinki for help with references and stories about Karelia. In particular, Katja Uusihakala gave me a copy of her grandmother's book, and Pertti Alasuutari, Anna-Maria Viljanen and Minna Ruckenstein read the manuscript and helped with details about Finnish culture and language. Jukka Siikala's critical comments pushed me to rethink and revise the argument about Finland and national communities. In addition, the anthropology seminar was a useful forum for helpful comments from Cliff Sather, Michael Vischer and Greg Urban, and Juhani Lehtonen kindly suggested relevant sources in Finnish ethnology.

Finally, my thanks to the 'home front' for their practical support and loving encouragement: Brian, Delia, Annika, Kai, Kate and Zöe.

A NOTE ON SOURCES

My primary sources are the printed memoirs and copies of original letters provided to me by Rauno Pärssinen. To date, Rauno has edited and personally published five books of family memoirs. I have read four of them. Some quotations come from number 2; I quote sections mainly from 4 and 5.

1. The Wartime Pastor's Memories, 1941–1943 (*Sotapappina – muistelmia vuosilta 1941–1943*). A limited edition edited and published by Rauno Pärssinen; I have not seen this but some of it has been reprinted in number 2.
2. The Parsonage's Family during the Continuation War (*Pappilan Perhe Jatkosodan Jaloissa*). Joensuu: Rauno Pärssinen, 1992. Some quotations from this book are marked AP, for Arvi Pärssinen's writings, or Rauno Pärssinen for the sections he added.
3. The Youth of My Parents: Life Changes 1907–1936. (*Vanhempieni Nuoruus: Elämänvaiheita vv. 1907–1936*). Joensuu: Rauno Pärssinen, 1992.
4. The Winter War on the Home Front (*Talvisota Kotirintamalla*). Joensuu: Rauno Pärssinen, 1993. Many of the quoted letters come from this book and are cited by date.
5. Helena Kuisma: My Own Life: Memories of Life in Kirvu's Inkilä and the Evacuation, 1880–1956 (*Helena Kuisma: Miu Omast Elämästäi: Muisteluksia elämästä Kirvun Inkilässä ja evakkotaipaleilla vv. 1880-1956*). Joensuu: Rauno Pärssinen, 1996. The quoted sections from this book are cited HK, followed by the page number.

1
EVENT AND MEANING

A series of events – which I collapse into a national event – took place in
Finland between 1938 and 1944 that are still being discussed today in private and public locations. This book is about that circulating discourse,
based on the written memoirs of one extended family. The national event of
war and loss of territory, which is the background to the writings, presents
a political situation ripe for nationalist rhetoric, in a nation state often
described to be very nationalistic. I will argue that, while there is a national, and nationalist, discourse in Finland, there are levels of discourse that
persist and evade nationalist rhetoric. In fact, there is a fairly consistent
story about place and kinship, which is linked at times to the national
events when they are refracted through society in the form of novels, films,
television documentaries, newspaper articles, and other forms of public discourse.[1]

The context is, very briefly, that between 1939 and 1944 Finland fought
two wars with the Soviet Union, the Winter War (1939–40) and the
Continuation War (1941–44). The eastern Finnish region of Karelia, bordering the Soviet Union, was a site of intense fighting. At the end of the
wars, in June 1944, the Finnish population of Karelia – about 420,000 people, nearly 11 percent of the national population – was evacuated behind
the newly drawn Finnish border.[2] When the final peace accord was reached
in September 1944, the total number who died in the wars was 91,500 and
Finnish Karelia and other portions of Finnish territory were ceded to the
Soviet Union. Because Finland had been allied with Germany, Finland had
to pay reparations to the Allied governments while at the same time resettling the Karelian population. This was an important moment in twentieth-century Finnish history and one experienced, in one form or another, by

most people living in Finland between 1939 and the end of the restoration and reparation period in the 1950s. It was a central event in the grand narrative of Finnish history.

The evacuated Karelians had to rebuild their lives in a new environment. Many of them could not accept the loss of Karelia and there has been constant talk, either personal or in the media, about getting Karelia back and whether or not it is feasible. The war years and the topic of Karelia lend themselves to a discussion of nationalism. For one thing, the territory of Karelia was central to the imagination of the cultural nationalist movement of the nineteenth and early twentieth centuries. Karelia was the region where the national epic poem, the *Kalevala*, was recorded, and the region claimed by some folklorists as the cultural homeland of the Finnish population. During the early twentieth century, after Finnish independence in 1917, Karelia was the focus of a conservative political movement that aimed to expand the national boundaries of Finland to include northern regions of Karelia that had never been part of the Finnish nation state.[3] More recently, since the war years, there is a Karelian Association with a building and offices in Helsinki that works to keep Karelia visible through its cultural programmes.[4] Periodic debates about Karelia occur on the letters page of the largest circulation newspaper, the *Helsingin Sanomat*, and documentaries and films about Karelia are shown on a regular basis. One mention of Karelia and people know some version of this history. Karelia can easily be seen as the symbolic centre for Finnish nationalism, the issue that could stir up sentiment regarding state sovereignty, national boundaries and imagined communities. That is part of the story, but not the whole story, as I will argue, based on the firsthand accounts of a Karelian family.

The meaning of an important event, according to Paul Ricoeur, has the possibility to transcend the conditions of its production and to be reenacted in new social contexts (1991: 155). The significance of this national event continues to circulate and be reenacted in contemporary Finland. In order to demonstrate this, I have to give many specific details. But the general point – and the comparative value of this study – is that culture is found in, and travels through, discourse (Urban 2001). Political rhetoric does not simply use or reconstruct the past to justify the present. It is most effective when it connects to systems of logic and meaning, to culture.

Benedict Anderson's theory about the rise of national communities has generated a lot of subsequent research. Anderson argues provocatively that nations are imagined communities: imagined because, although the members of the community will never know or meet most of their fellow members, 'yet in the minds of each lives the image of their communication' (1983: 15). According to Anderson, the rise of nationalism was encouraged through national newspapers and other print media. The media produce an abstract group 'we', and this in turn has the effect of creating the sense of a shared space and time in the nation state. This model is anthropological, according to Anderson, because nationalism emerges from (and in opposition to) the cultural systems (like religion) that preceded it, although he is not saying that nationalism supersedes religion (ibid.: 19).

A related question raised by Anderson, and one which he cannot adequately answer, is why people are so willing to die for such limited imaginings. His answer is that nations inspire 'self-sacrificing love' (1983: 129). Because one feels attached to one's nation through birth and parentage, belonging to the nation is 'natural', based on 'disinterestedness', and for 'just that reason it can ask for sacrifices' (ibid.: 131). For Anderson, a common language unifies people and allows for communication about the community through print; likewise, poetry, songs and national anthems play a part in generating loyalty to the national community (ibid.: 132).[5] Language is therefore central to generating a sense of nationalism and patriotism, but Anderson does not analyse what is said and he does little to distinguish nationalism from patriotism. Perhaps wondering about why people are willing to die for limited imaginings is appropriate for people who fight in foreign wars – war is ironic when it is not the imagined glory (Fussell 1975) – but the Finnish wars were at home. It can be as easily asked, what is it about place – friends, hills, fields, cows, sawmills – that holds the imagination so deeply?

The concept of patriotism – a team of British researchers could only agree that it is attached to a notion of the local and 'common man' (Samuel 1989: xi) – is an elusive one. Is not everyone in some ways a patriot (both in opposition and support) and does not everyone have a home, whether or not it is an actual dwelling place (Jackson 1995)? Gaston Bachelard (1969 [1958]) proposes that one's childhood space establishes a sense of home for the rest of one's life, and anthropologists have long recognised the central position of kinship for social relations and in transmitting culture.[6] While Anderson recognises, correctly, the potency of passion, he fails to recognise that nationalism and patriotism are related differently to the collectivities that compose the imagined nation state and home.[7]

Anderson's model has generated many positive and negative responses[8] and theories of nationalism have been reviewed thoroughly by Paul James (1996). I want to pursue the idea of imagined community, following Bruce Kapferer's (1988) refinement of Anderson's basic point about nationalism as political culture. Kapferer's (1988) comparison of nationalism in Sri Lanka and Australia aims to pick up where Anderson left off in order to explore more thoroughly the force of the nationalist imagination. To this end, he argues that there are specific nationalisms and he demonstrates how meaning is connected to the historical, social and political context in the two cases. Kapferer argues that nationalist ideologies are not surface phenomena but are based in systems of deep significance, which 'act in the very being of those who participate in them' (ibid.: 218), not unlike religion. Conceptually, what happens with national political culture is similar to the way significance is produced in ritual through its ability to summarise multiple levels of structure (Turner 1967). For Kapferer, past events are not simply used in the present; the present and the past are connected through a common logic, although past and present events may not necessarily share a common meaning (Kapferer 1988: 213). Significantly, Kapferer argues that nationalism moulds various messages into a singular form, into a 'highly distilled' culture, that is the 'essence' of the nation (ibid.: 209). The essence defining the nation then conditions what it reflects (ibid.: 4).

The problem of ontological worlds being united into a national political culture is also a problem of how culture moves in the world. Certain cultural elements make up the distilled essence of national political culture, but the puzzle remains, which ones and how does it happen? The views of recent linguistic analysis are useful here. The way in which culture is created and disseminated through language has been the focus of the work of Greg Urban. Urban has analysed how discourse is central to culture (1991; 1996) and the role of metaculture in disseminating culture (2001). For Urban, discourse about community reproduces the community and creates culture (1996), and culture is constantly moving, or changing, in 'restricted' or 'accelerated' ways (2001). The concepts and methodology used by Urban, combined with ideas about political culture from Kapferer, allow for more nuance in understanding the imagined community. Linguistic evidence in written texts – how and when the 'I' becomes 'we' – offers insights into how the experienced world (the restricted-empirical 'we') and the imagined national community (the generalised-essential 'we') fit together. If Kapferer is correct that cultural elements become distilled to signify a national political culture, as I believe he is, then self-generated texts reveal how individuals carry culture and offer clues as to how that distilled cultural essence comes about.[9]

These memoirs were generated by a forced diaspora and loss of place. Their relation to the past is therefore special, and distinct from the relation of past and present in other Finnish communities. Because of events, they do more than describe a situation; they project a world (Ricoeur 1991: 166). As the shared experience of Karelia fades into memory, the meaning of Karelia changes. It is no longer the phenomenal world, the shared, lived place, but a recollected world. Transformations occur on many levels as the once lived-in world becomes a memory, or virtual, world. Disruptions of this kind have implications for social theory because the memoirs of a diasporic group throw weight on the symbolic relations of society. The lived experience of Karelia, following Martin Heidegger's concept of 'being-in-the-world' ([1926] 1996) and Pierre Bourdieu's (1977) description of habitus, is central to the way in which people organise and understand their world.[10] However, for Bourdieu (1977; 1998), the habitus and distinctions created through symbolic capital circulate in a space defined by the boundaries of society, or more frequently, the French nation state.[11] The situation of diaspora challenges this view of bounded habitus. The world described by these writers is not confined by the spatial-temporal boundaries of the nation state; habitus moves with them.[12] This would be true of any group although the practical habitus of Karelians is particular; there are other types of historicities (Sahlins 1985: 53).

The portability of a world, of habitus, is evidenced most clearly in this material in the genealogical data, indicating the significance of kinship beyond practical social relations. David Schneider (1970) recognised the symbolic aspect of kinship and its possible connection to nationalism many years ago. In his work on American kinship, Schneider argues that culturally formulated symbols define and differentiate a system of social relationships. Schneider proposes that the pure domains of kinship, nationality and religion are domains of 'diffuse enduring solidarity' and that the diacritical marks of one domain should be found in another (1970: 120).[13] Anderson finds also that the family is linked to the nation through metaphor and the concept of 'disinterestedness' (1983: 131). Both authors provide clues to a relationship that is complicated by the component of time and space. Through memory and memoirs the past is significant in the present because of analogical and paradigmatic messages, which provide different logical possibilities for an individual (Valeri 1990). And when kinship extends beyond national borders, as with diasporic groups, where does the 'diffuse enduring solidarity' lie? The Karelian diaspora is a special situation, but it offers clues as to how these domains are connected.

Other studies of national culture often emphasise unifying symbols of a different order. For example, Michael Billig (1995) argues that the nation is 'flagged' through daily symbols, such as the 'we' of the media, sports events, currency, flags, anthems, and so on. And in Finland shifts in language can signal a symbolic connection to the nation, as when *suku* (lineage, line) shifts to *kansa* (people), or *koti* (home) to *kotimaa* (homeland) (Keryell 2000). But the way in which local actors perceive national symbols differs according to how meanings are socially experienced by various sectors of the population (Norton 1993). There can be points of resistance where the 'we' has no currency and the message fails (Urban 2001: 10). I am following the 'discursive pathways' of culture (Urban 1996) to look at what 'we' the writers refer to; I am not arguing for a national or ethnic 'we', a Finnish-We. Based on these written memoirs, it seems that perception founded in concrete social relations and practical activities influences meaning and identification with a community more than the classification of being a citizen of the nation state.[14]

Inkilä, 1997

Inkilä was a Finnish village with a population of about 800 people on the Karelian Isthmus before 1944. More specifically, it was part of Kirvu parish in the county of Viipuri. In June 1944 the civilian population was evacuated to other regions of Finland because of intense fighting with the Soviet Union. In September 1944 the region was ceded to the Soviet Union and the Finnish Karelians were resettled in Finland proper. For three decades it was not easy, often not possible, for Finns to visit their former villages. Then in the 1980s, with the *glasnost* policies of President Gorbachev in the Soviet Union, it became possible for people to travel across the border and visit the places where they had formerly lived. Such trips have become a common form of pilgrimage.[15]

I knew about Inkilä (now Zaitsevo) mainly through the life story written by Helena Kuisma. Helena died in 1957, having never returned to her home in Inkilä after the evacuation. Her daughter, Sylvi Pärssinen, also never returned. Sylvi refused an invitation from her children to travel back to Inkilä because she did not want to see her home occupied by strangers. On a hot day in June 1997 I travelled to Inkilä with two of Sylvi's sons, Rauno and Kari, Sylvi's granddaughter Maarit, and respective wives and husbands. We arranged a guide in Imatra, a city near the Finnish–Russian border where Sylvi had lived and where three of her children live, and early in the morning we drove across the Russian border into Karelia to see Päivölä, the former family home.[16]

Our first stop was the city of Viipuri, the county centre for Inkilä, where village property titles and other documents were registered and stored. It was also the nearest city where Inkilä residents sold farm produce, shopped for special items, and did their banking. Situated on the Baltic coast, Viipuri (Vyborg) had been an international city. It was established with a castle along major trading routes in the Middle Ages, a Hanseatic League city in the sixteenth century, and was one of the four commercial and cultural centres of Finland in the early twentieth century. In the 1940s, Viipuri was the site of 432 factories, 25,000 industrial jobs and 25 percent of the hydro-electric power of Finland (Paasi 1996: 114).

After Finnish independence in 1917, Viipuri experienced a period of expansion 'accompanied by a fine degree of sophisticated cultural awareness' (Spens 1994: 18), although there is little evidence of this today. The once grand train station, designed by the Finnish architect Eliel Saarinen and intended to rival Saarinen's famous and still used train station in central Helsinki, was destroyed during the Second World War. The large Jewish merchant's house on Red Square is a reminder of Viipuri's commercial past and of the once lively and now scattered Jewish community that had lived there. Also standing is 'the most advanced town library in the world' (ibid.), designed by Alvar Aalto and completed in 1935. The modernist library was designed to distinguish the newly independent nation of Finland stylistically from Russia and Sweden. During our visit, the library was in a state of disrepair. Only the once grand reading room, with its sophisticated system of skylights to cast light but not shadows, was open, but there were no patrons, few chairs, and a small number of old books. Along with the city of Viipuri, the library has been neglected.

From Viipuri we drove approximately fifty kilometres to Inkilä. In Inkilä Kari gave the driver directions, telling her to turn at a large apple tree near the train station, and from there the dirt road wound through the village to Päivölä. Although both Rauno and Kari had heard stories about Inkilä as children, Kari was our group's direct connection to the evacuation. In June 1944, at the age of eleven, Kari rode out of Inkilä in a car with his Pärssinen grandfather and whatever personal goods they could fit into the car. He does not remember being afraid, only that he was fascinated by the planes flying overhead. When I asked, 'Did they know they were leaving for good?' he answered, 'Yes, they knew.'

There is another view of Kari's visit and the uncertain departure in letters written by Helena at the time. It was a family pattern that some of the grandchildren would spend the summer in Inkilä. On 19 May 1944 Helena wrote to her grandchildren to thank them for the Mother's Day flowers they had sent her, reminding Kari that it was his turn to visit. On 12 June, Helena wrote to her daughter: 'So Kari is here – but now he is with the Pärssinens, not with us, although he promised to come here.' This letter, two days after the Soviets began a heavy military attack on the Karelian Isthmus, supports other evidence that the Karelians were not expecting an evacuation (Paasi 1996: 113).

Two weeks later, on 25 June 1944, the evacuation began quite suddenly and Helena did not know where Kari and the Pärssinens were. She wrote to Sylvi from Punkasalmi, the first stop on their journey. In the middle of the evacuation, described with a Christian reference, she wrote of her immediate concerns for Kari's welfare, with a few comments about the last hours in Inkilä and, characteristically for Helena, a small detail about her grandson Esko to illustrate how sick he was.[17]

> Well, now begins again our second *ristintie*[18] [evacuation] and we are now as far as Punkasalmi.
>
> First I'll talk of Kari. Kari was only with us one week. They had his clean clothes at Pärssinen's, he left Saturday night to change them and said that he would go with Aunt Mari on Sunday to Aunt Toini's[19] wedding, where he was. After that I haven't seen Kari. Now they say *ukko* [grandfather] Pärssinen is here in Punkasalmi. Although I have looked and asked, I haven't found him. I would have taken Kari with us. I would have gone to the Putikko station to look for him but my ankles are so swollen that I couldn't walk 7 kilometres and so I did

not do it. Now I am very worried about Kari. Here we thought that maybe Kari went with ukko to you at Tuupovaara. Mari came to ask us on Wednesday morning how are we leaving, by what vehicle, but then we didn't know yet and she said she would care for Kari, and they say he was going here with ukko by car [towards Punkasalmi].

We left home on Wednesday at 9 in the evening. We couldn't stay there because the windows were rattling and the Ruskie [*ryssä*][20] planes were overhead, although they only dropped two small bombs near the station, but often the gunfire from the planes spread death around. In the evening we thought we would leave by foot, pushing the children in carriages, and then Wäinö came to the *tupa*[21] [the main room] and quickly loaded us into the car for the journey, and then at 1:00 at night we were here. Oh how I worried about Kari but there was nobody who could have run to Pärssinens [and asked for him]. We are now waiting for Esko who is in the Kirvu field hospital because he had a high fever and diarrhoea. Esko was too weak, so that we were afraid of the worst. We even had to lift him onto the chamber pot and hold on.

Here there is congestion on the roads where everyone is – horse carts with women and children on top, cars with goods, cows walking, men on bicycles and soldier traffic, even a long line of Russian prisoners who are being taken to old Finland.   (Helena to Sylvi, 25.6.1944)

Kari knows many details about Inkilä from his childhood experiences, through the family's memoirs, and because of two books published in the 1980s by former villagers. Following Kari's instructions the van driver drove past several Finnish-style wooden houses, but the house we were looking for, called Päivölä by Helena and Päivälä in the land records, was gone. It had been torn down two years before so that a factory manager from Viipuri could build a summer house on the land. There were some foundation stones for the new house but the project seemed to be languishing. In a pile of rubble Kari found a piece of the house's wallpaper; most of the other buildings were gone. Only the concrete foundation of the cow barn, where Israel hid his business papers from the Reds in 1918 (during the civil war) and where Sylvi's brothers took shelter from Russian planes bombing the mill in 1940, is still standing. The two washing rooms, where there was a stove to heat water so women could clean, have become home for the old Russian grandmother who was evicted from the main house when it was torn down. She had been moved to Inkilä in 1945 by the Soviet state and had raised five children there. While we walked around looking at what was left, she returned with her middle-aged daughter and they invited us to come and talk. In our group the guide knew some Russian and could translate, and the Russian women knew a few words of Finnish.

The washing rooms were only big enough for a bed, a table and chair, a cooking stove, a trunk with photographs, and a storage closet. The closet and table came from the main house and originally belonged to the Kuisma family. This, a wood shed, and the large lilac bush which Helena and Israel posed in front of for a picture, is all that is left. On that day in June, the table was carried outside and we all had tea, bread, cheese and ham. The Finnish women had brought food for our group, which they gave to the grandmother, along with some packages of coffee for her daughter. The Russian women showed us pictures of their children and grandchildren. They also had two pictures of a visit several years earlier by members of the Pekurinen family. Pekurinen had been the Inkilä stationmaster and a family friend; he was with the Kuismas during the final evacuation. In one of these photos we could see the kitchen of Päivölä with a 1994 calendar on the wall. At the end, Kari gave a toast, with his arms around both Russian women, saying that their family missed their house, the home of their ancestors, but that he was happy that such wonderful people had lived there.

From there we walked a short distance along the dirt road to where the family mills had been. Nothing was left but the stream that had supplied water power. Kari and the others washed their hands and faces in the stream water and we looked for old artefacts but found none. Near the house the women dug up small wild flowers to take home. Before leaving, we climbed the hill across from where Päivölä had stood, called Revonharju by Helena. Revonharju is now a small cemetery used by the local Russian families; most graves are marked with the communist hammer and sickle.

There were no cars or buses in Inkilä during our visit, no radios that we could hear, no power tools. Occasionally a man on a motorbike with a sidecar, converted into a trailer for carrying bricks, drove from one end of the village to the other to move bricks to a building site. But otherwise there was the deep silence of the countryside, almost as if time had stopped sixty years before. Most of the wooden houses have not changed much - they have not been painted or repaired since the days when Finns owned them; where one Finnish family lived it is said that two or even three families now live. One house stood out because it had recently been painted bright blue[22] and remodelled; it was said to be the summer house for a family from Viipuri. A small train of four or five cars still runs on the rail line and there are some piles of wood to be loaded for transportation to a sawmill, as would have happened also sixty years ago. The train station, built at the turn of the century by V.R., the Finnish National Railway, is the same in style and construction as those built elsewhere in Finland at that time. These wooden structures, restored and updated, are commonly painted yellow in Finland and usually contain a ticket office, kiosk, waiting room and possibly a café-bar. In Inkilä the station is unpainted, there is no obvious ticket office or waiting room, and much of the building has been converted into housing for several families. One small room is the village grocery and there is a pay phone on the outside wall. During our visit the station activity centred on children buying ice cream and no one seemed to be travelling on the train. In fact, Inkilä station, with people and taxis, looks much livelier in old photos in the *Memories of Inkilä* (*Muistojen Inkilä*) memory book published by former villagers in 1982.

The material evidence that remains – the railroad, the three village roads, the fields, the location and style of the wooden houses, the lilac bushes and apple trees that mark a proper house site – are all reminders of a Finnish presence far removed, although Inkilä is only about thirty kilometres in a straight line from the present Finnish border. What is not Finnish is the lack of attention to the houses and to the landscape. No one that day was working in the fields, no one was sawing in the forests, no one was tending small vegetable gardens near the houses. No one was working as they *should* have been. Our tour group members commented frequently on this and the lack of attention to the forests, the fact that the brush was overgrown and the fallen trees were not cleared, and finally one said: 'I recognise the nature but otherwise all is changed.'

We had a sense of being both in and out of time. From maps drawn of the village as it was in 1944 we knew which house had belonged to which family, we had the feeling that we knew the village. But the current surroundings were quite different. Coming from Finland, it seemed as if we had gone back in time and yet it was, of course, not true. We were constantly making an implicit comparison of then and now, searching for a past that we could recognise from the memoirs.

A central location in the rural landscape is the church and the nearby cemetery. Finnish rural parishes have a church village (*kirkonkylä*) as the centre for surrounding villages. The church village for Inkilä was Kirvu, about ten kilometres away. Kirvu had been a predominately Lutheran parish (Sallinen-Gimpl 1989: 29) and Inkilä had been a predominately Lutheran village. Today there is no Lutheran church in Kirvu and no visible cemetery on the church hill. On top of a cemetery one kilometre away, called the 'new' cemetery by Helena, the Russians have built a military camp. Three gravestones lay on the ground near this cemetery, knocked over and with the Finnish names scratched off. We could hear Helena's description as we looked at what remained:

> There, there were common row graves, where the dead were buried in rows unless their relatives bought a special plot.[23]   (HK, p. 29)

A key site has been altered and destroyed. The Lutheran church marked the rituals of village life and the stone memorials stood to hold memory in place, to link one generation after another. Recently, now that the Russian state allows it, a Finnish group put new stone markers with inscriptions to mark the location of the church and bell tower, the new cemetery, and to remember parish men who died during the war. In 1993, at the site of the former church, the Kirvu Parish Society, located in Finland, placed a statue of a woman that listed the names of the men who died in war with these 'original words of remembrance' (the words came from the statue or monument which was there originally):

> At the front these Karelian home parish victims walked to death in the name of the fatherland.

> This mound is the crown of heroes, so come to the grave quietly praying.

By 1997 the statue had been beheaded although it was still tended to with fresh flowers (Figure 1). The monument at the site of the former cemetery, also built by Finns, was untouched. This cross of concrete (Figure 2), just in front of the military barracks, has two lines of inscription in both Finnish and Russian:

> On this place was the site of the Kirvu cemetery.
> Lord, you are our protector, generation to generation. (Psalm 90: 1)[24]

As we walked around church hill looking for the outline of the old church and cemetery, Kari found a four-leafed clover. 'This is my lucky day,' he said. Then we left Kirvu to return to Finland.

We were not the only visitors in search of a past; these trips to Karelia have become quite common. In 1991–92, 1.26 million Finns crossed the

Figure 1   Beheaded statue, memorial for Kirvu soldiers, church hill, Kirvu

Figure 2 Cross of concrete in front of Russian military camp, Kirvu cemetery

border into Karelia (Paasi 1996: 283). Our trip – looking for a house, visiting the local cemetery – was very similar to 'the grand narrative of visiting Karelia' which has emerged in Finland since the border opened (ibid.: 281). Because the landscape is often destroyed and is certainly changed, visitors search for signs of home and return with small items of symbolic meaning, such as some earth for their parents' graves or some water for a child's baptism (ibid.: 295).

Crossing the border is a slow and bureaucratic process. As our group waited in line they began to talk to another Finnish group who were making a tour of their former homes near the town of Käkisalmi. Each group was interested in the other, where they had lived in Karelia, what they knew about the place now. Our van driver and guide, who is busy with the trips all summer, is intimately involved with Karelia and during the trip she delivered a letter to a village office and diapers, from Finland, to an old age home. She has compiled her own version of history from all the family stories she hears and she told us these histories about every village along the way.[25] Her mother was born in Karelia and the guide is an active member of the Finnish–Russian society to promote cooperation between the two countries. The topic of Karelia is again a topic for public discussion. In addition to these popular visits, there are water projects, Finnish societies to help Karelians, a project to restore the Aalto library in Viipuri,[26] plans to send food aid during the winter, and so on. It is even possible to buy back former houses.[27] The new role of Karelia is being discussed and debated in all kinds of places, from personal living rooms to university departments.[28]

Although Helena and Sylvi could not know current historical developments, their collection of memories about Inkilä has new meaning now that it's possible to go there. After the war and until the 1980s, the Finnish government discouraged public political discussion of Karelia in order to keep good relations with the Soviet Union and prevent them from thinking that Finland might try to reclaim the territory. With this new traffic there are new possibilities for thinking about Karelia, for reintegrating it into the national project. No one particularly wants to reclaim the territory, although this is debated, but the visits allow families an important link with the past. Belonging is connected to place. In one of Sylvi's notebooks she wrote a poignant reference to this in recording the dates of her mother's life: Helena Kuisma: born 5.6.1882 in Kirvu's Inkilä – died as an evacuee 2.8.1957, buried in Elimäki.[29]

Our visit had lasted one long day. When we returned to Finland we felt tired and exhilarated. We had made a connection to a remote past; we could almost hear the characters who had inhabited Inkilä before 1944, as described by Helena. At the same time, we had met the Russian inhabitants and we had shared memories with them. We had been *somewhere* even if we had not seen Päivölä. We had made a pilgrimage of sorts, not exactly a religious one, but to the sacred landscape of Karelia. We had travelled along routes marked by remembered sites, we had had a moment of communitas with the Russian women, we had been both in and out of time, and we returned to our normal world feeling somehow changed.

Victor Turner outlined such processes in his discussion of religious pilgrimages, and in fact other Karelians have described their trip back to Karelia as a pilgrimage and refer to themselves as pilgrims to the Holy Land or Promised Land (Paasi 1996: 295). In his exploration of the symbolic nature of liminality and communitas, Turner recognised that the religious could be connected to regional and nationalist politics through personal experience (1974: 212). Our pilgrimage was not specifically religious but it was linked to national politics, to the loss of Karelia. Our trip, like most pilgrimages, was a voluntary undertaking. Through personal experience we encountered Inkilä; we reversed the finality of evacuation by going back and through communitas we experienced a powerful symbolic connection to Inkilä, as Turner (ibid.: 207–208) recognised:

A pilgrim's commitment, in full physicality, to an arduous yet inspiring journey, is, for him, even more impressive, in the symbolic domain, than the visual and auditory symbols which dominate the liturgies and ceremonies of calendrically structured religion. He only *looks* at these; he *participates* in the pilgrimage way.

The experience of pilgrimage, like the experience of other dramatic events, often leads to a personal realisation of the inner meaning of one's culture. 'For many that inner meaning is identical with its religious core values' (ibid.: 208). Sometimes such personal quests appear to challenge the existing structures, for example such trips to Karelia might mean a resurgence of political support for claiming the territory again. But, more likely, Turner points out, although they might seem to be challenges, 'in the long run [they] show themselves to be among its maintenance mechanisms' (ibid.: 228). As a pilgrimage to a symbolic landscape, personal memories recalled political defeat and personal loss. As a mnemonic tool, the Karelian landscape allowed us to put what we knew of the past onto present sites.

Community Discourse

In the materials here a particular historical period and a particular outcome of war become the basis for thinking and talking about other people and the nation. To be Finnish is to know the codes and be able to enter the story.[30] This is not about 'the Finns' but about how Finns talk about themselves and their society. Michael Herzfeld (1997: 9) makes much the same point about how Greeks 'argue about what Greeks do'. People construct their communities through the stories they tell and the lessons they pass along to others (Urban 1996).

Many researchers have studied Finnish folk culture, folklore and history. I have relied on a few of the well-known general studies, updated with contemporary media reports, in order to explain themes or events that these writers talk about. There could be many more details but I have followed the leads in the family's texts, discussing things which they discuss or giving the context for what they have selected. Using their words, rather than my interpretation, I try to show how they make sense of their world. At the same time national events and discussions of events, the metahistory, pull them into a national project.

The memoirs are a unit as historical documents for the family but they are narrative documents in distinctive ways. As I use them, there is, first, the memory of the home village of Inkilä. This narrative of recollection is found mainly in the life history written by Helena Kuisma (1882–1957) after she was evacuated from Inkilä and was living in Finland proper, although she had written several essays while in Inkilä for the national folklore archives.[31] She was working on her life story in 1953 and some of the writing was intended for national collections:

> During the fall I have sent to the 'Dictionary Foundation' the writings they wanted, 'My First Evacuation' and 'My Life Story'. I still plan to write 'My Second Evacuation'. (Helena to Sylvi, 11.1.1953)

14

Second, there are letters between Helena and her daughters, Sylvi Pärssinen (1909–91) and Toini Linjama (1911–94), typed from the originals and edited by Sylvi in the 1980s. These letters are primarily from the years 1938–44, the period of the wars with the Soviet Union. Sylvi's diary entries are interspersed with the letters in chronological order to make an historical document ('what this time has been like'). Two letters explain that she was thinking about this project in 1941 and that Helena sent letters and photos ('from that time') to Sylvi as requested in 1946:

> Yesterday afternoon I received the first letter you sent from Inkilä.[32] It did not have the Inkilä stamp, otherwise I would have kept it as an important historical memory. Surely you are saving all these wartime letters? I think that I would like to have them back, because I wrote so many letters and not so much in my diary, just because of the letter writing. One day the children might learn from them what this time has been like. Some of the children will remember, with the exception of the war baby, Ilkka-Elias.   (Sylvi to Helena, 10.10.1941)

> Now I sorted out all your letters from the wartime and send them to you, the older letters were left at home when we left during the first evacuation. As were the photographs. I always thought to send them too but I never did. It's pleasant to look at pictures from that time and remember past times that now seem so bright compared to this time that we now live.   (Helena to Sylvi, 24.2.1946)

These are contemporary narratives that have become history for the following generations. As such, they are very often about everyday life and reciprocal relations between family members.

Third, the life story and letters were reproduced and edited again by Sylvi's son Rauno Pärssinen in the 1990s. When Rauno edited, he omitted some sections and occasionally added a fuller explanation. His interpretation shows how the material becomes replicated and understood by later generations.

Like other researchers who use diaries to illustrate a period (Ulrich 1990) or temperament (Fairburn 1995), I use personal writing to explore collective patterns. Writing is not spoken language, it is discourse, and discourse is addressed to someone, about something (Ricoeur 1991: 145–50). In particular, I track the 'I', 'you', 'we' and 'they' of referential speech to see how the writers position themselves relative to the object of reference and the interlocutor (Hanks 1996: 236–37). This process aims to find clues about culture and how 'we' communities are constructed in self-generated texts.

The personal 'I' is able to join a group 'we' when the individual recognises common experiences which allow him or her to feel part of the group (Carr 1986; 1997). An individual has the possibility of belonging to many groups so long as he or she can make this shift in perception. Accordingly, a text must be open so that others may enter and make the shift from 'I' to 'we'. In addition, in order to be part of an ongoing discussion, narrative material has to be able to join a circulating discourse. A circulating discourse is one that flows from one person to the next and gets replicated over the generations. It 'lay[s] down the pathways for other discourse' and 'people are interested in this kind of talk because of how it conceptualizes community' (Urban 1996: 143). However, not all discourse circulates, not everything is of interest to others. In fact, very little actually moves into circulation. What circulates best is talk about experiences from the concrete world that can be linked to existing discourse (ibid.: 246).

All of this raises questions about who the community is and what is being talked about. In fact, a discourse about a community cannot be too specific because the community is always diverse and one opinion is not generally recognised as speaking for the whole. '"We" typically implies a not- "we"', an exclusion of some (ibid.: 55). In order to build community and to avoid exclusion, individual experience must undergo a conversion into referential meaning. In these materials personal experience is often joined to grand narratives either by analogy or by paraphrase as a way to avoid exclusion. With replication in either of these two ways, personal experience (news) gradually migrates in the direction of myth. Most stories do not, however, reach the level of myth, 'the vast majority dropping out before they reach this pole' (ibid.: 247).

These memoirs were written for the family and that qualifies the topics, intended audience and circulation. Family throughout this work refers to an extended family structure. In the introduction to his 1992 edited book, Rauno Pärssinen explains why family memories are valuable. More specifically, Rauno begins with a universal 'people' and then defines 'we' as 'the descendants'. In the text genes and culture are passed on to future generations. The frequency of 'we', 'us' and 'our', and the parallelism in their use, creates a repetitive refrain which serves to clarify and establish the group 'we' of family (my structure and emphasis):

People have always, in fear of death, imagined immortality.

Most *people* have not understood that this immortality is a fact that has been accomplished.

Our male and female ancestors live in *us, the descendants*.

We carry in ourselves thousands of years of genes, of culture, even habits and things *we use* are part of the whole.

It changes and evolves all the time but the most essential ingredients from it *we pass on* to our children, grandchildren, and even farther away generations. *We will come to live* in our descendants.

We are part of the unbreakable generation chain.

This is *our* immortality.

The knowing of family tradition, getting to know about the lifestyle and surroundings of the *generations before us*, helps *us to understand ourselves* also and *teaches us to see* our life as part of a [long] time [span] and cultural whole.

Only rare families have a chance to get such broad memory material as *we* do.

This inheritance, more valuable than everything else, has to be saved and guarded with care. It must be broadened with information that involves *our own generation*.

This family inheritance must be moved on to the *generations that come after us*, to the children and grandchildren.

They must also take care of passing along the tradition. There cannot be a more valuable motive for this writing!

I give this collection to the Pärssinen and Kuisma family's use in honour of *the previous generations*.

Rauno Arvinpoika Pärssinen[33]

The micro-flows of 'we', 'us' and 'our' in the text parallel the family's continuity over time (Urban 2001: 104). Rauno begins with two references to general people (human kind). The next section makes a transition from past to present ('our ... ancestors live in us'). Then there are ten references, following in a steady rhythm, to the 'we' and 'us' of the present generation. In the middle of these there is one reference to the past ('generations before us') and at the end, two references to the future ('generations that come after us', 'they'). It ends with a reference to both the future ('I give to') and the past ('in honour of'). The collectivity assumes an existence in time, if only in the text, and the text in turn contributes to the creation of the collectivity.[34] Rauno follows the pattern of community-building narratives; he establishes the 'we' of the family, emphasises continuity, and extends the collectivity into the future.[35] It is not the family institution of the nation state, but an extended family that includes past and future members. This is the meaning of family as I use it in the following text.

The Historical Context

There are many history books about Finland and this region. My interest is in circulating culture, not history. What follows is a brief outline of the historical events that the reader should know in order to understand the topics in the memoirs.

Finland had been the eastern part of the Swedish Empire for six hundred years, until the War of 1808–1809, when the Swedes lost the war with the Russian Empire and Finland became a Grand Duchy under the rule of the Tsar of Russia, from 1809 to 1917. In the nineteenth century there was a nationalist movement that focused on developing Finnish language and literature and educating the folk population. By the end of the century there were developing national institutions (banking, education, etc.), a programme of land reform, major developments in mercantile capitalism, and increasing social unrest.[36] On 6 December 1917 Finland was granted independence by the newly formed Soviet Union, which was followed by a civil war in the winter and spring of 1918. The civil war split the Finnish population into 'Reds' and 'Whites', as well as those who did not commit to either side, and cast its shadow on social relations for four decades to follow. During the 1920s and 1930s, a general effort was made to organise the new nation state. These efforts at consolidation were disrupted by the war years, 1939–44, the central time period in the memoirs.

The following is an explication of the events, following discursive pathways, to see how experiences moved from sense to reference, and the significance of that shift for analysing national political culture.

2
SUBJECTIVE MEANING

Looking from the top down, as it were, hegemonic national projects both include and exclude certain communities, while promoting an ideology of equal citizens within the nation state. But hegemonic projects are never totally successful. Quite often studies of nationalism or the nation state fail to appreciate the different levels and institutions of society, the different communities, collapsing them all into one (successful, national) project. This ignores the fact that the social community consists of nonpolitical institutions as well, a fact about politics pointed out by Radcliffe-Brown (1940). These materials reveal an 'imagined community' of a different level, based on social, rather than purely political, motives. Rather than assuming a commitment to the state, I want to look at where interest lies and how it comes to include the state.[1] One way in which this happens is through the repetition of rituals and practices that build a sense of community with other people who, themselves, repeat the same rituals and practices. This was Durkheim's (1969 [1912]) general point about religion; in the memoirs one place comes to symbolise social relations. Church hill was, and continues to be, a significant place in the Kirvu landscape.

The nation state is defined by national projects and national borders but something is always added to this in the practices of the people.[2] Subjective meaning is given to the space (the territory) of the nation by its various participants and they do so based on known systems of understanding. Descriptions of Karelia usually include descriptions of places and how things were done – foods cooked, the design of nets, types of fish caught, etc. – because this local knowledge is crucial for practical reasons and for understanding the world. The lived-in world is significant because it is the site for learning this knowledge through the corresponding social relations.

Significantly, the domestic unit is where important knowledge is learnt and repeated through practical application. The knowledge learnt, accompanying social relations, and particular locations where these were practised, are all ingredients for a sense of belonging.

The importance of this social and practical knowledge – what James Scott labels *metis* – and its replication is at odds with the bureaucratic thinking of nation states (Scott 1998). Along similar lines, Bruce Kapferer (1988; 1995a; 1995b) recognises that the imagined community of the state glosses situational differences, and he places this process in the context of the development of particular political systems. Kapferer (1995b: 66) has coined the term 'categorical imperative' to describe the abstract system of bureaucratic operations characteristic of modern political systems (and this includes Finland). He argues that, for bureaucratic purposes, the individual is an abstraction, broken down into classifiable parts, appropriately called on according to the bureaucratic task, and he demonstrates the significance of this for ethnic discourse in Australia (1995b). There is, therefore, always a tension and a dialogic relationship between the imagined community of the state and various actual communities. Everything in these materials points to the fact that, as Kapferer recognises, people live in embodied and significant worlds, not in disembodied or empty categories. The diasporic situation of the Karelians means that they emphasise the significance of place and social relations, and thus reject, or modify, the empty bureaucratic category of citizen, although they may be quite loyal to the nation as a community.

The evacuated Karelians left suddenly in 1944, carrying what they could bring along: a few mementos, food, their cows, some furniture, pictures and clothes. The houses with most of the furnishings remained behind, in some cases burnt by their owners.[3] The continuity of living in Karelia was broken. Writing is one way to recollect the absent place and absent people and to relive what was lost. The discourse about Karelia is therefore always loaded; it is selective and given significance. The significance is built upon recognised abstract structures and these abstract structures are local, national and, in the case of Christianity, global.

Routines and Rituals

A study of memory, like history, is a study of the processes by which patterns change while at the same time they are reproduced (Sahlins 1981). One thing that is apparent throughout the writing is the repetitive nature of certain work and ritual routines in Finnish daily life. Life in Inkilä, as in much of Finland today, was marked by an annual cycle of seasonal changes, work patterns, holidays and special events. The common holidays across regions were Christmas (*Joulu*) and Midsummer (*Juhannus*) and common family rituals were weddings and funerals (Vilkuna 1964: 164). Because women wrote much of this material, there is a focus on the celebration of family rituals, in particular how women organised them and how food and presents were exchanged and were central to the process. David Sabean argues that women governed the dynamics of kinship in the nineteenth-century German village of Neckarhausen. It was women, with their letter writing, their organisation of family rituals, their coordination of children's visits and gifts among family members, who were 'at the center of an alliance system that stressed mutual reciprocity between lines rather than patriarchal authority' (1998: 490). The women writers here describe similar moments, for example, parties for children and the many coffees shared with visitors in the course of a year, which show in the small details how kinship alliances worked and how cultural values and memories are instilled through these repetitive patterns.

Holidays in Finland follow a set pattern even though there are regional differences. In fact, there are comments in these writings that indicate that life outside Karelia is 'somewhere out there', even if they are talking about central or western Finland.[4] But there is a commonality in that the same holidays are celebrated throughout Finland and in such a ritualised fashion that everyone from the region, at least, knows the songs and the routine about what will be served, when, and who should be served first. These patterns are learnt in the household, in the schools and by attending public events. As a foreigner I have had to learn the routines as well, by imitation at academic parties, in Christmas and spring parties at the day-care centre and school, and at friends' parties to celebrate a child's graduation. Children learn how to present the coffee and how to dress and perform properly for these celebrations in the day-care centre. Later, in school, they are taught how to properly set the table and how to prepare the expected *pulla*[5] and cream cakes. It is hard to live in Finland, especially as a woman, without knowing something about these celebrations. They occur as a steady beat, setting the times of work and leisure, repeating again and again throughout the years.

Through these family-orientated events, culture seems natural; it is embedded in the most ordinary daily routines, which Pierre Bourdieu (1977) has described as habitus. Following Bourdieu, this means that a person is 'endowed with categories of perception' through practice and that he or she is not 'indifferent' (Bourdieu 1998: 9). The patterns of daily existence are, in part, why people feel Finnish; it is not an imagined common history but a lived reality for all classes. While this family may have differed from others in the details of their celebrations, or from their Orthodox neighbours, they were celebrating the same holidays and the same family rituals as other Finnish Lutheran communities. The 'we' therefore includes other

Finnish Lutherans in practice. The talk also reproduces at times central ideas in the mythopoetics of global Christianity.

The calendar of the Lutheran Church marks off holidays and cycles of the year, with the two most important holidays being Christmas and Easter. Helena wrote about Christmas and Easter in her childhood. In these short descriptions she refers to local variations of common practices in Finnish folk culture. The temporal reference is to the past, her childhood, and therefore it implies tradition, an interest of Helena's, something she wants the reader to know. This is cued by comparing it with today ('same as today' and 'during that time') and she assumes that the reader does not know Inkilä's traditions, but that there is continuity. The 'we' of these descriptions is 'we children' and the domestic group, although it includes the 'they' who didn't know how to eat raisin soup.

> For Christmas, holiday foods were special, (the same) as today, even though they were different [foods]. First there was the Christmas Eve soup boiled of a pig's head (potato soup), potato- and barley pies, barley bread, pulla, and oven-roasted meat (what is today called Karelian stew).[6] On Christmas Day raisin soup was cooked, though during that time one did not know how to eat it but they would taste it anyway.[7] On Christmas Eve, after sauna, a straw bundle was brought into the tupa. First stars were made out of it and then cones. They were made so that the straw was bent in half and tied together on the side that was bent, the ends cut off, and a stick put on the tied side. It was put in a gap in the wall.[8] The star was made the same way but the straws were spread in a circle. I don't know if the cones were intended to ask blessing for the growth of the grains and if the star meant the Star of Bethlehem. The rest of the straw was spread on the floor where it remained over new Christmas [New Year] but not over *Loppiainen* [Epiphany].[9]
>
> During Lent a normal daily life was lived at our place regarding both food and clothing. But on *Kiirastorstaina* [Maundy Thursday][10] my mother read: 'At the Last Eucharist Jesus sat down at the table to eat Easter lamb, and so on', the same on Good Friday: 'The earth trembled, the rocks split and the graves opened, and so on' [from the Bible]. We children listened to it while holding our breath.[11] On Easter Saturday father made us children a swing, then we could freely swing the whole Easter holiday.[12] Certainly my home's old *mummot* [grandmothers][13] said that the sun dances on Easter morning, though I wonder if anyone really took that as truth.   (HK, p. 22)

Christmas and its traditions were not only recollected, it was written about in letters exchanged at the time. The following letter about exchanges between family and close friends is the first entry in Sylvi's book of memories. Christmas was important; every Christmas was noted although some were more joyous than others. Christmas is the 'we' of the family group.

> We thank you from our hearts for the gifts! We did not have a cake server so this one is received with pleasure. Mamma sent me a salmon pink slip, mittens to the

children, socks to Arvi and some sweets for everyone. I got a set of light green silk underwear from Santa, a low upholstered rocking chair, a case of make up (!), chocolates, and a crocheted cloth from Hilja. From Aira I got a wool cloth that will suit the top of the bookcase. The children got toys, two dolls for Helena, one from Mamma and one from the doctor's wife. Arvi didn't get much of anything from Santa. ... The parish gave the whole family socks and mittens.   (Sylvi to Toini, 8.1.1939)

Following her description above of Christmas and Easter, Helena refers to the Midsummer holiday, which marks the longest day of the year. Her brief mention assumes cultural knowledge by the reader, both regarding the burning of Midsummer bonfires, which is still done by many people, and a more vague reference to leaves on the floor.[14] Again, Inkilä is distinguished; 'we' didn't use birches 'at our place' before the habit was brought from outside and leaves were not used on the floor.

The birches were not used at our place during Midsummer before the Karelian [train] track was built, but that custom was brought by the builders from elsewhere in Finland which, however, remained as a permanent custom. Leaves were not used on the floor.   (HK, p. 22)

A wedding was always a special event, highlighted by the special foods, and amounts, eaten. In 1937 Helena's son Wäinö was married to Aira Pekurinen, the Inkilä stationmaster's daughter. Because daughter Toini was unable to attend the wedding in Inkilä, Helena wrote a detailed description in a letter. The wedding was on Sunday and after the wedding Wäinö and Aira went to their own home where everything was already in place. The family had purchased a radio for them, which brother Eino had put in the house. Other family members had given silver: two oatmeal spoons, a cake server, a half-dozen large eating spoons and a half-dozen smaller coffee spoons. Sylvi and her husband Arvi gave a prayer-book and a book series consisting of ten books. Helena added: 'Your present was visible also. Many times they missed you [pl.], asked why you [pl.] didn't come.'

Toini would have enjoyed this news of the presents and she certainly would have recognised the wedding celebration and the foods in Helena's description. This 'we' is a family event and the 'they' includes all who were there, the two families and the Läherintas.

Now Aira's and Wäinö's wedding is over and it went well. No trouble to remember. Sylvi and Arvi came here on Friday evening and left Tuesday morning on the mail train. Sylvi visited Viipuri on Monday and bought small things – shoes for herself, mittens for the children, and so on.

So about the wedding then. There were no other guests except the Läherintas – Hanna, Sylvi and Eino – not including Miss Helvi.[15] From our place we departed on Sunday a little before 2:00 to Aira's home with two cars. I will list who we were: Father, me, Wäinö, Itti, Jenny, Sylvi and Arvi. First before we went we had

coffee, cream cake, two spice cakes, four different sorts of cookies, there was a
lot of it. Then the wedding [ceremony] followed (the bride was not shown before
she came to be wed).

The marriage ceremony took place in the large living room (the one that has
a writing table in it). There were candles in a five-branched candleholder, the
candles were lit, [and] flowers were plenty. The bride [in] a white dress down to
the floor, a ring of flowers on her head, and a veil at least a couple of metres
dragging on the ground (it was so long).[16] A beautiful bride and, why not, also
the groom. Wäinö had a new black suit. They said that Aira had never been so
beautiful. After the wedding there came the congratulations, first by the mother
of the bride, then me, then the fathers, and then whoever followed.

After that juice was served with cream cake. Then following a couple of hours
after that there was a dinner. Oh, all the food, first a smorgasbord, whatever
courses, then liver casserole with gooseberry jam, along with potatoes, rice casserole and carrots. After that was served bouillon with meat pie, and finally for
dessert cooked rice and pieces of almond and sliced banana mixed into whipped
cream – that too was good. Well that was the dinner. Except for the end, still coffee. Then after everything, Arvi gave a beautiful speech to Aira and Wäinö.

We came home by foot; when we arrived at home it was already 10 o'clock.
On Monday evening we invited all of them to us for evening coffee. All the others came also, except Läherintas; though Hanna came. (Helena to Toini,
16.11.1937)

These moments where people gather, have coffee and cakes, eat special
meals and give speeches in honour of each other are part of the way in
which culture is replicated, and they are repeated with similar ritual
behaviour at various points in the life cycle – baptisms, confirmations,
graduations, weddings, funerals – through the years. In 1998, one hundred
years after her own took place, Helena's great-great grandson had his confirmation. It was celebrated with the customary gathering of family and
friends, a speech, servings of juice and cream cake with strawberries, pas-
tries, Karelian pies, and coffee.[17] Reading Helena's account today, those
who know present-day Finland can easily imagine what it was like to be at
the wedding celebration some sixty years ago.

The Lutheran Church in Kirvu

The memoirs contain constant references to the church and church hill and
to certain ritual practices, and the writers use metaphors that reveal a deep
religious belief. Helena's basic description of the church reveals how it
influenced village life; this contextualises the impact of religious metaphors
when the writers write about other topics, especially war. The Christian
Church established itself in Finland by joining church rituals to existing
markets and patterns of work and exchange (Vilkuna 1964). Helena pro-

24

vides a description of the practices of one historical period, which in turn incorporated older patterns of socialisation.

The Lutheran church at Kirvu, situated on church hill, was a dominant symbol in the landscape as well as being a dominant influence in organising the social life of the surrounding villages. Although religion is referred to throughout the fifty-nine pages of her life story, Helena has written ten pages specifically about the Kirvu church and church activities, making it the second longest subheading after the sections about her family. The memories of the church shift constantly between then and now because religion continued in Helena's life even though this particular church did not.

Karelia is a region with two predominant religions, Lutheran and Russian Orthodox. The Lutheran Church is an integral part of the Finnish state, the demographically dominant state religion, and the majority of Inkilä residents were Lutheran. The Kirvu Lutheran church and its rituals were an important part of Helena's life and the routine of the family. The church is also an opportunity for her to talk about tradition and traditional practices in Inkilä. In this short paragraph Christian symbolism is incorporated into everyday life. To the outsider, although someone local could probably make sense of this, there is also a non sequitur as she moves from baking to talking about a cross in the field. There is an implicit comparison to a place or a time when crosses were put in the field, although it is not clear where or when.

> My mother had this custom when she would bake. After the dough was emptied out, [she would] sprinkle flour on the bottom of the dough, make a cross on the flour, and say 'Jesus blessed'. In the field I don't remember a cross being made anywhere. (HK, p. 22)

The Kirvu church was built in 1817, and after a general history of the church, Helena tells that people wore their best clothes to church. Those who did not have good clothes could borrow some from someone else in the village but 'it was said that the lazy wore borrowed clothes', the 'it was said' cuing gossip and the 'lazy' underlining the importance of work. The trip to church was marked by two resting places, the first at a large rock called *Leppuokallio* three kilometres from Inkilä. The second resting place, called *Saarnoja*, was almost at the church and it was here that the women changed from their walking shoes to their (better) church shoes. There was no heat in the church in the winter and it was the custom that men and boys sat on the left facing the altar while women and girls sat on the right. The boys could be noisy and occasionally the minister would tell them to be quiet in the middle of the service. One time the minister saw a woman sleeping; in the middle of his sermon the minister said in a loud voice, and Helena quotes him, 'Get up you [sing.] who lie down and rise from the dead, then Christ will enlighten you [sing].'[18] The direct quote emphasises the position of the minister and brings the reader into the story.

Helena includes details of the service, how the hymns and prayers were listed on the wall, as is the Lutheran custom even today, and various procedures. She relates that outside the church Liena Wehviläinen sold her home-baked pulla and 'Rinkel-Yrjö' sold water-*rinkeliä* (pretzel-shaped dough), small details which reveal the importance of the church as a place for social gatherings. Polite greetings were required, as for any social occasion, and greetings were sent back to Inkilä. The greetings mark the local because they are in Kirvu dialect; they also report a distinction between young and old.

> Back from church, the greeting was,
> '*Terveisii kirkost*' [Hello from church].
> To which young people answered, '*Kiitos*' [Thank you].
> But old people said, '*Terve tuojal, toine lähettäjäl*' [Hello to the one who brings the greeting and another hello to the one who sent it]. (HK, p. 24)

The church bell, housed in a separate bell tower, was significant in the past and still in the present. In the past it called the people to church, marked off the special time of Sunday, noted funerals and weddings, and sounded an alarm in case of fire or trouble. It was also a way to talk about the difference between the 'we' of the Lutheran church and the 'they' of the Orthodox ('Russian church bells'):

> We had a hired church bell-ringer. Mother said to us as kids that the bells played '*pou pouuu, pouuu*' but the Russian church bells played '*pilipali, pilipali, pilipali, pouuu*'. (HK, p. 28)

Moving to the present, the church bell was moved during the evacuation to Orimattila, where many Kirvu residents settled after 1944, 'where now it is rung only when someone from Kirvu is buried' (HK, p. 28). When I visited Orimattila in 1999 to look for the bell, the church secretary confirmed that the Kirvu bell is hanging in the bottom part of the old bell tower, with a long rope attached that makes it possible to ring the bell. Several people passing by said that they had 'heard stories' that it was the Kirvu bell but no one that day knew if the bell was ever rung, or had much to say about it. In the nearby cemetery there is a large monument for the Kirvu people who died during the war years. The bell and the monument signify Kirvu for those who claim a connection; to others they are merely reminders of historical events.

The church was an active agent in the local community, but it was not *the* community. On 20 December 2000, there was a news report on Finnish television about a man who repairs church bells in Finland. He said that two or three days before he brings the bell down to repair it, he puts a notice at the church so people will know. According to him, many people come to see the parish bell when it comes down. The Kirvu bell is in Orimattila, but not other parts of the Kirvu church, such as the altar. The bell, which stood in the tower on church hill, is significant because it marked communal events and could be heard by everyone, the inclusive 'we' of Kirvu.

The topic of burials leads Helena to a discussion of funerals in Inkilä, and there is an implicit comparison with the present and how funerals are conducted in other parts of Finland.[19] When a person died, the body was washed and laid out in the burial clothes, black clothes but not special ('the same as for the living'). They did not wear shoes, only socks and gloves, and the men wore hats while the women wore headscarves. 'For one rich *isäntä*[20] in our village they had put a ring on his finger and a watch in his pocket, and when taking the body to the church they were setting the watch' (HK, p. 28).

> When a person died the whole body was washed and death clothes were put on the body, then the village's jointly owned body board was fetched and the dead person's body was lifted onto it. Then they sang some death hymn for the body and carried it to a drying barn [*riihi*] and also there they sang some verses. Dead children were taken to the clothing storehouse [*vaateaitta*].   (HK, p. 28)

The body, in a coffin, was then taken from Inkilä to Kirvu by horse. The dead were either buried in the first cemetery, near the church itself, or later in the new cemetery one kilometre from the church. On the way to Kirvu from Inkilä the cart pulling the body crossed a river, called *Äksjoki*, which marked a boundary for the souls of the dead. The trees with crosses described here are known as *karsikkopuu* and this folk habit was found in many regions of Finland (Sarmela 1994: Map 6). The social collective is 'we in Inkilä' and the 'they' were the villagers, close kin and others, who accompanied the coffin and cart. The social collective is also we-the-living, carefully marking the border with the souls of the dead. The temporal markers ('before', 'in the time of my memory') again emphasise tradition. The 'you' in the second paragraph is a co-participant in this local landscape.

> For us in Inkilä it was about 10 km to the church. Before, the deceased were transported by horse to the church. The coffin was lifted into the first sleigh or cart, on top of it sat the horse driver and the singer, after the coffin [came] the close kin and other mourners. Before, they were singing for the whole journey to the church, the singers just were changed in between, but in the time of my memory [they were singing] only when passing through a village or near a house. At present that custom [the singing on the trip] has faded away completely.
>
> Almost half way to the church from Inkilä is Äksjoki, after you drive over it, on the right side of the road, there are large [old] pines and on the bark there have been drawn crosses. Driving to the church my mother showed [me] them there and said the mourners had drawn them so that so far the souls of the dead can return homewards but not further from there [not after the trees].   (HK, p. 29)

Finally, there are a few criticisms about various Kirvu priests who did not do their job as well as people thought they should, or who asked too many questions about who was drinking, who was dancing and who was playing cards. There is a complaint about changes in the revised printed editions of the Bible.[21] And then Helena turns abruptly to the present, after the evacuation, in the mention of hymns.[22] She writes as a member of a special community 'the evacuees from Karelia', for whom these hymns are important:

> Now my present favourite verse [hymn] is Verse 171, 'Lord Jesus is here with us' [*Herra Jeesus kun täällä vain kanssamme on*]. That [hymn] has been adopted by the evacuees from Karelia as their own hymn which was sung on several occasions. My other hymn at present is Verse 600, 'Oh Lord, when I am a traveller on earth' [*Oi, Herra, jos mä matkamies maan*]. (HK, p. 23)[23]

Nancy Munn (1995) proposes that Kaluli songs put the displaced dead people back into place, although the Kaluli themselves are not displaced from their homeland. In a similar way, a frequently quoted song, found often in Karelian obituaries, places the displaced person back in Karelia:

> Oh, the Karelian forests have leaves on the trees,
> Oh, the Karelian birches are getting thick again,
> Cuckoos call there and it is spring,
> My bottomless longing carries me there.[24]

These stories of Inkilä are intended for the family. At the same time they repeat what everyone knows: to be a member of the community is to know about and participate in the annual calendar. As a mnemonic device, these celebrations recall the symbolic intervals of everyday life in Inkilä; they describe culturally significant events in that place. As a performance, there is continuity in the life cycle rituals; they are still practised today.

Residual Structures

Festive practices were central to social activities in Inkilä and they were of long duration. Finnish ethnologists have described the many different days that were celebrated in different Finnish regions (Vilkuna 1994 [1950]). Each locale had its annual cycle of festivals, usually in the summer, where people would gather. This pattern extended back to the Middle Ages or earlier and such festivals were usually connected to the annual cycle of work (Vilkuna 1964).

The pre-Christian folk concept of time was established around a calendar that divided the year into four equal sections based on weeks (thirteen weeks in each). This system, found in other parts of Scandinavia, divided the year into two seasons, winter (14 October) and summer (14 April), with midwinter (13 January) and midsummer (13 July) marking the middle of the seasons. These distinctions continued in South Karelia, with the four quarters marked by Christmas (25 December), Lady Day (17 March), Midsummer (21 June) and Michaelmas (29 September) (Talve 1997: 207). Helena's life history refers to Christmas, Easter, Midsummer and Michaelmas as important days in Karelia at the end of the nineteenth century. These days were important in the seasonal variation of farm life. They marked the rhythm of life, 'the successive phases of increased and decreased intensity, of activity and repose' (Mauss and Beuchat 1979: 78) according to the work of the season.

In Karelia church festivals brought people to the church at least once a year and each church village had its feast day or *kihu*, which was accompanied by markets where people would sell food and handicrafts and trade horses. The church feast in Kirvu was on Midsummer, on Trinity Sunday[25] in neighbouring Räisälä, and on the tenth Sunday after Trinity Sunday in neighbouring Antrea (Vilkuna 1964: 166). A person might travel to three or four feasts in a summer, especially the young people hoping to get married. Kustaa Vilkuna's description of the patterns in Karelia for the parishes around Kirvu echoes that of Helena:

> The ninth [festival day] was the great raspberry Sunday of Ruokolahti which was then celebrated for three Sundays in a row; the first to make their counter visits[26] were the Kirvuans, the second were the Jääskeans, the third the Joutseners, and Rautajärvians.[27] The raspberries were already ripe. Those [the raspberries] the girls brought in [small, birch] baskets to the church hill and offered to the boys they fancied as signs of their favour. That one of the boys who took the basket demonstrated with that his will to continue courting with a proposal in mind. (Vilkuna 1964: 167)

The festivals were popular in the nineteenth century, although Helena writes that they died out in the beginning of the twentieth century.[28] In these descriptions the social collective who share the event is the community, not the nation state, and these collective events relate to important aspects of the social structure. The *kihut* (pl.)[29] were gatherings of special interest to young people because it was where 'your own and the neighbouring parish's young people' could become engaged. The social group of 'your own' and 'they' is the parish in this case, not the village:

> Church festivals took place in Kirvu and the neighbouring parishes still at the beginning of this century, although in the final years people almost forgot about them. Every parish had its own church festival [day]. For Kirvu people it was Midsummer, in Räisälä on Trinity Sunday, other parish's festivals I do not remember. I wonder if the festivals had any other meaning than for your own and the neighbouring parish's young people to meet and become engaged. They drove horses up the long church hill, those who had open carriages. The horses foamed at the mouth from pulling the heavy load. Only a few young people had time to

go to church, they just walked along the long church hill. It was always the same at every parish festival. (HK, p. 24)

The landscape of church hill connected personal experience – the narrative 'I' – to that shared by the local community. After leaving Inkilä the recall of social gatherings, the church festival, a wedding or Christmas dinner, both distinguished and included Inkilä in collective representations. Inkilä, as part of Karelia, had its regional traditions but similar celebrations took place in all regions of Finland.

The surnames of people in Finland can often be traced to a particular topography or type of work. The house and the place identified the individual.[30] Likewise, places had names that indicated topography or events that took place there. When Helena describes the church she includes the place, church hill (*kirkkomäki*). Inkilä itself is always placed in Kirvu parish (*pitäjä*), a civil administrative unit, so that it is commonly called Kirvu's Inkilä (*Kirvun Inkilä*). The district court for any area is called the *kihlakunta* and the social community of the church parish is called the *seurakunta*. The church hall where gatherings are held, such as for the meal after a funeral, is called the *seurakuntatalo*. All of these are terms in common usage in Finland today and all have origins which reveal central organising structures of Finnish society (Vilkuna 1964).

These terms have their roots in patterns of social organisation dating back to the Middle Ages and sometimes earlier. Vilkuna argues that the markets and feast days were older than the Christian Church and that the Church (first Roman Catholic, then Lutheran) fitted its ritual calendar to these festivals and markets (1964: 182). For example, in Turku in 1292, the one day for an official marriage ceremony performed in the church (*vihkimispäivä*) was also the day of the market, 18 June (ibid.: 170–72). The markets held during the summer were important days for trade, for dancing, for arranging marriages, and for servant girls and hired men to change positions. The verb *kihuta*, which in Karelia becomes *kihupyhä* (church festival), implies a circle, days to move around, and people travelled to several markets in their region. In one summer a Kirvu person might go to Antrea, Hiitola and Rautjärvi, each on a different day (ibid.: 176). The importance of these markets for exchange, and especially to make marriage alliances, as recognised by Helena, meant that church feasts were mostly attended by young people and the church hill became a key place for young people to meet. Although *kihlakunta* is today the region served by a district court, the verb *kihlata* means to become engaged (and *kihlat* in plural is a sign of engagement). Kustaa Vilkuna (1964) and Väinö Voionmaa (1969 [1915]) both recognised that the old parish, law and tax districts were the same area, and this area was the region of marriage exchange, where most people found their marriage partners.

The church in the Middle Ages was the governing arm of the Swedish king, responsible for recording the population and for collecting taxes. It also defined the region of the local district court. The *pitäjä* (civil parish) designated an area where people worked the land together and paid taxes, often paying in crops such as barley (for beer brewing). It implies as well a group with whom one shares reciprocity in food (Vilkuna 1964: 135–36). Finally, the words *seura* (group) and *seurakunta* (congregation) are common words today with links to old meanings of working together. There were groups (*seurat*) formed for forestry work, for hunting, for fishing, for slash-and-burn agriculture, and so on. Each person who took part in the work got a share of the product. These old work groups, where one was paid with a good meal, were an important part of Finnish social structure (ibid.: 137) and are echoed today in *talkoot*, temporary work groups to clean the yard of the house or to organise the anthropology department.

The festival pattern was much older than the Lutheran Church and central to reciprocity, trade and marriage alliances. Although patterns of social organisation have changed over the centuries, marriage, trade and voluntary associations are still central to Finnish social relations. In exploring the roots of these words, Vilkuna uncovered basic patterns of social organisation that still have meaning but are not thought about in everyday usage. Kinship organised social relations and the marriage alliances and market exchanges that took place at the annual festivals outside the church were central to the domestic mode of production. Kustaa Vilkuna's insight shows the continuity of structural elements recalled by the name of a location, church hill. However, although there is this continuity, to paraphrase Sahlins (1985), every reproduction is a transformation.[31]

When Helena writes of the church and the church hill, she is talking specifically about Kirvu at the time she lived there, to preserve the memory of it. At the same time, her choice of topic can only be appreciated by understanding the central importance of the markets and exchanges that took place at the festivals outside the church door. Church hill was significant to Helena; she reproduced stories about what happened there. However, she did not reproduce the traditions, she reproduced the significance of the place; both the place and the former practices are changed (and would have changed in any case). The political situation means that the reproduction of events on church hill took a turn to memory, to recollection, and this turn gives church hill in Kirvu a different meaning today, although it remains a place endowed with significance.[32]

Abstract structures of long duration allow the possibility for people to join their personal 'I' to the 'we' of the community. The connection can happen because there is significance; it does not happen through the empty bureaucratic categories of the modern nation state.

3

SIGNIFICANT WORLDS

Personal experience and personal memory is strongly linked to the collective through social interaction and particular landscapes which are given significance. In part, the landscape is a setting, especially as the concept has evolved within the European context; through painting, landscapes came to have meaning and to be described as 'picturesque' (Hirsch 1995). In part, certain landscapes are perceived to be special or commemorative, and a setting may serve to reify memory (Halbwachs 1992). The commemorative aspect is typically found in pilgrimage sites, as Halbwachs wrote about the Holy Land, and Karelia too has become a site for pilgrimages, a site of commemoration. Church hill was a place in Kirvu with long-term significance in the social landscape. Other places have a different kind of significance, one connected to daily routines. These are spaces known more intimately to the narrator because she has dwelled there.

In Inkilä, and elsewhere, place names are part of the referential aspect of discourse that makes it possible to summon persons and events long gone and far away (Urban 1996). Spaces known intimately are spaces that are possessed by the writer. In the Kaluli songs analysed by Nancy Munn (1995), place names and the social relations depicted in the songs were two key elements for recollection. Something very similar happens in the Inkilä material, where place names and social relations highlight the Karelian landscape. Place names are scattered throughout Helena's writing, central to the memory books, and preserved in the 1938 maps still sold for returning visitors to Karelia. In hearing a place name, people can remember particular people and events as they experienced them, even if their experience was different from Helena's. Munn's model proposes that a homeland, as a symbolic space, is the place where one may go to find oneself. To remember the homeland is to be able to visit it, and at the same time to re-contact the self in the place where one belongs (Munn 1995: 90).

The landscape is invested with social relations. Work was an integral part of everyday sociability in Inkilä, although it was distinguished from time spent at school or church, or at special events such as weddings and funerals. It seems as though this distinction was made and enforced by the church more than by the locals. Helena's life story mingles work and ritual events but she notes that some Lutheran ministers checked to see if people were working on Sunday and she includes two tales told by her mother about people who worked on Sunday (*työnteosta kirkkoaikana*, work during church time). These are part of a genre known in Finnish folklore studies as taboo tales or warning stories (Talve 1997: 247). Such type stories circulate in Finland and are made local by attaching them to known people, places or events (Siikala 1990). The subjects in the stories here are anonymous ('one old man', 'two women') but the stories are linked to local practices ('my mamma told', 'Haikko village') through a temporal reference ('during the time of my childhood').

> My mamma Anna Rantalainen (*née* Wornio) told the following stories about work during church time. It was absolutely forbidden still during the time of my childhood or it would be punished, as like what happened in the following stories:
>
> One old man from Haikko village went fishing [with a line and rod] on a Sunday during church time to Mustjärvi in Paavilansalo. He fished for a while but didn't catch anything but a few small fish. The old man became fed up with fishing so he threw the fish back into the lake and said: 'This is for you, Mustjärve Pirkko' [guardian spirit of the lake]. At the same time a long-bearded old man rose from the lake and climbed into the bow of the boat, where he sat down. The old fisherman became scared and started to row to the beach as fast as he could. Then as the bow of the boat touched the shore stones, the old man who came out of the water jumped back into the lake.
>
> Two women went during church time to the forest to pick berries. They met a man in the forest, who asked of the first one: 'What will you do with the berries?' The woman answered: 'I will sell them and buy my children bread [with the money].' The man did not do anything to this woman. He asked the same question of the other: 'What will you do with the berries?' This one answered: 'Sell them and buy myself a beautiful necklace.' And suddenly there was a snake that wrapped around her neck and she could never get it off. This was the penalty for working on a holy day. (HK, p. 27)

In her talk of work, Helena begins with a description of cow-herding practices in the 1890s, the work of girls, based on her own childhood experiences. The cows were kept in stalls during the winter, where they had to be fed, milked, cleaned and cared for daily by the *emäntä*[1] and other women workers. In the summer they were put out to pasture or in the forest in order to graze. In the annual cycle, Michaelmas (*Mikkelinpäivä*) on 29 September was the day to put the cows in the winter stalls and they were put outside again in May on a designated day (*karjanuloslaskupäivä*), although the exact day varied by region (Vilkuna 1994 [1950]: 131). Talve (1997: 210) reports that 23 April (*Yrjönpäivä*) or 1 May (*Vappu*) were the days in the south and east when the cows were put out. Putting the cattle out often involved magical practices to protect the cows from wolves and bears. Helena's history of village life joins the work of girls to this annual cycle and to places in the landscape.

The girls were responsible for tending the cows and bringing them home. Helena tells the reader about this, and includes the reader in the local world by using dialect when quoting what they said. They knew the sound of the bells for each house's cows so that one would shout (*huuu huu*) to another cow herder, 'Have you seen Eskola's [the house name] cows?' with the answer 'no' or 'there on the Linnamäki side'[2] (HK, p. 20).

A few lines later the narrative shifts in style. It is now without dialogue, entirely local in references. The 'we' of the story is 'we herding girls', the ones who know the landscape and the cows in it, although this is only clear at the end. In order to keep the translation as close as possible to the Finnish, I have kept the passive voice. Hence, 'was listened' refers to listening for the bells of the cows, as described above. The title is Helena's.

On the Path of the Herder

At that time, the 1890s, there were no fenced pastures for the cows of *Kirvu's Kuismala* village, but cows could wander in the forest lands as far as they wanted-ed.

At my birthplace's forest lands there were five small lakes; they were *Wiijenlampi, Kärmelampi, Matolampi, Heinlampi* and *Lamssiilampi*. *Äksjoki* [a river] divided *Kuismala's* and the church village's [*Kirvu*] lands from each other and the road leading to the church from *Sairala* village's lands, though if the cows wanted, they could freely go even there. Then the cows were milked three times a day. In the morning they were milked early and then herded to the forest. The herder was woken up at about six in the morning, given a sandwich in the hand, and then to the forest to search for the cows. Before noon the pastures were near the house, but towards the evening they managed to get deep into the forest as far as 4–4.5 kilometres away in the forests around the village.

The herders' footpaths led from hill to hill. Near the village there were, though, two hills, *Riihimäki* and *Kotimäki*, but they were so close to home that the cows were never there. Before noon the herding areas were the following: going on the road by the side of *Likasi's* field, then behind *Siltasi's* field climbing the path up *Suontakkaisel* hill, it is a half-kilometre-long ridge, and from where always on the highest hill the [church] bells were listened to. To it belonged [pasture lands] from the side of the rail line *Lillikkoro*, surrounding *Pinomaa* and *Honkamäki*. At the end of the ridge there was *Kevätaijoi* hill, and there the *Kultamäki* side was listened to. Over *Martikorpi* peat land one rose to

34

Martikorpi clearing and from there over the road leading to the church to *Halkomäki* [hill]. Now one turned more towards the lands of *Laalo* village to *Ruokko-oksii* and *Siltasi* hill, there one listened toward the side of *Linnavuore* and *Keihäskivi*. If until now the cows were not found, then one came along the *Siltasi* road to home. Then the pasturing cows were not milked and the cows were left [swollen] till the next day.

Towards the evening the village's herders gathered together at about 3–4 and they went together until the one who found their cows left the group. Now the group went along the road towards the church for two kilometres. At the border stone one left the road up the foot path to *Soikallio*. There it was said that on a clear day the *Kirvu* church tower was visible from seven kilometres distance. At *Soikallio* towards *Leppuokallio* and *Rötlähtie* was listened. Then again the journey continued along the path and rose up to *Mykkylä* hill, it was the kind of hill that one could not climb up from any side but by crawling. There *Joro* forest, *Tetrsuo* and *Äksjoki* banks were listened. From there it was a short trip to *Tikkamäki*. Then one climbed down a steep hillside and over *Lammioja* [stream] and *Suoportai* hill. *Lammioja* has its source in *Wiijenlampi* [small lake] and flows into *Äksjoki*. A short distance away in *Matarahol* one climbed up a large rock and listened to the side of *Kärmelampi* [snake pond]. Again one climbed down to the path and up *Portinrinta* hill, it was a lofty, high and wide hill where one always stayed a longer time. We girl-herders practised dancing there on smooth rocks and in the summer turning to fall we went to *Matolampi*'s stony shore to pick juicy raspberries. Then the journey continued by the side of *Lehmäkuoppa* grassland to *Paalakallei* hill, where the sides of *Linjatie* and *Lammaspiiri* hill were listened to. If until this the cows were not found one went home. It was not yet good [*sillä hyvä*, meaning the job was not done]; then one still had to leave with some older person to the forest to look for the cows. (HK, p. 20, my emphasis)

How does one make sense of all these names? There are no cardinal directions in this description; in fact, in the memoirs, only Ilmari's description of Inkilä, for the people 'who have not lived in the village', includes a mention of 'in the south'. By drawing a map of Inkilä it might be possible, through homology, to make more sense of this. One could try to be scientific and produce a model of the landscape, but still one would be lost. While seven of these named places are on a map drawn by villagers, most are too local even for their map. For example, whereas Helena has named the roads, the villagers' map has no named roads. What is important in all the accounts, is the named houses and social relations. The directions are social; the girls move through a landscape of hills, ponds, fields and stones, between villages and houses. And the collective depicted is differentiated - it is not the anonymous collective of Durkheim; everyone is not the same. This is the perspective of young girls, with the recognition of difference between gender and age. Such descriptions are not factual descriptions of the earth as a territory; this is a description of a different ontological order. It is a description of a world.

The language itself, in the use of the passive voice, indicates continuity, an event repeated many times, not just a one-time occurrence. At the end of the passage it is easier for a nonparticipant to get some meaning. Here the reader can imagine the dancing and the berry picking of the girls and the need to finish an unfinished task if the cows are not found. Otherwise, Helena's 'we' includes only those who shared the empirical experience of the writer (Urban 1996: 46). In fact the 'we girl-herders' at the end would be a very specific group in age and gender but it is opened up in the 'herder' of the title and by the emphasis on habitual rather than personal behaviour. Other locals can understand and be included because they know the habitual landscape of herding around Inkilä. Only at the end, with the dancing and berry picking, are some (males) excluded. It is a narrative of a very local world, known intimately to those who participate. Outsiders are excluded because outsiders do not know either the landscape or the habitual practices.

The narrative is unusual for Helena in comparison with her other writing. It has stripped away people and events, leaving place name after place name. It does not link places to legends or connect the landscape to historical events. This written passage does not recall a mythical landscape, rather in its structure it resembles a myth itself. The starting point for systems of knowledge is in the 'organization and exploitation of the sensible world in sensible terms' (Lévi-Strauss 1966: 16). By converting herding girls into a general type ('the herder'), by using the passive ('was listened'), and by focusing almost exclusively on features in the landscape, the narrative makes a structural pattern from the known world of cow herding in the same way that myths utilise knowledge of the known world (ibid.: 33). Helena's narrative, based on the sensible world which she knew intimately, creates a structure – name after name – from locations in the landscape which, now that it's gone, narratively places Inkilä in a time and space known intimately only to those who lived there. It reveals the deep knowledge of the landscape known to those who habitually worked in it.

When she continues her description of herding a few paragraphs later, Helena incorporates common folk beliefs. This is her introduction to the story:

> Sometimes it happened that the cows were not found even though they were being looked for. Then it was said that they were in the forest cover [*metsänpeitossa*]. At the time when this happened I was only ten years old but I remember very well one event.

Although this is presented as a personal account, there is a genre of such stories (*metsänpeitossa*, hidden by the forest) in Finnish folk narratives. Matti Sarmela (1994) has a map showing the distribution of these stories and Helena's story contains all the components of the narratives that he distinguishes. As she continues, there is a reference to the animal in the forest cover and to a specialist who has the ability to release it. Direct quotes add emphasis and bring the reader into the story.

> One time the heifer cow did not come home in the evening with the other cows. It was looked for for many days, all the possible danger spots, edges of ponds, ditches, and all the marshes, but they could not find it. Finally they came to the conclusion that it was probably in the *metsänpeitto*. Kiveri's Olli-ukko, who was related to the old people from my home (Eskola), was still alive then and living in Ylikunnu village. He was known for always getting the animals out of the *metsänpeitto*. There was nothing else I could do except go ten kilometres away to get Olli-ukko for help. After he came and entertained, he went into the woods, I do not remember what else he wanted along other than tar. After a while he came back and said: 'It seems that something is sitting on the back' ['*Näkkyyki oleva oikei kahareisi seläs*'].[3] He wanted a knife along and then went back into the woods, and said: 'Now we'll find that cow, dead or alive' ['*Kyl se lehmä nyt löytyy, löytykyö elävän tahi kuollien*']. (HK, p. 20)

But they didn't find the heifer immediately with Olli-ukko and they heard later where she was. The behaviour of the stray heifer fits the second distinction in Sarmela's map: animal trapped and bewitched. Sarmela notes that in Karelia this often puts the animal in the form of a stone, stump or tree (1994: Map 53) and that a specialist (sorcerer) could be called to find it and release it. In the story, Olli-ukko was the local specialist and he suspected that the cow was held down by some force. In her conclusion to the story, Helena reveals that she knows of the folk beliefs ('they said').

> In the evening the village shepherds came home with their cows and brought the word that your[4] heifer is at Martinkorva's field, right beside the dirt road. They went to get it away but it couldn't get up with its own strength so it had to be pulled home with a horse. In its hunger, it had eaten the top layer of grass all around [where it was lying]. During that time they said that a beast in the *metsänpeitto* turns to stone [so] that the human can't see it. And if you hit it with some hard object, it will hurt the animal. (HK, p. 21)

The personal experience, presented as remembered reality – this happened when she was ten, Olli was from her house at Eskola – is part of a genre of stories. Helena mixes the two so that folklore becomes lived experience. In that respect, she probably accurately recounts how people talked about events in Inkilä when she was young. At the same time, she fits personal memory into a common story-telling format and into more general folklore motifs (Siikala 1990).

To know the landscape is to be situated and in place. In this sense the landscape is a dwelling, a place where people lived and worked and, 'in so doing, left something of themselves' (Ingold 1993: 152). There are no clear boundaries for dwelling (ibid.: 155). Knowing the landscape is a form of knowledge that the 'we who lived there' know. To dwell in a place implies that one is 'familiar with', 'accustomed to' and is in a position of 'looking after' it (Heidegger 1971: 147). In this dwelling, one engages with and cares about the world through daily interactions and experiences.[5] The peasant woman is secure in her world, as described by Martin Heidegger (ibid.: 34), because she has practical mastery of it. A similar deep knowledge of one's world is found in Helena Kuisma's writing. Knowledge of the landscape and of one's place gave people a sense of security, which by analogy extended to the idea of home. Home is where one dwells, where one is familiar, accustomed to the place, and where one puts one's care and concern into the daily activities of farming, having coffee with one's neighbours, and so on. Helena's narrative about the paths of cow herding is so direct it is like singing. 'To sing the song means to be present in what is present itself. It means existence' (ibid.: 138). For Karelians, memory recalls the dwelled-in landscape, the place where the family belonged. The current political situation is one of displacement and the tension between belonging and displacement is central to Karelian memories.

The following passage, which occurs later in the life story, is quite different. This time the description is of a landscape of people and events – a war, the Russians, a girl named Katri – which the reader can make sense of through a general knowledge of history and human relations. Here certain geographical features serve as a motif attraction for the story of Katri. In motif attraction stories, as well as with jokes, it is possible to find similar stories in different villages, and that in fact happens in the Karelian materials. *Wartiovuori* (*vartio*, to guard; *vuori*, mountain) was a place that was important in the 1808–1809 war, when Sweden lost the war to Russia and ceded the territory of Finland to the Russian Empire. In this section Helena makes a shift to the narrative 'you', including the reader ('after you have climbed up you realise'). Now the addressee can take part. Here the 'we' is those who know the landscape and 'you' who participate with them.

About 7 kilometres from Inkilä station, between Ihaksela and Worniola villages just by the roadside there is a small knoll named Wartiovuori.[6] It doesn't attract the attention of passers-by because of its insignificance but after you have climbed up you realise that it's worth its name. From there opens a wide view upriver stretching all the way to Löylölä village twelve kilometres away. In the same way the borderlands of Räisälä parish are visible seven kilometres away.

Wartiovuori had been an important place in the War of 1808–09. There there had been the Russian soldiers' favourite camp and watch place. It was easy to guard because from the mountain there was a vast view over a wide area, there the road moves alongside the mountain very close, which was dry pine forest. Kuunjoki [Moon River] flows on one side and on Ihaksela side was Katri's-ditch gorge (which acquired its name because in former times a certain Katri-named girl killed her child and threw it in the gorge), where at the beginning of time a heavy stone bridge had been built. Over the river the Russians had built a bridge, the stones of which were still on both banks. (HK, p. 41)

These rocks and hills and gorges were a way in which past events were experientially present in the landscape (Sahlins and Kirch 1992) and an integral part of peoples' working and socialising experiences. Whereas the Hawaiian landscape described by Sahlins was 'the mytho-praxis of the people's alienation from the existing authorities' (ibid.: 35), Helena's landscape reflects an authority that is not so openly oppositional as between commoners and kings. Her landscape is a border territory marked by the work of girls, the wars between competing empires, the presence of the Lutheran Church, and the failure of some individuals to live up to community expectations. It is a landscape inhabited by the inclusive 'we' of the past which 'you' may participate in.

Inkilä was a place of work, leisure and ritual events, and such places have no boundaries. But of course, larger events were taking place that affected the local community. Eventually institutions that were at the core of building a Finnish nation, even before independence, came to Inkilä at the end of the nineteenth century. Helena's story includes her perception of some of the changes that occurred in the Finnish countryside after 1860. For one thing, the decade from 1860 to 1870 saw a rise in the number of rural landless. The years 1867 and 1868 were years of famine, which resulted in death for eight percent of the population (Talve 1997: 317) and the implementation of reforms that led to industrialisation, especially in the timber industry. In the area around Viipuri, the sawmill and timber industry offered work for landless peasants. This was a period when transport lines were expanded (canals, railroads), when the Finnish mark became legal currency (1860), when elementary schools were established (1866) and employment reforms (1865) gave workers freedom of movement (ibid.). The Finnish language was granted official status, second to Swedish, in 1883 and numerous organisations, sports and workers' groups for example, began to spread to rural areas. These general changes happened during Helena's youth and her descriptions of Inkilä sometimes refer to them to inform her readers.

One of the important marks on the landscape was the rail line built through Inkilä from the town of Enso in the west to Käkisalmi in the east. Before the railroad, Inkilä was a quiet place of fields and farming. The only machine was a machine-saw, which was so special that many people came just to look at it.[7] The railway, begun in 1890, brought modern life to Inkilä and at this time, Helena claims, Inkilä became more integrated into Finnish life. The first line workers to build the railroad arrived in Inkilä 'shortly before Christmas 1889' and lived in the village until the entire line was finished in 1911. The arrival of the workers presented an opportunity for new trade for Inkilä's women and girls.

> Inkilä's women started a new trade: they cooked coffee that the small girls took in bottles to the work place. When the men saw the girls coming, they sang, 'Hey

39

you pile drivers, the little girl brings coffee.'[8] That was the greeting for coffee break. (HK, p. 41)

The wives of the railway workers brought a new skill that they taught the women of Inkilä. This generates an aside in the text into which Helena inserts her personal experience. 'I' indicates that the speaker inhabits the discourse and this provides for a connection across time (Urban 1996: 50). It brings the reader from the past to the time of the writing.

> I am happy about one thing. The railway men's women brought the skill of lace making to Inkilä. I found a lifelong favourite hobby in this. During the days of my youth I did not have much time for that because of my household chores, but later in Elimäki, being in the care of Aira and Wäinö [her daughter-in-law and son], I crocheted many a lace for sheets. (HK, p. 42)

With the railroad and three other public buildings (the school, the Youth Hall and the Workers' Hall) by the end of the nineteenth century, Inkilä was gradually being integrated into a national Finnish pattern of community life. For Helena, an important event was the singing contest in June 1898.

> One summer the three-day singing festival was in Inkilä; then there were people in Inkilä from all around Finland. (HK, p. 32)

Although Helena's text emphasises how Inkilä was being integrated into Finland, Finland was in fact a Grand Duchy of the Russian Empire at the time. She notes that local people were travelling back and forth to St Petersburg for work and trade and that they were paying for things in roubles, but other than that, there is almost no evidence of Russian rule in her writing. The one mention is part of a story about the Great Strike of 1905. The general strike of 1905 in Russia had a counterpart in Finland. In Finland the strike resulted in social reforms for workers, including the franchise for women, Finland being the second 'country' in the world to grant women the right to vote.[9] According to Talve (1997: 236), 1905 also marked the end of folk Christianity and the deep roots of the Lutheran Church in household practices. Helena doesn't say much about the general context of the events of 1905, focusing more on Inkilä and her household but in the story the Inkilä station manager opts for the Finnish flag if given a choice. The 'I' of the writer again provides a connection across time.

> At that time the Finnish blue and white flag also had the red cloth of Russia. I do not remember if the red was on the top or bottom edge of the flag. The former Inkilä station master of those days [of the strike], Kopperi, was excited and ripped off the red cloth and hoisted the blue and white flag to fly on the station's flagstaff. Soon however the news came that the general strike didn't succeed, and the emperor is the ruler as before. Now the station manager was in a hurry to sew the red cloth back on the flag.

At my husband's home there were large-sized pictures of the emperor and empress on the sitting room wall. My father-in-law [Aadam Kuisma] wanted to take part in the general strike in his own way. He took down the pictures from the wall of the sitting room and put them on the wall of the cow shed. I do not know where he put them after the general strike but they did not appear on the wall of the sitting room again.   (HK, p. 33)

In this short passage a historical event is recalled through the 'I' of personal experience and the activities of two local actors, the station manager and Helena's father-in-law. This period of Finnish history is often described as the time of passive resistance. Through personal experiences people participate in collective events, and through the memory of particular persons they are linked to the event itself. Whether or not Helena intended it, the story illustrates the period.

Topogeny

One common theme in people's descriptions of Karelia is the landscape: the flowers, lakes, trees and animals of Karelia. The landscape is known now only through stories or from short return visits but it remains a central feature in how people talk about Inkilä. At a family reunion in 1999 several people had photographs of their return visits to Karelia. In most cases the original house was gone but there were pictures of the land, the birch trees, the rocks, and the remaining apple tree which marked the home site. When I mentioned that I too had visited Inkilä, one man's immediate response was, 'Is the bridge still standing over Kuunjoki [Moon River]?'

Inkilä is described by Helena as a village cut through by four roads which lead to such places as Kirvu, Räisälä and Kaukola.

It was said about Inkilä station that it is the most beautifully located station on the Karelian railway. From the station opens up a beautiful view to Alajärvi [lake], to villages surrounded by fields and grasslands, of which seven are visible. Along the Räisälä road are the villages of Paksujalka, Kuismala, Niukkala, and a part of Ihaksela. At the end of the lake, where Alajärvi ends, is the Kuolitoksen bridge. There over [across the bridge, on the other side] a road begins along the lake edge back to the station through Paavilanmäki, Merola and Inkilä village, where the road crosses over Sahajoki, at the far end of Koposilta. (In my home the old ladies told that the bridge was named for the Koponen who built it.) The original bridge was old in the time of my youth, and later made new, but the name remained the same.

Between Kuismala and Niukkala villages is the high Hiijenmäki, which is crossed by a road, which is so steep that the horses could not drive a carriage except with at most a driver. Later the village built a new flat road between the hill and the lake. That station was the large Pärssinmäki, where before burned Juhannus bonfires. In the same area on the other side of the road was Liputmäki;

41

it was a swinging hill for the village's youth, where the youth met on holidays to enjoy themselves and boys swung girls. (HK, p. 31)

The names are significant points for exegesis. Along these roads are named houses, settlements, bridges, rivers, lakes, hills and rocks, which are in turn linked to people's names or to special events. Areas of the village had different names and these names typically were linked to house names and personal names. Helena gives the example of her mother, Anni Wornio, who lived in Juonpää (dialect for Joenpää, head of the river). She was known as Juonpää's Anni, or, adding her house name, in Worniola, Juonpää's Anni (*Wornialassa Juonpään Anni*). As an old woman, this same Anni was referred to as Ylioja's grandmother (*Yliojan mummo*). Another man was called Harjun Matti; he was distinguished from other Mattis by being especially strong. Here is Helena's description of him:

Harjun Matti

The first men to work on the railroad came to Inkilä in 1889. They lived for a short time in my birthplace [house], Eskola, then moved to a house neighbour-ing the station. Some of these men carried knives – they brought some bad habits from the rest of Finland. As a result, some locals did not greet them.[10]

There is one event that I remember – Antti Westerinen's wedding in Läyölä vil-lage. Six or seven line men went to the wedding feast and they were a little drunk when they arrived. The *isäntä* told them to leave because they were not invited and they started to quarrel. There was a well-known 'strong-man' ['*voimamies*'] from Kirvu named Harjun Matti (Matti Inkinen). He threatened to throw them out if they did not leave peacefully. He did throw one out the window in the dark. The man hit a stone and was sick from that. The others went back to Inkilä.

Harjun Matti had a small cabin about two kilometres past Ojajärvi station near Läyölä. Matti lived there with his wife and children. One time a man who had heard about Matti's strength asked at Ojajärvi station, when he was a little drunk, how to get to Matti's cabin. He went to find Matti. Matti asked the man what was his business and the man said he came to see the powerful man who did the floggings.

'Come into the cabin', said Matti, 'and I will show you a thrashing so you can tell others.'

Then Matti said, 'If you come a second time, that's what I will do to you.'

The man promised that he would not come again or tell where Matti lived.

Harjun Matti met his fate in Heikki Suutarinen's sauna in Ojajärvi. The men were playing cards there, and there, it's been said, Lehtola's Jussi stabbed Matti and he died from the wounds. (HK, pp. 34–35)

This named landscape, including the people, is an important part of ref-erencing local talk and understanding. Helena writes many details like this; they are a key part of knowing Inkilä. These personal and landscape names are carefully noted in the *Two Sides of Koppo Bridge* (1986)[11] memory book about Inkilä, where each name is followed by what the person was called, such as, Inkinen, Juho (Torpan Jussi) and Kuisma, Matti (Ukon-Matti) or the specific names on the map of Lake Kuunustainen, which notes 53 islands, coves, points, beaches and rocks by name. The book includes personal recollections, photos and interviews with former residents, and a series of maps that list every house by name and its residents (by name) at the time of evacuation. By mapping the village and recording the names of the people and the houses, the population is fixed in Inkilä as it was last known just before the evacuation.[12]

The memory books do not repeat a nationalist mythology; they do not write about the origins of the Finnish nation. They write about their home-land: the houses, friends, churches and cemeteries they had to leave behind. The descriptions include nature, a known landscape marked by place names, and a landscape of social relations, of people known and songs sung. Social life was marked by the rhythmic temporality of Karelian natu-ral cycles and Karelian nature is often the beginning of a description of Karelia. The following paragraph was written by Helena's son[13] in his intro-duction to the 1982 memory book about Inkilä. The speaker recognises that the 'best expert' is 'every resident' and he does not claim to know more than they do; he includes himself with them. Instead, he addresses the out-siders, 'the people who haven't lived in the village', and because they are outsiders, he includes cardinal directions and factual information.

> The best expert about the village is every resident [*kyläläinen*] themselves but for the people who haven't lived in the village I will tell about its nature. From a bird's view, Alajärvi [lake] was in the middle and Alajärvi broadened in the south into Hiidenselkä. The clearing of the village was surrounded by high moraine ridges that were covered in forest. There was a village road at the edge of the for-est and along the village street the yards of the houses were decorated with gar-den trees, lilac bushes and apple trees. The fields sloped down to the beaches of the lake. At the edge of the fields there were sheds which had grown grey under wood-shingled roofs. Kuunjoki's [Moon River's] canyons and the deep channels of its streams gave the scenery a wild tone. In the middle of the wild forest there was the broad, dark, clear-watered Kuunustainen [lake] and a group of smaller lakes and ponds. The lake was 80 metres above sea level and 35 metres deep. With its islands and fjord landscape, this lake was part of wild, untouched nature. From this lake the surging Lehter River rapids flowed through the town. (Ilmari Kuisma, Preface, *Muistojen Inkilä* [Memories of Inkilä], 1982)

Topogeny is the recitation of an ordered sequence of place names that mark the journey of an ancestor, the migration of a group, or the transmis-sion of an object (Fox 1997: 8). This idea is expressed in a book written by Kaarina Uusihakala (1989) about her personal experience of leaving Karelia, called *One Road, Many Paths*.[14] One road was the leaving, many paths was the many directions into which the Karelian population scattered, the breaking up of the community. Such topogenies are central both to the memories of living in Karelian villages and to the descriptions of leaving Karelia. Recollection depends on concrete spaces, images and objects, what Pierre Nora has called 'lieux de mémoire', the embodiment of memory in certain sites (1989: 7). To know a place is to be able to walk through it in your mind, to map the sites where specific events took place. 'I remember every curve, every hill,' one woman said about her former home in Karelia (quoted in Paasi 1996: 278).

There are two classic mnemonic principles: (1) to imprint on the memory a series of loci or places; and (2) to rely on sight as the strongest of the senses to produce visual memory (Yates 1966: 32). The recall of a named landscape can serve as a locus to hang or locate one's memories. Places noted in the landscape are often places where culturally significant knowledge is stored, which offer points in the narrative for a more detailed exegesis (Fox 1997: 13). Helena Kuisma used local places, such as lakes, fields and hills, as well as certain people, as cues in her narrative. She wrote for readers who shared some of what she knew and her recollections are loci on which others can hang their stories. To describe nature, to list the place names of Inkilä, to remember the associated stories and songs, is to recall Karelia and its relation to Finland. The place names and stories of characters known to the writers evoke a past sociality and a lived-in landscape very different from the current regime (Sahlins and Kirch 1992: 17).

The persistence of tradition in a village follows the paths of the landscape, resides in household interiors, is passed along to children at the cemetery, and is continued in practice through marriage alliances and daily reciprocity (Zonabend 1984 [1980]). These repetitious patterns of daily life provide continuity and the impression often that rural life changes slowly. Certainly such patterns characterised Inkilä as people carried out their daily activities and incorporated local knowledge through their activities. This process of daily activity, where past and present are constantly intertwined, no longer exists in Inkilä for the Finnish Karelian population. It is only when one realises the extent of the practice of dwelling, the ways in which people are linked to place, that dislocation has meaning.

The landscape remains important for people looking for their past in former Finnish Karelia. Today the forests are not considered to be properly cared for, although, importantly, it is the same nature to the Finnish visitors.[15] Most place names have been changed to Russian names, so when the Finns visit Karelia they use the 1938 Finnish maps to find old roads and former villages. There are still people living who were part of the 1944 evacuation, although the numbers are declining. For these people and their descendants, Karelia remains the landscape of home, a landscape imprinted by their activities and those of their ancestors. The trips to Karelia are organised to find former homes, to collect stories of all the former Finnish villages, and to visit cemeteries in order to look for one's ancestors or a husband's or child's grave.[16]

The commemorative landscape has involved confrontation and this has happened on church hill. To ensure the success of their occupation of the Karelian Isthmus, and in line with Soviet policy on religion, the Soviet government destroyed most of the Finnish churches and cemeteries. In Kirvu the church and cemeteries were destroyed and a Soviet military camp was built over the new cemetery. During the 1990s, Finnish groups were allowed to place commemorative markers at the sites of churches and cemeteries. In Kirvu, the commemorative marker for the new cemetery and the plaques to mark the former church and bell tower are in place. But the memorial to the men who died in war has been beheaded. War memorials are a potent symbol of nationalism and sacrifice (Rowlands 1993: 145), and that message was defaced by the population currently residing in Kirvu. Because of the historical timing of events, the Karelian experience can always be linked to the collective memory of the war years, but this is a history still under revision. For example, in a documentary about Karelia shown on Finnish television during 1999, a Russian historian argued that Karelia was Finnish, not Russian, and should be returned. History has in a way doubled back on itself as new issues continue to focus on the site of church hill in Kirvu.

The Text as a World

Ethnologist Kustaa Vilkuna (1975) recognised that Finnish culture did not have clear boundaries (certainly not the boundaries of the nation state) and he readily listed distinctions in climatic zones (north/south), religion (Lutheran/Orthodox), language (Swedish/Finnish), material culture (west/east) and trade that created different boundaries. The world of the narrative is not a microcosm of Finnish life, nor can it be. It builds a picture of those who participated in events together in Inkilä. It is not a strictly bounded 'we'; it includes at times other villages and parishes. It is a Karelian 'we', although it recognises, through comparison, that others practise similar rituals. It is certainly a temporal 'we', a pre-1944 'we', not the 'we' of the present inhabitants of Inkilä. To occupy the world is to name it, to participate in it, to describe it. Inkilä's landscape, marked by place names, was the setting for the 'I' and 'you' and 'we' and 'they', the social relations of the community.

It is the nature of writing to preserve discourse as an archive available for individual and collective memory (Ricoeur 1991: 107). But writing converts the 'saying of language' into the 'said of discourse' (ibid.: 146), and in this turn the known world is interpreted. Inkilä as lived becomes the memory world of Inkilä. Activities and people, described to preserve a view of Inkilä, become a template which structures the biographical remembering of others (Munn 1995: 87), as happened to us during our 1997 visit. A text must 'open out' in order that reading is possible; in the process of reading a new discourse is conjoined to the discourse of the text (Ricoeur 1991: 118). In this manner, the reader/interpreter reactivates what is said by the text and understands something about him/herself. Memory likewise engages the subject. In remembering former places and activities, a person makes the past his or her own. But just as it becomes 'my past' there is the recognition that it is gone, that it is no longer 'mine' (Munn 1995: 89). This contradictory field of mine/not mine, or of a past that cannot be reconciled, marks the written memoirs and memory books.

The recollection of Karelia continues to circulate because it can be linked to the biographical remembering of others. This was apparent to me during a seminar I was teaching on how to analyse field materials. To demonstrate my presentation, I used three of the narratives from this material. During my talk, one young woman had tears in her eyes because, as she explained, these were the stories her Karelian parents and grandparents told her over and over during her childhood (two others nodded their heads in agreement). At that moment the general story becomes one's own, same and different are linked, and that enables discourse to circulate. One example here (On the Path of the Herder) does not open out; the girl's experience in the landscape cannot easily be repeated by others. But other stories are genre stories or stories about people and history that the reader can understand. The written text opens out when the world it describes can be compared with the world of the reader, and in this interaction between self and other, that world can be interpreted by the reader, although the reader and writer may give it a different referential meaning.

4
GENEALOGICAL NARRATIVES

The territory of Karelia has been a recurring political issue since 1944: how to talk to the Russians about it, will Finland get it back, and more recently, would Finland want it back? Karelia has been, at various times in history, the focus of Finnish nationalist politics.[1] The national discussion focuses on questions of territory and national sovereignty, while the Karelian discussion is more about home. The Karelian claim to place is a phenomenon of a different order than the claims of the nation state. One question raised, therefore, is on what bases do the memoirs make a claim for Karelia, and how is this claim different from claims of national sovereignty? Anthony Cohen argues that nationalist rhetoric and symbols have to have a meaning that can be recognised by the experience of the audience, and his focus is on the actors' experiences and understandings of national representations (1996: 812). I am also interested in personal experiences of nationalism, but I begin with personal narratives to see what themes they focus on and how they include and discuss national events.

Benedict Anderson (1983) recognised that the abstract community often linked blood to place. It is this aspect of the abstract nation that I explore here. Genealogies link notions of blood (genes) to place. Does one find narrative expressions of an imagined national community in genealogical narratives?

The memory of Inkilä is transmitted often through genealogical information and related stories about the family. Genealogical memory focuses on status, property and the social relations of Inkilä village. It places the family at the centre of alliances that were not shared by everyone. The 'I' and the 'we' in a genealogy are specific; it is not the 'I/we' of Karelia or Finland. There is surprisingly little about national politics in these materials. And yet the 'we' of genealogy is somehow open.

In all societies there is a tendency to find justifications in the past for the present. In analysing the claims of Hawaiian kings, Valerio Valeri (1990: 157) distinguished genealogical charts from narratives, each with its own message, which he called syntagmatic and paradigmatic. A syntagmatic relationship is temporal, based on a chart of names or a list of events. A paradigmatic message, found in narratives, is about instantiations of the rules (ibid.). In Hawaii both are used to legitimate the succession of rulers. In a similar way, the Karelian genealogical charts and narratives are used distinctively to make a claim for duration. As a syntagmatic record, there are excellent church records in Finland of everyone born, baptised, confirmed, married and buried, by parish, going back to the sixteenth century, which can be used to make a genealogical chart. The narrated genealogy, as stories of human actions, exemplifies the paradigmatic: who 'we' are, 'our' values, what distinguishes 'us', and the continuity of family life. The different possibilities in the messages allow several possibilities for interpretation. This is important, as Valeri understands, because it means that both types of message operate as a charter or as a set of possibilities for future action, although neither determines absolutely.

I am circling around the issue of legitimacy and the question of how, when and why individuals might consider themselves part of a political community. Years ago, Audrey Richards (1960) explained how the legitimacy of a Bemba king was based on an historical charter passed from generation to generation. This charter was made up of a series of names of people and places, myths and legends, although it was devoid of detail. However, as with mnemonic systems in general, one detail stimulates memory of other details. Richards argued that the classificatory kin terms were linked to the system of 'positional succession', which in turn put the whole system into place through only a few names or details. Much the same happens with the Karelian stories: a few names of people or places, a joke or story, are enough to stimulate the memory of a whole system. This is a claim for Karelian legitimacy, although the names and stories are about quite ordinary people, not kings or chiefs. Karelian genealogies, since 1944, are more significant than genealogies in other regions of Finland. Genealogies are origin stories, and in territorial politics, origin stories are a central narrative in claims to legitimacy; they tell who has the rightful claim to place. Landscape is one element of the memory system; genealogical charts and narratives about kinship and marriage alliances are another central aspect of the mnemonic system of legitimacy.

Looking at how Helena writes about the community opens questions about the ontological significance of the nation. People do not live in abstract notions of social reality. They live in concrete situations, understood structures and actual events. The genealogy outlined in Helena's story centres on the memory of certain individuals while many others drop away, similar to research in Ireland about how the Great Famine was remembered by remembering specific individuals (Silverman and Gulliver 1997). There is an assumed understanding about Karelian house society, key social roles, and important sites in the ritual landscape. It demonstrates that discourse is about the world, but it is also in the world (Urban 1996: xiii).

There is also a structuring structure, a social context, for genealogical information. As in spoken language, the written description of the family is intelligible only through an understanding of the social organisation, although this might not be mentioned (Hanks 1996: 164). Genealogical memory assumes known patterns of social organisation in order to be intelligible, even if these are not the obvious focus of transmission. It is not a description of social organisation but it offers a key to understanding the structure at various points in the narrative. And that structure itself is an important aspect of personal identity, of knowing where one belongs. There has been a lot of literature about invented traditions and their rela- tion to political claims, following the work of Hobsbawm and Ranger (1983). If there is tradition, it is in these narratives, and it is not invented or static.

Marriage and Alliance

Kinship rules always include some people and exclude others through rules of descent, alliance and residence. Church hill was an important place because of its connection to engagements and marriage alliances. Marriage was a central organising institution for the production and reproduction of social relations, although it was part of a larger system of reciprocity, as both Väinö Voionmaa and Kustaa Vilkuna recognised in the word *seurat*, work groups. In European cognatic kinship, the rules for marrying are based on negative restrictions, who you should *not* marry (Sabean 1998). Unlike unilineal systems, systematic continuing relations between groups should not take place; thus the youth of one village look for suitable mar- riage partners from other villages. However, in Finland before the end of the nineteenth century, marriage was not a random event. Young people were expected to obtain their parents' consent for marriage or they could be denied a dowry or inheritance. Only after 1864 were they allowed to marry whomever they wished (Talve 1997: 192).

The named house was a central feature in Karelia and people were iden- tified by house. A person was linked to a house; his or her name often reflected the house name (e.g., Anni Wornio of Worniola), taxes were paid by the house, and the continuity of the house took priority over individual members. Väinö Voionmaa (1969 [1915]) argues that the need for labour in the slash-and-burn economy was the reason for the predominance of the

Karelian extended family household (*suurperhe*) and for the central importance of the house. There were clear laws about tax responsibility and regulated procedures for succession. Ownership of the land (and therefore the distinction of partible and impartible inheritance) was not as important as the organising role of the male head of the household (the *isäntä*), who directed production and was responsible for paying the taxes. His counterpart, the female head of the household (the *emäntä*), organised domestic work and the resources of the household, in evidence daily by the keys to the storage rooms that she carried with her. It was a bilateral system of descent, although there was an 'agnatic twist' in the naming system and in the practice of fathers and sons or brothers working together as the heads of the extended family. Both women and men inherited property, which characterises European kinship systems in general (Goody 1983).

Origins

The life story written by Helena Kuisma is the central text for providing genealogical information and the foundation for the family's knowledge about itself. The personality of Helena Kuisma, her experiences and general attitudes shape the selection of topics and the story. But personal narratives are given form according to collective models. During Helena's lifetime, Finland was predominantly an agricultural society with a historical tradition of clearly demarcated cultural distinctions between east and west (Sarmela 1994). Karelia is in the east and the traditions of Inkilä reflect its location there. Helena wrote most of her life story in southern and central Finland and she knew about the interests of Finnish folklore and ethnology. Her writing reflects discussions in Finnish folklore and history about how the various tribes and regions of Finland were both distinct and related.[2] During her lifetime, she submitted several essays to the Finnish Folklore Society about Kirvu customs and collected a list of 183 proverbs and folk sayings in local dialect.[3] She uses these ideas of regional distinction, sometimes through direct description and sometimes through implicit comparison, to highlight the memory of Inkilä.

It has been claimed that a concern with tradition is a characteristic of modernity, that 'the awareness of such things as traditional is itself a definitive mark of modernity' (Herzfeld 1997: 52). Certainly, recalling past events and values 'underscore[s] the historical contingency of the modern' (ibid.). And the way in which past events are recalled and presented as history may be particular to European, or Western, thought. The subject of Michael Herzfeld's ethnography, Andreas Nenedakis, 'demonstrates his modernity through his explicit engagement in traditionalising talk – talk that emphasizes its own orality even when it is written' (ibid.: 291–92). Helena does much the same when she switches between proper written Finnish and Kirvu dialect. But this seems less a sign of that elusive concept, modernity, than a way to think in terms of differences: past and present, regions, self and other. As a folk ethnographer, it is more likely that she was simply following an old ethnographic method of comparison, comparing how we live and how others live, and at the same time echoing a national (mainly academic) interest in folklore and regional specialities.

The Kuisma name is linked to the founding of the village and to ideas of precedence based on the original houses. Helena explains that the village was first settled by two men from Ingria, one named Inkinen and one named Kuisma. Inkinen settled on the east side of Alajärvi (lake) and on that side, during the nineteenth century, there were thirteen houses where the *isäntä*'s name was Inkinen. Kuisma settled on the other side of the lake and eventually there were nine houses on that side with *isäntäs* named Kuisma. 'When I was young, the old grandmother in our house, *Ellimummo*, showed me the place where the first houses were.' And she ends the section by emphasising the break in history: 'There before the evacuation trip began in 1944 was the village named Inkilä, and before that [it was named] Kuismala village' (HK, p. 8).

Väinö Voionmaa's (1969 [1915]) research on the history of Karelian families, based on tax and church records, indicates that Helena's description is generally correct. It was common practice that a place grew up around one house or *talo*, and that everyone shared the name. Helena's recollections reach back to the beginning of the nineteenth century, based on what she knows from her mother and two old women in her childhood household. This is similar to what Anna-Leena Siikala (1990: 149) found for folk memory in western Finland, where people generally began their history with the Swedish–Russian War (1808–1809), and to recollections of local history in Ireland (Silverman and Gulliver 1997), which are based on personal stories of people known to the narrator or at least the narrator's family. It is also possible that this family's history in Kirvu began about the beginning of the nineteenth century. The family story says that they came from Ingria to Inkilä and, in fact, local populations moved frequently in the greater St Petersburg area during this time (Alapuro 1987). The church records indicate that there was a small population in Kirvu in the eighteenth century, which grew rapidly in the nineteenth century due to people moving in from other areas and through natural increase. In general, the population of Finland increased rapidly during the nineteenth century, from 830,000 in 1800 to 1.7 million in 1867 (Talve 1997: 311).

A House Called Poja-Aatam

After a general introduction to the village, Helena sketches the genealogical line of her husband's Kuisma family. She gives a bare outline of the male line and relies for the rest on stories that she has heard. The structure of the information is about marriage alliances and people moving from house to house because of work and marriage, and the narrative emphasises continuity.

Her husband Israel was the son of Aadam and the grandson of Niilo. Niilo and two of his sons, Simo and Aadam, traded small wares in St Petersburg. To illustrate this, Helena tells a story about one of their trips where they were lost in the cold and dark and finally found a house where they were taken in. There, a caring old grandmother nursed Aadam's frozen fingers. Eventually Aadam became the hired hand to Matti Jortikka in Inkilä and when Matti died, Aadam married Matti's widow Maria. 'Aadam proposed to the widow Maria, who did not say no.' Aadam then became the *isäntä* of the house that included Maria's two sons, Niilo and Yrjö Jortikka. From that time on, the house was called Poja-Aatam. Aadam and Maria had one son together, whom they named with the biblical name of Israel. Then Maria died, but Helena adds a key detail: 'The house needed an *emäntä*. The *emäntä* was thought as necessary as some essential thing in the house.' Aadam therefore married a servant girl named Susanna Ollonen, who had been born at Parikkala,[4] and they had three children. Aadam and Susanna and the children of three marriages, plus servants, lived in the one house. Helena concludes with the information that Niilo Matinpoika [Jortikka] was a bachelor who died at his birthplace. Yrjö Jortikka married Hanna Läherinta, changed his name to Läherinta, and their son Eino had a shop in Inkilä before the evacuation in 1944.[5]

One anecdote tells about village politics with a paradigmatic message. Aadam Kuisma was in a high position as the village elder for many years. Helena describes the inspection of the villages, which was done by the Lutheran minister and his assistants, and the position of the village elder. Aadam's story is an example of how one achieved high status in these rural communities by organising work, through literacy and knowing the laws, and through connections with the church.

> The pastor, dean, head pastor, organ player and bell ringer drove with the horse from the church if there was no possibility to stay overnight near the previous examination [of reading and biblical knowledge] place. Before the proceedings, the pastors were given coffee, after that the pastor sat down behind the long table of the *tupa* and led a prayer. Then the dean instructed who should lead the reading of those attending the confirmation school and those intending to go to the school in the fall, and who should lead the reading of the children below the confirmation school age. The dean stayed leading the reading and questioning the grown-ups about the Bible. Sometimes small funny mistakes happened to the one

[person] reading; it was even reported that when one old person was told to read the sentence in the Bible, 'They went to Jerusalem where the synagogue [*synagoka*] of the Jews was', the old person read, 'where the sins of the Jews were gathered [*synnit koossa*]'.[6] Several who were not literate complained that they cannot see to read anymore. In every reading circle a 'village elder' ['*kylävänhin*'] was elected, who was always questioned at the end of the reading about the news of the village and if [there were] any complaints. Aadam Kuisma from Kuismala village was a village elder for several years. He always had complaints: in which house spirits are used, in which house dancing and card playing is done, and so on. The villagers did not like that and the village elder got many mocking names. (HK, p. 23)

Aadam Kuisma's achievements are stories told for the family. But there is some confusion in the story about his house, which illustrates how genealogy aims for continuity and unity. Helena says that his house was called Poja-Aatam (from *poika*, meaning boy, or son-Aadam), and this is the house she moved into as daughter-in-law. In the story, it seems that Aadam married the widow Maria, nine years his senior, and moved in with her and her sons. But the church records report that Aadam's son Israel was born at Paxujalka No. 2, Aadam Kuisma's birthplace, and Helena says that Niilo lived out his life at his father's Jortikka house. Both of these facts indicate that Aadam did not move to Jortikka house. In a book about house names in Kirvu (Lehikoinen 1988: 183), there is a note that Poikala house (Paxujalka No. 2), the home of Niilo Kuisma, broke up in 1873 and that the house went to his son, Aatami Niilonp. Kuisma.[7] The house is recorded as 'Poja-aatamila'[8] under the name of Aadam Kuisma in 1874 (ibid.: 182). It was common that a house would split, that the other two sons would move elsewhere, but the narrative does not give these details, emphasising the unity from father to son rather than a split between brothers.

The Central Story: Eskola House

After forty pages about Inkilä, Helena returns to her family at birth and traces the Rantalainen family genealogy. I quote her story at length because it becomes the basis for later family memories. As with the previous narratives, people are linked to place and she repeats how a house had to have an *emäntä*. There is a side story about houses when the old house with its ten people is contrasted to the more modern Päivölä, 'our last home'. The verbs shift between present and past because the 'I' of the speaker inhabits the narrative and provides a connection across time. The ethnicised 'we' ('we Finns') is not found in narratives like this because such stories, like myths, were never meant to include everyone (Urban 1996: 49). I have highlighted inserts about national events in the text.

I am born the 5th day of June 1882 in Inkilä, Kirvu parish. More exactly said in Kuismala village, but nowadays was called Inkilä for the whole railway station region. Inkilä village according to the church records is about one kilometre from the station on the other side of the lake. *There was our home at the time of the evacuation journey. It was our last home, Päivölä, in Karelia.*

My mother gave birth to me in my home's sauna at the time of making whisks,[9] as my mother used to say. Then it was said the children were found in sauna under the benches. I don't remember if it was believed or not. The mothers of those times lived with their child in sauna as long as three to four weeks before they came to the tupa, even then they weren't allowed to come to the same table to eat with others before the child was baptised and the mother was 'churched'.

I am from an old Karelian farm *suku* [family].[10] My father is Tuomas Matinpoika Rantalainen, whose mother is born in Kirvu at Rätynkylä [village]. My mother Anni Aatamintytär Wornio, whose mother was Mari, is born in Kirvu's Worniola.[11] The year of the birth I do not know. My father Tuomas Rantalainen came as *kotivävy* for Samuli Inkinen's daughter Wappo to Inkilä. After its [her] death my father brought another wife, my mother Anni Wornio from Worniola village. To them were born four daughters: Helena, Katri, Wappo, and Anni (the youngest died small).

My natal home, Eskola, was quite close by Inkilä station by the road leading to Räisälä. My last memory of my natal home was sad. *One boy from the village had taken a picture while the area was reclaimed [from the Russians], in which my old home was a smoking ruin.*

Earliest Memories from Childhood

My father was good-hearted. I don't remember him ever whipping us children. But if the games turned out to be too rough, [he] said only 'Now quickly, one [child] into one corner, the other in the other [corner].' I remember well how I sometimes was allowed to sit on father's knee 'horseback' ['*kopoteltavana*'] if a bad feeling made one cry. And father sang 'Cuckoo, cuckoo, far away cuckoo ...' ['*Kukkuu, kukkuu, kaukana kukkuu ...*']. My mother though was ordinarily a tough person. It did not take much cause before one got grabbed by the hair or the master of *koivuniemi* came to visit and beat your legs red.[12] If she told you to go for an errand then immediately you had to leave. You already had to be by the door when you were told where to go. Otherwise, well, my mother was just and religious. At his arrival from Viipuri, my father always brought *pulla* or *Wiipurinrinkeli* [pretzel-shaped breads, a speciality of Viipuri], and those mother divided among us equally, for everybody the same amount. Usually families hoped for sons but in our home it was said, when one girl after another was born, that 'even a girl is good into an empty hand'.[13] And in Eskola Tuomas had a boy, Samuli, from his first marriage.

I remember once when we four small girls sat on top of the oven of the *tupa* quietly giggling and chirping like a crowd of grey finches in the bush. I as the oldest one had to take care that the younger sisters – Katri, Wappo and Anni – do not fall when everybody eagerly tried to peep to the floor. This was around 1890.

I was eight years old, the others younger than that, and Anni almost a baby. We were waiting for an exciting drama and soon a nice clopping was heard from the doorway and father led the horse into the *tupa* to be shod. At that time it was common that during the winter the horses were shod in the *tupa*. The horse was tied by the reins to a ring in the wall. During the procedure we girls had climbed up on top of the oven, there one saw well this 'merry' ['*lustig*']¹⁴ event. Anyway, the horse scared us small girls. Father shod [the horse] and brother Samuli held the burning shingle, because the small light in the ceiling did not give enough light.

[We were] living in Inkilä in Tuomas and Anna Rantalainen's (*Yliojan mummo*)¹⁵ house at Eskola. In the house there were two living *tupas*, [with] a hallway [*porstua*]¹⁶ in between, but one *tupa* at a time was lived in. The one [diminutive] *tupa* was a storage [area] in which was stored food and the dishes ('*kolittimet*')¹⁷ needed in the house. Occasionally the *tupa* was changed. In the same family were living also older generations. There were El'ämmä and Mar'ämmä who were already in their eighties when I was a small girl. Their husbands, brothers Antti and Hemmi Kuisma were former *isäntäs* and already dead. Antti's and Mari's only daughter, Katri, lived with her husband, Samuli Inkinen, who had come as *kotivävy* [son-in-law]. Their only daughter, Wappo, with Tuomas Rantalainen also taken in as a *kotivävy*, continued running the house. To them was born a son Samuli but Wappo died after a few years. In the house there had to be a young *emäntä*; Tuomas brought Anna Wornio from Worniola village to be his new *emäntä*. These were our – the small girls who climbed on to the oven – parents. Samuli who held the shingle was a stepbrother. Our family of ten persons lived in a single *tupa*, which during the winter was so wet that the corners were quite mouldy. (HK, pp. 46–48)

This is predominantly a story about the family. Inserted into the story are comments about the national events of war, such as the smoking ruins of the house, the evacuation from Inkilä, and leaving Päivölä. Stories of individual people form the basis of the narrative and stories about the same individuals occur elsewhere in the life story. For example, in another section, there is a humorous story about El'ämmä, titled 'Eskola's old women':

The Lutheran pastor visits El'ämmä when she is on her deathbed and tries to talk to her. He asks her how far she has been and wandered the roads on the earth. She answers that she has not been further than Jääske Bridge and Hyppölä mill, and then he asks, where does she now want to go, to the joys of heaven or to the fires of hell? She answers, 'Old people don't mind the joys, they are happy wherever it's warm.'

Despite the availability of precise records, each generation focuses on only a few key individuals and their stories as points in the memory system. The small details of individual lives are more important than long lists and dates that include everyone. Only recently has Helena's grandson Kari Pärssinen attempted to draw a complete genealogical chart.

Greg Urban (1989: 49) has argued that an indexical-referential 'I' alone is essentially unsocialised, and he proposes a chart of types of discourse 'I' and their relation to sociability (ibid.: 43). In particular, the 'I' of myth, the projective 'I', is where the speaker-narrator assumes the 'self' of the original ancestor. This move aligns the speaker-narrator with past 'I's' and with the original (mythical) narrator. There is a similar move in what I call the genealogical 'I', although it is different from the projective 'I'. Helena uses an indexical-referential 'I' in her narrative ('I am born', 'I am from', etc.) and she does not assume the self of an original ancestor. But when her text is read today, or when the stories are replicated, Helena's 'I' becomes a genealogical 'I'; it is the 'I' of 'my' ancestors. The reader is not the 'I' of the author, as with the narrator of myths, but because of genealogical ties the author is 'mine', and the two 'I's' become 'we'. The continuity of culture occurs in this turn between the indexical and the genealogical 'I' (Urban 1989: 45). The turn is a subtle, but crucial, move in establishing legitimacy through genealogical narratives.

In May 1999 the Rantalainen family held its first family reunion since the 1944 evacuation in the small town of Mäntsälä, about forty kilometres north of Helsinki. The area around Mäntsälä is where people from Inkilä and Kirvu parish were resettled in Finland after the war. About eighty people came to the family reunion, mainly the descendants of Samuli Rantalainen (the father of ten children), Helena Kuisma (née Rantalainen) and her sister, Katri Korte (née Rantalainen).

The reunion was held in the main room of an old manor house that is used for such parties. The event centred around an opening ceremony, a main meal, music, a presentation of family history, a group photograph, and coffee and cake. In the centre of the room was a memory table: a table with photos of Samuli Rantalainen and his wife, old photos of their farm and house, called Pyymäki, a map of Kirvu, small Kirvu and Inkilä pennants, several memory books written about Kirvu parish, and a text written about Rätynkylä, the village of the Rantalainen family. On a table at the entrance to the room was a guest book to sign and a book of photographs taken by members of Samuli Rantalainen's family during their visit to Inkilä in the mid-1990s. One photo on display at the memory table showed a horse, a man and two women working in the oats field, with a log house in the background. This photo was juxtaposed with a second photo of the same place now that the house is gone, the land is untended and scrub birch trees are growing in the former field. The photo of weeds and scrub trees was titled 'my birthplace'.

The programme opened with songs of Karelia and Inkilä[18] and then with stories about the family ancestors. A grandson of Samuli, who introduced himself in the Karelian manner as Erkinpoika (Erkki's boy), talked about the family at Rätynkylä No. 2, the farm at Pyymäki, and how Tuomas and

Samuli had worked with horses. Samuli, who died 3 July 1944, just weeks after the evacuation of Inkilä, was a self-taught animal doctor for the local animals. After the meal Helena's grandson used an overhead projector to trace the family links to Tuomas Rantalainen, Wappo Inkinen and Anni Wornio. He also repeated the story told by Helena of the two old widows, El'ämmä and Mar'ämmä, and showed an old hymnal dated 1831 which, according to Helena, had belonged to Maria Kuisma, the Mar'ämmä of the story. When he was finished, people came to look more closely at the book and to copy genealogical information into their own notebooks. After coffee and cake was served, the event was over.

Karelian House Society

Some of what Helena wrote involves contextual information understood easily by the family and other Finnish speakers through the language, so that they would not even think to explain it at the family reunion. In this narrative there are two important contextual references, one to the naming system and the other to residence patterns. Both refer to the larger structure of the Karelian *suurperhe*, or extended family. The Karelian *suurperhe* shares some of Claude Lévi-Strauss's distinctions for what constitutes a house society: the house has a name which is linked to location; it is perpetual over time so that in the absence of a son, the son-in-law succeeds his father-in-law; the group traces their descent from ancestors who founded the houses; it is not individuals who act, it is the house which is subject to rights and duties; and the naming system is combinatorial or features periodic returns (Lévi-Strauss 1999 [1979]: 163–87). A 'dialectic of filiation and residence' is common in house societies and descent cuts across different modes, transmitting material and immaterial wealth down a real or imaginary line, which is expressed in the language of kinship (ibid.: 174).

Patronymic names were used in recording the Lutheran Church records and the naming system featured periodic returns. The Karelian custom was to name the oldest son after the paternal grandfather (Voionmaa 1969 [1915]: 191) and a younger son was often named for the maternal grandfather, although this system was changing at the end of the nineteenth century. The same naming system could be used for girls. Since the name of the earliest residents often became the name of the village, and everyone commonly shared the name of the house and the village, it is important to know the patronymic in order to trace a family's genealogy. Helena uses the patronymics so there is information about three generations in her account. More importantly, she tells the names of the mothers and the place where they were born because, although many women moved to live with their husbands at marriage, it was possible that a man would move in with his wife. From Helena's story, we know that Tuomas Matinpoika Rantalainen was the son of Matti and that his mother was Helena, born in Rätynkylä. Likewise Helena's mother, Anni Aatamintytär Wornio, was the daughter of Aadam Wornio and Mari, born at Worniola. Since the church records, some of the oldest and most complete records in Europe, link a birth to a place, place is important for tracing the genealogical record, in particular because of residence patterns after marriage.

A second important distinction in the language is the term *kotivävy*, found twice in the narrated genealogy and four times in the researched genealogy. *Kotivävy* means literally 'son-in-law-at-home', which indicates that the customary residence pattern – wife moving to husband's house – was not followed. Instead, the husband moved to the wife's house, where he became a full participant with equal inheritance rights as a son, provided there was no son at the house (Voionmaa 1969 [1915]: 390). When he left home, the *kotivävy* brought his inheritance of personal items with him, such as clothes, a horse, some cows, tools and whatever he might need for his work (ibid.: 379).

This residence pattern was not uncommon in Karelia. According to Voionmaa, the swidden method of agriculture, relying on slash and burn to clear fields, was labour intensive (1969 [1915]: 108) and residence patterns were adjusted more because of labour requirements than because of inheritance itself, although the movement of men did alleviate pressures on the land if a family had many sons. In the narrated story, Antti and Mari Kuisma had only one daughter, Katri, so her husband Samuli Inkinen moved to Kuismala No. 1 as *kotivävy*. In turn, Katri and Samuli had only one daughter, Wappo, whose husband Tuomas Rantalainen came as *kotivävy*. This is where Samuli Rantalainen was born on 2 August 1878. After Wappo died, Tuomas stayed on and brought his second wife, Anni Wornio, to this house. Samuli Rantalainen, named for his maternal grandfather, became the *isäntä* of Kuismala No. 1 through his mother Wappo and her mother Katri, although he later moved to another farm.

Claude Lévi-Strauss claims that house societies are marked by dualism and a tension between patri- and matri- principles. The *kotivävy* reveals a point of tension in the Karelian system. Although he succeeds his father-in-law, his children succeed him in their mother's house and kin group. The ideal Karelian *suurperhe* has been described as being patrilineal, patrilocal and patriarchal (Mannila 1969: 10). In fact descent could swing between the two sides. In patrilineal systems the wife-taker claims the child for his group. In house societies, there is the possibility for the wife-giver, the maternal grandfather, to claim the child (Lévi-Strauss 1999 [1979]: 186). Väinö Voionmaa (1969 [1915]: 471) insists that the *suurperhe* was not a kinship or land ownership institution but an economic institution for joint production and consumption in swidden agriculture. This, and Matti

Sarmela's (1987: 258) speculation that Finnish swidden society was matri-archal, is not at odds with Lévi-Strauss's idea of house society, remember-ing that 'the transmission of material and immaterial wealth is expressed in the language of kinship or affinity, and more often, of both' (1999 [1979]: 174).

Helena mentions that ten people lived in the house of her childhood. According to Voionmaa, there could be as many as sixty people in the *suurperhe* (1969 [1915]: 409). There was a strict division of labour by gen-der so that men worked in the fields and forests and with their horses, while women worked at the house and yard, cared for their cows, and helped in the fields. Both male and female work was crucial for the household and men and women remarried if widowed because the house 'needed an *emän-tä*' as Helena writes, or conversely an *isäntä*, so that the hired hand, Aadam Kuisma, married the widow Jortikka.

The *isäntä* held an important position as the head of the house, especially in earlier centuries. The house carried his name and if the *isäntä* changed, the house name changed (Voionmaa 1969 [1915]: 188). The *isäntä* was responsible for paying the taxes and the rent on the land to the Swedish Crown, although these fees were split within the house among the mem-bers. The requirements of shared economy and work were more important than inheritance, which tended to be personal, and the death of an *isäntä* or *emäntä* caused more problems regarding authority and responsibility than regarding actual land or house ownership. Ownership of property and inheritance laws were clearly delineated and focused on private items and what one had created through one's own labour. The *talo*, or house, was a communal space, shared by the extended family. However, each nuclear family had a small building outside called an *aitta*, where personal goods were stored and where people could sleep in the summer. Each person had their own bed and clothes and women had their own jewellery, linens, cat-tle, and two or three sheep, which they brought to the marriage as their dowry. The dowry cows (and sheep) remained the woman's property although the house might have its own cows too. Her cows were returned to the house of her parents if she died without children (ibid.: 485). Unmarried girls were entitled to the same goods as married daughters even if they stayed at home (ibid.: 488). Men had their clothes, horse, and rights to the forests and fields that they worked (ibid.: 368) although Karelian women also had rights to land through inheritance, especially if they worked it (ibid.: 492). A woman's daughters would inherit from their moth-er and a father would pass his goods along to his sons. An old couple or person with no family could adopt a younger man, an *ottopoika*, who would care for them until death and then inherit from them (ibid.: 373). If a husband died and the couple was childless, the woman moved home again since it was expected that a widow would be taken care of by her son.

Childless widows often worked at their brother's home and her brother would pay for her funeral (ibid.: 505–506).

Mar'ämmä and El'ämmä of the narrative were the widows of two brothers, Antti and Hemmi Kuisma. These two brothers were the two *isäntäs* of Eskola; their wives were the *emäntäs*, the women in charge. The *suurperhe* was most frequently headed by two brothers, although it could be a father and son or even a man and woman not related to each other. The *suurperhe* included male hired hands and female servants. 'Loose' men or women who were employed seasonally in the farm and forestry work were counted also as part of the house. Voionmaa's data indicates that there was a high percentage (80–97 percent in 1901) of rented land on the Karelian Isthmus and around Viipuri so that there was little possibility in this region for servants and hired men to go off and establish their own farms (1969 [1915]: 401–402). By 1901 there was a decline in the *suurperhe* because of changes in land ownership, agricultural practices and other opportunities for work. Nevertheless, the numbers were still high in rural areas around Viipuri and Kuopio (ibid.: 414).

When I wrote an article based on these materials (Armstrong 2000), I used the name Rantalainen and the house name Kuismala No.1 from the church records. After the article was published, Rauno Pärssinen translated it into Finnish. Ilmari Kuisma, Helena's youngest son, read it and wrote two pages of comments. He objected to the names Rantalainen and Kuismala No.1, and his corrections reveal how the logic of house society prevails over the logic of blood relations. Ilmari corrected the house name to Eskola. It was the Karelian practice to name a house for the first name of the founding male.[19] In the church records, the marriage of Eskill Nilsson Kuisma and Catharina Andersdr. Janduin on 10 December 1811 is the earliest record I find in Kirvu.[20] Eskill in Swedish is Esko in Finnish – the name he would have been called – and the house was named Eskola after him. Following the logic of house society, filiation and transmission went through Eskola, not family names; the blood relative concept was weaker in Karelian house society than it might be in Finnish kinship reckoning today.

The *suurperhe* changed by the end of the nineteenth century although the gendered division of labour continued as well as certain rights and obligations regarding property. The narrated genealogy is an example of how people lived in the *suurperhe*, how the houses worked, and how members split off and came back together through marriage. The narratives exemplify rules that are relevant for the present by analogy, even though they are not directly reproducible. Valerio Valeri (1990: 157) recognised that an event in the present can stand for one in the past and be treated as its sign either metonymically (because they belong to the same syntagmatic chain) or metaphorically (because they belong to the same paradigm). However, there is a further distinction because of the genealogical 'I'. Family members are linked metonymically as part of the list of names. They are also linked in the turn from the indexical to the genealogical 'I'. This is different from the way other people relate to the genealogical narrative through metaphor. Other Karelians can relate to the narrative metaphorically, by analogy; these ancestors are not 'mine' but 'mine' also lived in Karelian house society and have been exiled from 'our' place. However, that is another order of 'we'.

Names and people were closely linked to place. There were no strangers in Inkilä and this is part of the subtext of displacement. To be evacuated was to break these structures and ties that crosscut the community. The names stand in the church record, much as the oral genealogies placed the Bemba and gave legitimacy to their social structure. Classificatory kinship and positioned succession were key signs in the Bemba system; in Karelia, house names, house society and genealogical charts and narratives represent and legitimate a community that once existed there.

Genealogical narratives refer to a collectivity of people who may not be known to the present-day subject. This collectivity is not necessarily the nation state; it often lies outside the realm of governments, national territory and notions of citizenship. Sylvi's husband, Arvi Pärssinen, expressed this when he wrote, 'Whether Swedish or Russian, there have been Pärssinens in the church and tax records of Pyhäjärvi [Karelia] since 1594' (Rauno Pärssinen 1992: 4). Genealogies emphasise origins and continuity and therein lies the symbolic message, a claim to place. This is a reason why they are important for diasporic groups. The situation of diaspora helps to clarify that a genealogical 'we' is a particular 'we'. A transference of a different order happens for the genealogical 'I' to become a national 'we'.

5
KINSHIP AND NATION

In the last chapter the genealogical narratives did not include references to a national community. And yet people were living within economic and political structures that influenced their lives. When Arvi Pärssinen wrote about his family living in Karelia for five hundred years, he wrote that his ancestors can be found in the church and tax records. The Karelian population was governed for centuries by one empire or another. As I have mentioned, the Swedish Lutheran Church records are extensive and these records were part of a system to monitor the population for taxation and for recruiting soldiers for the army of the Swedish king. In a study of a village in Germany, based on extensive church records, David Sabean (1990) found that marriage and inheritance were central events in the ability of families to amass and distribute property.[1] Likewise, marriage was an important moment of contractual exchange in Karelian village life and one that brought people into contact with the laws of the church and empire. It was a legitimate (heterosexual) union that defined roles and determined the status of children. In that sense, it established a grid for social relations (Godelier 1998). As expected, there is some evidence of governing institutions in family stories regarding marriage (church) and inheritance (taxation).

There is no doubt that people live within conjunctures of particular historical and economic events. I do not want to downplay this aspect, but there is simply not much about it in the memoirs. There are a few references to institutional structures and national politics and these are positioned through referential language; much depends on knowing the historical context.

In a book about fertility and demographic change, Jane and Peter Schneider (1996) outline historical events which influenced class structure and the ideology of family life in Sicily. They describe the effects of capital-ism on class structure and the hegemonic discourses about sexuality that circulated in Europe and influenced private lives. They conclude that lower birth rates occurred in Sicily among the *bracciante* class only when con-trolling birth rates was perceived as 'maintaining or achieving a culturally desired – that is, respectable – standard of living' (1996: 272). More gener-ally, they conclude that innovations come from multiple internal and exter-nal sources and are 'selected or rejected and substantially reworked in local context' (ibid.: 273). This material makes much the same point, without the emphasis on class: that multiple influences are reworked in the local con-text. The structure of the narratives is a clue as to how these processes happen.

The genealogical narratives recount the story of the family. When nation-al events are mentioned they are peripheral; they are brought into the nar-rative, they do not determine it. But one further caveat: genealogical narra-tives are about kinship and kinship is a symbolic system that can include or evade the nation state.

Getting Married

At the end of the nineteenth century in Karelia there were new opportuni-ties for education and changes in land ownership, which led to new busi-ness possibilities and the emergence of a rural upper-middle-class popula-tion. These changes are apparent in Helena's life story when she talks of her marriage to Israel. After marriage the young couple lived in the house called Poja-Aatam for six years. Then they borrowed money and moved into their own small house. They were distinguished from their neighbours because they were not dependent solely on farming, although they still grew crops and managed land. Helena's schooling was very important to her and this too distinguished her from some women of her generation. She enjoyed going to school and later she made sure that her two daughters were sent for higher education, while the sons were trained to follow their father in business. Her love of education was a story that was repeated at the fami-ly reunion by her grandchildren, particularly her granddaughter Pirkko, who knew her well.

Helena's parents were uneducated, as was Samuli. Tuomas had basic read-ing and writing skills, while Anni could read and write only her name. When the children were young, Anni sat on the bed every night and taught them prayers and songs from the Bible and other religious books. They were also taught by travelling teachers who went from house to house and received room and board in return for teaching the children to read and write. And then, exceptionally, when the church opened a school (*kansakoulu*) in Kirvu,

Helena was the first student from Inkilä. She attended this school from 16
September 1895 to 8 May 1897, completing the four-year course in two
years. This was a high point in Helena's life; she loved school, 'it was for
me a very wonderful time, when I was a student for the whole week' (HK,
p. 51).

Remembering the general through a particular incident, she describes
how she and her sister Katri walked the ten kilometres to school each week
in the snow. Their father gave them twenty-five kopeks to buy pretzel-
shaped buns at Matti Lähde's store. A long walk in a snowstorm and
another special event stand out from winter 1895–96:

> The male teacher (Antti Juho Wartiainen) took those students who had skates
> ice-skating at Kirkkojärvi [Church Lake]. Somehow the teacher went too close
> to the mouth of Alajoki[2] [river] and fell in. He cried for help but the students did
> not know what to do. There were no boats around. People who came to help him
> threw ropes to the drowning one, but even when he had a rope in his hand, he
> could not hold on because his hands were so frozen already. Finally the son of
> Jaakko Wiime's Minna [*Wiimein Jaakon Miina*], a poor widow, (I do not remem-
> ber his name), took a rope, went near the open water and tied the rope around
> the teacher's hands and pulled him out. After that the teacher gave the boy nice
> clothes and fed him dinner every day all winter.   (HK, p. 51)

After school ended, and required in order to be married in the church,
Helena attended confirmation classes in Kirvu. As was the custom, Helena
was expected to go for two weeks in autumn, 1898 and two weeks in
spring, 1899. However, her father died on Sunday night in September
before the classes began on Monday. She joined the classes late and
returned home for her father's funeral, which is noted simply: 'my father
was buried on Michaelmas'.[3] One year later on Michaelmas Helena was
engaged to Israel Kuisma. The 'I' of the story provides continuity over time
into the present; national events inserted into the story are highlighted. The
title is Helena's.

Getting Married

> My husband Israel Aataminpoika Kuisma, is also born in Kirvu's Inkilä [on the]
> 28th day of June 1876. We were, with my husband, hearth neighbours [*tulisija*]
> as the old people say, only the border fence in between.[4] There it was easy to get
> to know each other already since childhood. Already while on the way to school
> this neighbour's son, Poja-Aatam's Israel, had been watching this lively girl from
> the window of his house along the road, thinking, as he later told to me, that if
> he had dared to he would have asked his father for a horse and driven me to the
> church [village] every Monday morning.
>
> There was innocent dating developing between us, even an exchange of letters.
> I saved a small bundle of love letters in the drawer of the chest of drawers *until
> almost to the war time* but then I destroyed them.
>
> In the spring at seventeen years old I finished confirmation school, our engage-

ment was made public on Michaelmas Sunday in 1899 and in the fall, on 5th November 1899, we had a wedding. The farewell party [was] in my home and the wedding in the groom's home. The short distance from us [our house] to the neighbouring house was done in a solemn manner by foot, first the marriage broker [*puhemies*], then the bridal pair, then the men on the groom's side, the singers [*nuoteet*], the bridesmaids [*kaaseet*], and then in a row the others according to their rank. Entering the *tupa* the people waiting for us sang '*Koko maailma iloit' mahtaa*' ['The Whole World Rejoices']. From that song we have had joy many times though I do not say it mockingly; at that time it was reverence.

I received from Israel handsome presents: silk scarves, a golden brooch which had a cross, a heart, and an anchor,[5] a watch with a long chain and rings so broad that even the wedding pastor Paavo Pakkanen admired them. *These lovely rings I gave in 1940 to a nationwide collection and received iron rings in return.* The wedding dress was beautiful, light grey cashmere, on the shoulders fashionable 'puffy sleeves', in front small pleats and lace. The skirt was made of several panels, almost full length.[6]

I kept my wedding dress in our clothes *aitta* up until the 1920s. Then the dress suddenly disappeared. My daughter Toini secretly took this protected dress, ripped open the seams, and cut it with scissors for doll clothes.

The silk scarves frayed, so that one hardly could touch them with [one's] hands anymore. The thick black scarf frayed in many pieces. The silver grey woven-patterned scarf has remained (in one piece). I gave to my daughter Sylvi.[7]

So I became Poja-Aatam's daughter-in-law [*miniä*] for almost six years and good it was. My mother-in-law, though she was my husband's stepmother, had a nice attitude towards me but my father-in-law was very often hostile towards me. I think I even know the reason. My father and my father-in-law, the border neighbours, had developed a disagreement about something pointless and about that I think there was enough grudge even against me.

Living in a big family did not please us however. We broke off from the big Poja-Aatam in 1906 and bought a small cottage near it. We did not have a lot of money and we had to borrow 50 marks from Juho Hänninen for supplies from the shop.

My husband Israel had never liked farm work. He wanted a different career which would suit better his lively nature. Already when young he had been interested in a businessman's career. First he established a water mill with Tuomas Lankinen and acquired at the same time in his possession the whole *Myllykoski* [Mill Rapids] estate. He also supplied timber to St Petersburg [*Pietari*][8] and *after the border closed* (between Finland and the Soviet Union) *to the state of Finland.*

In St Petersburg at that time there was a high demand for firewood. Israel began to buy their forests in gross from the landowners.[9] In addition he made delivery contracts with the sellers of forests. During the economic booms he bought in and his working sites extended to all of central Karelia. He had pine and birch *halkos* [firewood][10] cut and transported by horses to the railway station storage areas to dry. The dry pine halkos were transported by train to St Petersburg to warm up the bakers' ovens and the birch halkos to heat up the houses. The Russians were in general fair buyers. In St Petersburg Israel had his own halko storage and a multi-lingual man selling halkos to buyers. The roubles he earned he first exchanged to gold and the gold in Viipuri to [Finnish] marks. At its largest [when it was most expanded], in Israel's forest business 1,500 men and 750 horses worked [hustled].

Israel made it to every place where it smelled of money: buying the forests, having them cut down, measured, and paying salaries. As his purse he had a money bag reaching up to his elbow. As the reason for the length of the bag, he gave the fact that the fingers were never able to reach to the bottom of it. (HK, pp. 53–54)

As the boys grew up, Israel expanded his mill so that at the time of war in 1939 we had two modern grain mills. (HK, p. 55)

This is generally an account of how they set up their family in a separate house, how they moved into business and no longer lived in the *suurperhe* farm-orientated household. But the description of the marriage ceremony reflects communal practices. The couple was engaged on Michaelmas. As Ascension Day (*helatorstai*) in May marked the time to get ready for summer, so Michaelmas marked the time to get the crops in and to get ready for winter in the annual cycle (Vilkuna 1994 [1950]: 278). It was a time for the autumn harvest festival, a time to move the cows and horses to their inside stalls, and a time for marriages and engagements. On Michaelmas Sunday, the pattern was to attend a service at the church, then to move outside and have a market, music and dancing on the church hill. Helena mentions the *puhemies*, the man who made the marriage arrangements between the families, and also the *kaaseet*, or bridesmaids. The *kaase* was a young married woman, usually a relative of the girl, who spoke to the boy for the girl when they met at the church hill. There is a description of this in a diary passage from another native of Kirvu, Aino Heikkonen, born in 1901 (quoted by Vilkuna 1964: 169):

There [at the church festival on church hill] the girls and the boys had the possibility to meet each other. The girls were accompanied by somebody married, a young woman, often a relative. This '*kaase*', which was how the chaperon of the girls has been called here, led and kept up the discussion with the boys and replied on behalf of the girls to the boys' witty remarks. The *kaase* also told the young men to buy gifts for the girl, at the stalls of the gift-peddlers, who always were present at these kinds of gatherings [of the people]. A popular girl was able to get a large bundle of gifts to take home. The boys took the girls home in their carts and often raced the carts on the road.

The two-part marriage system described by Helena was very common. Ilmar Talve's general description can be compared to Helena's specific description. Individual tastes and styles were part of general patterns in Karelia.

According to ancient tradition, best preserved in Eastern Finland (as in Russian Karelia), the first part of the wedding, the *läksiäiset* [farewell party] at the bride's home, was relatively brief. The bride's and the groom's relatives congregated in separate groups. The groom's party (the *hakujoukko*) usually set out for the bride's home in the evening. Two of them were sent to the bride's home as peace-seekers (*rauhananojat*). On the arrival of the groom's party, led by the spokesman, the spokesman proclaimed his mission in solemn formulaic language. The groom then had to seek out the bride, who did not immediately appear. Following a joint meal, they at once set off for the groom's home, where the wedding festivities began that very same night.   (Talve 1997: 196)

Although Helena describes her wedding as part of the traditions of Inkilä, these customs were part of centuries-old cycles of work and ritual activity, which the church gradually incorporated into its calendrical year. Kustaa Vilkuna traces the wedding scarves to old European marriage patterns, where a tent or cloth was put over the couple in order to mark the transition to married life and the significance of reproduction (1964: 234). Such continuities constituted the fabric of social life in villages like Inkilä.

Israel was an active businessman and an involved member of the community. He was a founding member of the Workers' Association and was elected to the Board of Education in 1905. He read many books and newspapers and people often asked his help in their business affairs. He read the Finnish law books so he often gave his opinion, 'even if the judges did not appreciate [look with a good eye on] this self-taught lawyer'.

My husband was very progressive. For this reason we had the first radio in the village. People from the village gathered to listen to church services on Sundays on it. Israel also had a typewriter. We bought the first '*voorti*' [Ford car] in the village. Our daughter Sylvi was Inkilä's first high school [*lukio*] graduate. Very early I got the first electric iron and the whole village knew when I was ironing because then almost everybody else was cut off [without] electricity. So weak was our electric company.   (HK, p. 55)

Israel's 'business blood' made him always move to a new home. When he had a good opportunity he sold the old one and we just had to pack our things and move. He did not ask me about these things. This was hard and stressful for the mother of the family. Seminar [*seminaari*][11] was only a far-away dream for me but I still wanted to read a lot. Thankfully, Israel valued reading and keeping up with the news [current events]. We got many newspapers and magazines at home, also some for me.   (HK, p. 55)

After this, she lists the six houses that they lived in at one time or another. And then there is mention of the evacuation: 'Now we took a sigh of relief and wished that we would not move anymore anywhere. And we did not move anymore, until we had to move out of the way of the war' (HK, p. 56).

As part of the national politics of the newly independent nation, the Finnish border was closed in the 1920s and trade with the Soviet Union ended. This meant that Israel and his sons focused on the grain mills and a sawmill that they owned. About 1926 things began to go badly in the family economy and, although not found in these memoirs, the family story is that Israel spent six months in jail because he had continued to trade in St Petersburg after the border closed. It was a time of financial depression in Inkilä. Helena does not explain exactly what happened; she describes instead the view from her position. Hers is a story of betrayal and her attempts to keep everyday matters under control.

> Israel's business affairs were not going as well as before. A general depression had come and many households were having money troubles. Selfish people started to take advantage of Israel's reputation and credibility as a 'good man'. No matter what kind of good-for-nothing man from somewhere,[12] then with the bottle, my husband would write his name on the credit note,[13] believing in the man's honesty. The credit sums got to be very large. Also his business partners used him as a straw-man and he got a scapegoat [cheater's] reputation when other people's betrayals were discovered. I heard a few conversations from which I discovered how my husband was being betrayed. Without getting too involved in these, I'll only say that the dirty avalanche that was threatening our home and economy almost crushed everything. My husband finally understood his position and gave everything to our son Eino when he gave up his business. But in name only.
>
> These times were difficult in our home. I was living every day under pressure. There was nothing else I could do except, quietly suffering, carry our family's burden and get the children to school.   (HK, pp. 56–57)

She ends this section by noting that the villagers were gossiping so much about this that she stopped inviting people for coffee except certain close neighbours, such as her sister Katri. Social relations with some members of the community were broken because of these events. Inkilä thus remembered was not perfect; it was a community where there was both harmony and conflict.

Inheritance

The family economy has to be deduced from the life story and letters; it is not often talked about explicitly. However, in the comments about the house and inheritance, and later about reciprocity between households, the reader gets a sense of this family's position in village society. Differences in status, as lived, are played down in Inkilä 'as remembered'.

The land maps for Päivölä and the mills have been saved by the family. These are the official Finnish state ownership documents issued in Viipuri; in a handwritten addition to the map, next to the house name, someone has written 'owned by the Kuisma family', not previously owned.[14] These papers are no longer valid as state documents; however they remain a significant sign of the place that once was theirs.

Helena and Israel were successful at establishing their nuclear family in a large house of their own in Inkilä. They could provide an education for their daughters and a business inheritance for their sons. Both daughters attended secondary school (high school) in Käkisalmi, and Sylvi went on to study architecture in Helsinki. Through business and education they established themselves as middle-class residents of Inkilä. When the Winter War began in 1939, Israel was sixty-three years old and Helena was fifty-seven. They had begun to turn their affairs over to their sons and they would have expected to distribute their estate equally to all their children.

The Finnish population had been strictly controlled by laws about property and taxes ever since the sixteenth-century consolidation of the Swedish Empire. Helena and Israel were subject to the marriage law of 1889, which stipulated that husband and wife owned property jointly although it was normally under the control and management of the husband. However, it was possible for either spouse to own individual property if it had been acquired before marrying or if he or she inherited it before or during the marriage.[15] Under customary law in Karelia it was the right of a woman to be given a dowry by her father upon marriage and, if her father was dead, by her brother (Voionmaa 1969 [1915]: 402).[16] A husband had no rights to his wife's dowry; it was her property to pass along to her daughters. Helena received the customary presents from her husband. The rings were important to her because they were outstanding enough to be commented on by others, and because they were part of her personal property that she donated to the national government to help the war effort.[17]

Under the 1889 Marriage Law – and therefore different from the customary *suurperhe* practice – after the death of one spouse, the widow or widower inherited half and the children inherited the other half. It was not uncommon for one child to inherit the farm and pay off the remaining children for their part of the estate and it was likely that daughters would receive their share of the inheritance in the form of livestock or money. Päivölä and the mills were the core of Israel and Helena's estate. Occasionally Helena writes to her daughters about the house and money affairs and these few comments indicate that the parents were planning to distribute their estate among the children.

In 1939 Helena reports that they are considering the sale of Päivölä. The last comment in her letter refers to inheritance matters and possibly to giving the two daughters money for their shares:

> Now our men again have a fever to sell the house. I am not against it at all. My age seems to go already there [to be such that] that doesn't require more than 'walking quietly' ['*hiljaa kävelemään*']. Antrea's sugar factory's boss offered 375,000 marks, but these men left it at 440,000 marks. I don't know if he will come over a third time. I have mentioned your and Sylvi's business [affairs]. (Helena to Toini, 27.5.1939)

In September, just before the war, Helena discusses the family economy in a letter, this time about the cost of the mills and how they have had to sell some land in order to make the mills more productive. Helena has a central role in the family economy, she pays debts and arranges credit, and again she mentions money for the two daughters.

> The mill men [*myllymiehiä*] are here as in other autumns. Both mills go around three times [shifts]. Now the money will come. Now I am going to seriously say to Eino that before Christmas we have to give both girls some money because now is the time to give [money]. I have not asked money for the girls though I mentioned earlier to Sylvi that I would do it, but then I had to send 30,000 marks to Sweden for the machines. I should have sent more there too. Now today I had to pay a 60,000 mark debt and then took 20,000 anew. I do think that this will work out but during the summer I thought it could become ugly. It helped to be able to sell these lands, *Suolahen* to Laurila's Tuoma[18] for 62,000 marks, fields to Matti Uimo for 23,000 marks, and fields to Topia's Tuoma for 32,000 marks. I don't want to check up on them [her sons], but I do promise that you will not be without anything.   (Helena to Toini, 25.9.1939)

The war changed all these plans although the family was eventually compensated by the state for their loss of property in Karelia. There is a final letter about the material value of the house from Helena to Sylvi after the war and the death of Israel, in which she relates what she knows and reveals that she has given directions about how the money issues should be resolved. The end of this letter again links kinship, people and place, but now, away from the place, 'you bump into people' without knowing that they are 'your own'.

> Matters of Compensation. I don't know anything else about those things except what Ismo [son] wrote to me. Eino [oldest son] had invited him there and had given him money – 17,000 marks - and Eino had said that the money from the mill had not come yet. They had gotten 100,000 marks from Päivölä. That was officially decided[19] and after that it [the total] would be 908,000 marks. I wrote to Eino about this earlier that the money of Arvi and Pekurinen should be given out first, and even a bit more.[20] After that there has to be a legal division with everyone and you and Toini can't be without any either.
>
> Esko [Eino's son] came here before and gave me 2,000 marks and now during the second week he gave me 4,000 marks.
>
> Ismo sent me a package last Saturday that contained all sorts of things. He had bought me dress cloth and sent money to pay the seamstress in the same package and told me to take it right away to the seamstress. I took it today to Jokela and it happened so nicely that the seamstress lady was from Hakolahti, her husband is a Suni, himself from Löylölä. That's what it is here in the world. You bump into people from your own village without knowing it.   (Helena to Sylvi, 25.11.1946)

Except for a few years during their childhood, Helena and Israel spent their entire lives together and yet they are buried far apart. Helena's grand-daughter explained how the displaced family moved around Finland after the evacuation. The oldest son lived in Suonenjoki, so Israel was buried there. After the death of Israel in 1946, Helena moved to live with her other sons and their families. In each place she lived in a small room. 'You can't imagine how modest she was, this woman who had once been the *emäntä* of a large farm and involved with all the business!' her granddaughter exclaimed. But things were never the same for the two oldest sons away from Inkilä. They were not skilled for other industry, they found themselves working in factories with strong labour unions whose politics they did not share, and they moved frequently in search of a better situation. By contrast the daughters and the younger sons fared better because they were trained in professions and could move into appropriate careers. The moving, and certainly the dislocation, is what Sylvi meant when she wrote that Helena 'died as an evacuee'.

Exchange and Transmission

The stories of Tuomas and Samuli Rantalainen and their horses, the old widows and the hymn book, Helena's education and passionate interest in folk traditions, and Israel's business problems were repeated to me on the trip to Inkilä, during visits, or at the family reunion. These are the stories that circulate. There is not much specific information about income or property in the life history because a life history is not intended to be a strict record of daily events.

Discourse is in the world; it reveals key conceptual ideas and it has to make sense to others. In the genealogical story, the experiences of the extended family link the group to a social structure, to particular cultural practices, and to a place. The stories give clues about centuries-old patterns of work and social organisation that underlie Karelian village society. When people talk about their ancestors today they know only part of the genealogical information and little about the social organisation. Their interest is in personalities and the fact that their ancestors lived at Eskola, Pyymäki and Päivölä. This information is replicated at the family reunion in a few stories about individuals and by showing everyone the iconic sym-bol of the hymnal. The stories and the material items sign membership in the group.

The loss of Inkilä was a material loss for these people. However, today they are more likely to emphasise the continuity and duration of their link to Karelia. This confirms the argument of Maurice Godelier (1999: 36) that society is founded on both contractual exchange and noncontractual transmission. Marriage alliances in Inkilä were part of a system of reciprocity and contractual exchange of long duration that was influenced by historical events originating beyond the region. New class structures emerged at the end of the nineteenth and the beginning of the twentieth century which influenced marriage and property relations. The genealogical narratives refer to these but their primary message is not about productive relations. Here Godelier's criticism of Lévi-Strauss is relevant: 'He has left unmentioned or has diminished everything in kinship which falls outside the area of exchange, which partakes of (imaginary) continuity, which is rooted in time, in the blood, in the soil, and so on' (ibid.: 35). It is, in fact, these noncontractual ideas of time, blood and soil that give meaning to the genealogies now. Genealogy is about transmission, and 'transmission is not exchange' (Godelier 1998: 408). Transmission is that added-on value given to genealogy by family members, the symbolic dimension of kinship.

The stories are persistent; they focus on the family's experiences, and national institutions and events are merely inserts. In a common model of imagined communities the nation absorbs kinship, for example in the way that the social welfare state absorbs family obligations. Etienne Balibar, using France as the model, argues that welfare state planning makes possible a nationalisation of the family, which in turn makes it possible to imagine the symbolic kinship of the national community (1996: 144).[21] The welfare state is very effective at connecting the family to the nation because it provides services formerly provided within the family. However, as Maurice Godelier argues, the state is not an abstraction; the state governs and it is what those who govern make it (1999: 3). Put another way, the state is increasingly called upon to 'recompose society' because a capitalist economy breaks the social fabric (ibid.: 2). What the state provides, and how it influences the population as a result, is a problem of kinship/state relations but it is different from the symbolic domain of kinship.

David Schneider originally made the point that the pure domains of kinship, nationality and religion indicate domains of 'diffuse enduring solidarity' (1970: 120) and his analysis of American kinship has been applied to the study of European kinship by others. For Schneider, kinship has the possibility to be inclusive or exclusive. Marilyn Strathern (1982) uses a similar argument to discuss kinship and village boundaries in England, although in a later work (Edwards and Strathern 2000: 158) the practical social relations and self-limiting aspects of kinship are emphasised.[22] In their work, Jane and Peter Schneider (1996) accept David Schneider's basic classification system of European–American kinship (as a 'native' system of classification) and show how it was reproduced in the discourse about fertility in Italy. John Borneman (1992) also recognises the central nature of kinship as an institution, and its relation to the nation and nation building in

Germany. Borneman argues that the state, mainly through family law, creates a sense of being '*zu Hause*' (at home), being among kin, in order to create a nation that people can call their own. Evidence of this is that people retell their histories in terms congruent with those the state uses (1992: 287). But Borneman finds also that state narratives may be challenged, or at least not accepted by various groups, in which case the state has to refashion the law. The law has to respond in order constantly to maintain the classifications that are used to define group membership regarding kin, nations and states (1992: 304).

In England, Italy, Germany and Finland the organising principles are slightly different and the local interpretations vary according to local experiences. All these studies indicate the central position of kinship and its various economic, legal and symbolic dimensions for the nation state in Europe. The memoirs suggest, however, that one must be cautious about the leap between the levels. For example, like Borneman's findings, Minna Lahti (2001) finds a repetition of state narratives in personal narratives about family violence in Finland and J.P. Roos (1987) has analysed narratives by generation to show how people of the same generation in Finland use similar metaphors and share a similar world view. All three studies generate interesting questions based on narrative materials. But all three use narrative sections as examples of themes, and all use a particular kind of narrative: public narratives, narratives constructed for an interviewer, or narratives written as part of a project. For example, one of Borneman's narratives begins, 'And I have to tell *you* that we were so naïve ...' (1992: 174, my emphasis). The intended audience (you) changes the narratives into what Pierre Bourdieu (1977: 16–22) identifies as outward orientated discourse. It is a different audience from the narratives used here, which are 'among us' and not constructed for another.[23] The different focus can easily lead researchers to conclude that 'memory selectively recalls the past as legitimate history' (Borneman 1992: 285) because the narrative situation requires this type of construction. In these situations, people do join their personal stories to grand narratives; it is how memory is used in this kind of narrative expression. By looking at narratives 'among us', I have been arguing that memory is more complex and this has important consequences for understanding memory and political behaviour.

There is still the problem of how the connection is made through personal experience. Cognitive theory suggests that humans have a model of a domain and use that model conceptually. Accordingly, Mark Turner argues that the metaphor of kin is a basic conceptual metaphor in European and American society, especially regarding the relationship of the parts to the whole (1987: 15–16). Because everyone has knowledge of kinship and everyday experience with it, kinship metaphors are used to understand relationships and to communicate that understanding. Following this logic, the metaphor of kin is a way to understand the relation of individuals to the nation state.

Within the narrow scope of this study, kinship provides a logic and plays a symbolic role in the Karelian diaspora. Genealogical narratives and charts offer the possibility for kinship to expand across time (to include people one has never known) and beyond the boundaries of the nation state. The politics of Karelia were discussed between four of the cousins during lunch at the family reunion. One man began the discussion with the rhetorical question, 'Will we get it back again? The government always promises a solution but they do not produce one.' Everyone at the table had an opinion on the subject – some were more cautious than others – and finally they agreed that there were many problems to solve, for example about the Russian settlers there now and the deteriorated economic situation in Russia, before anyone could think seriously about Karelia again. The 'we' seemed to be 'we Finns' and the 'it' seemed to be Karelia. But the immediate referential group was the group at the table and the family at the reunion. When the man at the table asked rhetorically, 'Will we get it back again?' the 'we' refers to the family at the table, not the 'we' of Finland, and the 'it' is the house and land once owned by the family. Such comments are a reminder that kinship is enduring and expansive, which is why it often causes problems for the nation state, for example regarding immigrants, diasporic communities, and homelands. The practical unit which makes up 'family' is part of particular state practices and structures, but the conceptual grid of 'kinship' extends beyond the spatial-temporal zones of the family as an institution. Benedict Anderson and Maurice Godelier both recognise the importance of imagination – that something added on to practical relations – in society. This added-on aspect of kinship is where one finds the possibility for an imagined community that can inhabit global spaces.[24]

The idea of domain and a metaphorical relationship of the parts to the whole is central to David Schneider's analysis. However, in diasporic situations the family evades national boundaries and the analogical relationship between kin and nation state is not so clear. Perhaps a further distinction made by Roy Wagner (1977) about 'analogic kinship' is useful here. Wagner begins, in contrast to earlier approaches to kinship, with the idea that 'all kin relationships and "kinds" of kinsmen are basically analogous because all incorporate the essence of human solicitude that we call "relating"' (1977: 624). Beginning with similarity, there are culturally specific rules of differentiation which create an analogic 'flow'. In the West, Wagner argues, the marriage of two people (collective joining) creates the appropriate differentiation from which all other relationships 'flow' (ibid.).[25] Marriage in Europe is the re-creation of culturally specific analogical relationships, and it is also central to economic and political relations. The recognition of kinship as an analogical system opens the way to propose a

link between the domains of family and nation. There is one further quali-
fication, however: while the metaphor of kin is a basic conceptual
metaphor, different salient features of the metaphor can be used in different
contexts so it will not necessarily be the same in all situations.[26]

A metaphor is a relation of four units, such that the relation of A to B is
similar to that of C to D. As narratives, genealogy (A) is to family (B) as history (C) is to the nation state (D). Both genealogy and history are constructed through syntagmatic and paradigmatic messages and both offer the
possibility of forming a 'we' community. Genealogy – in chart and narrative form – outlines social relations and the flow of proper kin relations. It
is a charter linking the family to a place and significant structures, but it is
not about the nation state. It is not rigid; it emphasises duration and it outlines the possibilities for proper action. It creates a genealogical 'I' and a
family 'we' that is exclusive and yet expanding. In an analogous way, history that tells a story of human solicitude – such as stories of war – connects the individual to a national 'we'.[27] The next chapter explores how par-
ticipation in certain common historical events contributes to the construction of a national 'we'.

6

WARTIME: A NATIONAL EVENT

❦

One of the attractions of Benedict Anderson's model is his focus on why the nation ('these particular cultural artefacts') arouses 'such deep attachments' and a sense of a community of 'deep, horizontal comradeship' that 'so many millions of people' willingly die for 'such limited imaginings' (1983: 16). For Anderson, the deep connection of the individual – patriotism – centres on language, specifically a mother-tongue 'encountered at mother's knee and parted with only at the grave' (ibid.: 140). I have been arguing that cultural structures and ontological worlds complicate the reasons for deep attachments. But sacrifice, war and death are central moments in forming deep attachments, and in this regard Anderson identified a clear moment when people imagine their membership in a national community.

The last days of living in Inkilä were the last days of the Continuation War. The Soviet Army began a major attack on the Karelian Isthmus on 10 June 1944. The Finnish civilian population began to be evacuated later that month and in September 1944 a peace accord was signed that ceded Finnish Karelia to the Soviet Union. These events are a significant part of the grand narrative of twentieth-century Finnish history. Pierre Nora (1989: 22) proposes that memory attaches itself to sites, whereas history attaches itself to events. But Sylvi made the connection between the events of war and the site of Inkilä by putting them together in her memoirs. The letter excerpts that form the basis of this chapter demonstrate the construction of collective memory and a national 'we'. Specifically, allegiance to a community (patriotism) gains its force through a circulating discourse about the community that both expresses and creates community.

Individual Voices and Collective Memory

During the 1990s the war years were a popular topic in the Finnish media. Almost every documentary shown on television in 1997 as part of Finland's celebration of eighty years of independence (the year's theme was 'Multicultural Finland') had something to do with the war years. The war themes in four of the documentaries resonated with current political discussions in Finland. Sometimes the media presented an image but no commentary, as when one documentary about Finns evacuated to Sweden during the Second World War ended with a picture of Somali refugees walking across the tarmac of Vantaa (Helsinki) airport in the 1990s, silently combining multiculturalism and the common experiences of refugees. A second documentary was about how the Finns moved Russian residents of Karelia into camps during the Continuation War. A third showed old men today in Russian Karelia who had fought in the Finnish army and can now receive Finnish veterans' pensions. The last film in this series (YLE, 15.10.1997) was about Lotta women, young women[1] who served during the war, cooking, nursing, and doing random necessary jobs for the army. For many, it was a significant moment in their lives. In a personal conversation, Meri Viljanen (b. 1919) told me how at the age of nineteen she left her job to volunteer as a Lotta. She, as a city girl, had to learn to chop wood, live in a tent, and do all kinds of work that was new to her. She was not alone; most of the nation was involved in some kind of war-related work. Those girls who were too young, or women who were home with young children, did other work such as knitting socks and mittens for the soldiers. The Lotta organisation was banned after the war as part of the armistice and the women were depicted as being either too politically conservative or as 'loose women' in a world of men.[2] Revealing the morality of the times, as if in anticipation of such comments, Arvi wrote about the Lotta women in his diary:

> There has been a lot of disparaging talk about the Lottas on the front, but probably in vain. Their moral strength is certainly better than on the home front in general. But, whether their presence here is beneficial for their later life, is another question. My impression is that feminine shyness and delicacy disappears here under the conditions at the front. The Lottas tell stories about how those Lottas visiting the front ask, for example, for the toilet. They are told you take care of your needs under a tree you regard as most suitable. The Lottas tell further how they have to take these civilian Lottas for their needs. These are further surprised – 'do we stay so close to the men' – and then the front-line Lottas tell that they themselves don't bother to go even so far away. Ordinary civilised [mannered] women would not talk about these things in the presence of men, but here the women become men. Gender differences seem to be completely forgotten. At least this is my first impression.   (AP diary, 12.12.1941)

The five women interviewed in the documentary wanted to set the record straight about the Lotta contributions to the war effort, which were considerable, as well as to recognise all women's work in the war. One woman, in a long segment of the film, described her job as a nursing assistant. The wounded and dying young men came in waves and it was terribly busy and confusing for the medical staff; the Lotta women tried to do whatever the doctors told them to do. A common job was to prepare the bodies of the men for burial. They washed the body and wrapped it for the wooden coffin. If possible, they collected personal identification and information from the body. The job of the chaplain, as Arvi writes, was to notify the family and return the personal items. He also supervised sending the body home for burial and performed the last rites.

However, the Lotta woman added, many times they did not know who the young man was, or he was too wounded to identify. In that case the body was washed, wrapped, put into a wooden coffin and buried in the nearest churchyard, in the heroes' section. She said that the Lottas wrapped the body 'with love' as a 'mother' or 'sister' would, giving him a last 'embrace', so that he was buried with love and friendship. Without saying explicitly, she told how they buried the soldier as part of a family, in this case the family of Finland, not as someone uncared for. As she narrated this, the film showed rows of crosses for unidentified soldiers in a church cemetery.

Documentaries about the wartime resonate in an audience that has experienced the same events or heard stories about them. The media helps to keep the stories alive, as do collections of family memoirs and photos. Personal letters are an accepted genre in the national discussion of the war years; many families have saved their letters, some have been published as book collections, others have been given to archives. Reading letters almost sixty years later is like catching fragments of a conversation, rather like being there in person, but removed in time. The letters and diaries are at the news end of the pole of discourse; they discuss daily events. In letters, as in daily conversation, what is of interest to people are both the sensible and the meaning of things. Ordinary life is contrasted to the extraordinary because the war created extraordinary situations. The writers do not reflect much on daily experience except in an instrumental way to explain what has been done or what has to be done. When the letters pick up themes of human tragedy or relate to historical or political events they become interesting to non-family members, especially those who have lived through similar events. Then 'we' have the possibility to understand because of 'our' own experiences.

The letters reveal how the writers slide between a nationalist discourse and a religious one. Ideas about God frequently serve as a metadiscursive device, that is, fragments of discourse that exercise regulatory effects over other discourse (Urban 1996). In the letters such ideas appear as: to live properly is to 'live a Christian life', to survive is 'in God's hands' and, in times of suffering people 'carry a heavy burden'. The talk about community gets its power often through tragedy. The language of the letters becomes most nationalistic and religious when the sacrifice of individuals is perceived to be for the survival of the nation. Michael Herzfeld has noted that the warring nation state frequently claims the loyalty of its citizens through the promise of immortality (1997: 82). But these people knew also about sacrifice from the Christian Bible, religious core values that may be connected to political behaviour in some circumstances (Turner 1974). In Helena's letter to Toini, which includes a poem she wrote, she connects herself with other Finnish mothers who are preparing to sacrifice their sons 'in God's name' for 'our country and our people'. Her language also reflects the discourse about nation, which was promoted during the nineteenth-century nationalist movement.

> Now they leave here together: Eino, Wäinö and Itti [three of her four sons]. They go in God's name. I am of course sorry, but also happy that Finnish mothers have such boys who will try to defend the border and save and protect our country and our people.

> Every man, every man, every Karelian man,
> If you are honest and in good shape
> Your country [*maa*] and nation [*kansa*] is calling you,
> Heart, mind and conscience.
> All for one, one for all,
> Every man a brother to another man,
> So stand up every man and defend again
> The country you were born in.

> (Helena to Toini, 9.10.1939)[3]

The Civil War and Its Aftermath

The wars of 1939–44 raised questions about the national community because of events twenty-one years earlier. The Finnish nation state was built on nineteenth-century ideas of the folk but a bitter civil war in 1918, shortly after independence, proved that there was no common folk after all. The wars of 1939–44 rekindled the discourse about community: was there a unified national community to fight the Soviet Union? Questions about the national community were in the minds of these writers and form the background for some of their comments.

By the end of the nineteenth century there was an active nationalist movement, based largely on Finnish language and culture. At the time Finland was a Grand Duchy in the Russian Empire, which gave it a special status, with autonomy in language, education and local political authority.

In fact, the territory of Finland was more developed than many other parts of the Russian Empire. The nationalist movement therefore worked more to educate the peasants and proletariat to become good citizens in the future independent state than to openly promote revolution. The ideal, promoted by statesman-philosopher J.V. Snellman and others, aimed to replace the existing upper-class Swedish language and culture with an upper-class Finnish language and culture. The Swedish elite in Finland took the lead in creating Finnish nationalism, which seems to be an odd position for them. Risto Alapuro (1989) argues that this weak elite needed the support of the peasants against the power of Russia and thus encouraged a national Finnish cultural unity while at the same time preserving sectors of their own cultural heritage and political hegemony.[4] In the nationalist endeavour, the Finnish-language peasants were seen as the core of the nation and the core of Finnish culture. These peasants were to be educated and guided by a patriotic intelligentsia, the local ministers and schoolteachers, in order that they could participate fully in the new nation. The end result would be the creation of a state with a unified national culture, which could better resist threats from either of the two neighbouring powers. The Finnish-language school system, established in 1866, helped to spread nationalism; one of the popular school readers was *Maamme kirja* (The Book of Our Country) by Zachris Topelius, Jr., which began with a line from the Bible.

Finland received its independence on 6 December 1917, shortly after the successful Russian Revolution in November. Although the Finns did not wage a war of independence from Russia, a civil war broke out from January to May 1918 between two factions in Finnish politics, the Reds (left) and the Whites (right). The names for the civil war reveal the different perspectives. It was called the 'war of independence' by some (usually Whites), the 'citizen's war' by others (usually Reds), and the 'Red rebellion' (by Whites), among other names. Briefly and superficially, but true to the way the story is remembered, the Whites were conservative, landed farmers and middle class, while the Reds were made up of social democrats, members of the workers' unions, landless rural farmers, and people sympathetic to international socialism (and therefore the Soviet state). In fact, many people, including these writers, could not be as easily labelled as being on one side or the other. The conflict, which began simply enough when the social democrats did not want to give up certain benefits that they had achieved (Alapuro 1988), quickly escalated into a national crisis. The Whites used the threat of the Soviet Union in their propaganda. They claimed it was a war of independence to preserve Finland's newly achieved state and they were suspicious of any political parties that could be linked with international socialism and the Soviet state.

By all accounts, the Whites were excessively cruel in the final days of the war. Both sides suffered losses during battle, but at the end of the war over

8,000 Red prisoners were executed, while about 12,000 Reds died in prison camps, often due to malnutrition, inadequate hygiene and poor health care (Paasivirta 1988: 145). The Reds were bitter about the excessive cruelty and the two sides remained suspicious of each other for many years. For example, Reds were buried often outside the churchyard at this time, as was the practice for suicides and criminals (Talve 1997: 204). As an easy code during the 1920s, any leftist ideas were read to be anti-nationalist, and any Red was labelled a traitor to the nation. Although the Whites won the relatively short war, the conflict raised severe moral questions in the new nation that were not openly talked about. Some people, such as the cultural-nationalist clergy and schoolteachers, often felt betrayed by the people they had prepared for independence. 'The activities of the educated class in the inter-war period and for a long time after the Second World War can be seen as a reaction to the traumatic shattering of their nationalist-populist self-image in 1918, and as attempts to reconstruct their lost contacts with the people' (Alapuro 1989: 155). Writing in the 1980s as she assembled her papers, Sylvi described her youth and the split in Inkilä, according to dance halls, in the early 1920s:

> We went to dances in the Youth Hall but we did not go to the Worker's Hall. The civil war with the Reds and the Whites was, you see, still too close. I later regretted that division.   (Sylvi's notes, 1992: II)[5]

Sylvi and her husband Arvi were children during the civil war. Later, as students at Helsinki University, they were members of the Academic Karelian Society although they never mention this society directly in the memoirs. The society had its roots in the nationalist movement and was especially promoted through folklore research that found Finnish national cultural roots in Karelia (Sihvo 1973; Wilson 1976). In the late 1920s and during the 1930s this was one of the most active student groups in Finland, quite conservative and later fascist in its politics, and outspoken about its goal of claiming the northern part of Karelia, which had never been part of the Finnish nation state, for Finland. Through images of a Finnish-language homeland in Karelia, the society promoted anti-Soviet activities and supported an attempted military annexation of Karelia during the Continuation War of 1941–44 (Alapuro 1973). The society was so active and threatening to the Soviet Union that it was abolished after the war as part of the terms of the peace agreement with the Soviet Union (as was the Lotta organisation).

These were the politics of the times. Sylvi and Arvi left the university before the militant days of the Academic Karelian Society. But as Karelians and professional clergy and teachers, they worried about a Soviet invasion and they coded their political suspicions in religious terms. Thus, they did not dislike poor people but they were suspicious of people who did not go

to church, who had no religion, such as communists. Frequent stereo-
typed references to 'Ruskies' in the letters repeat that they are 'Godless'
(*'jumalaton ryssä'*).

One of the problems they confronted during the war years was that of
the common soldier, who might very well be from a working-class, social
democratic or Red family. As key members of local society, and as patriots,
they participated fully in the war effort and met many soldiers who came
through their village to the nearby front lines. Finland was hard pressed to
fight a much larger and stronger neighbouring power and everyone had to
be drawn into the war effort. Old assumptions about traitors had to be
adjusted and the idea put forward that everyone would fight for the fatherland. At the end of the Winter War, the government declared a Memorial
Day for all veterans, as Sylvi noted in her diary, using the inclusive 'we'. The
'we' in this segment moves from the national to the church community, to
the family of the minister:

> It is Memorial Day for the dead heroes. Our War Marshall has changed the cer-
> emonies from May 16 to this day. Now we remember all the Finnish people from
> 1918 to this day who have given their lives for their convictions and fatherland,
> also those who died for the Reds in 1918.
> The flags are flying at half-mast. In the church we blessed two dead heroes. In
> the service Arvi did the liturgy and Pastor Lauri Hakamies gave the sermon.
> Cantor Stenberg played the organ. The dead heroes' relatives had their own
> reserved place in the church. Afterwards we had a memorial coffee. The officers
> invited Arvi and me to coffee – in our own dining room. Captain Mäki spoke to
> us and the officers' staff and Lottas gave us a coffee service. It was a surprise.
> (Sylvi's diary, 19.5.1940)

Sivistys

As the nationalist movement progressed at the turn of the century an
emphasis was put on the link between the individual and the national community. Positive values linking God, the fatherland, the Emperor, the family, and cultural and material progress, were preached in churches, youth
associations, and through the popular temperance movement (Alapuro
1989: 151). The Finnish national movement, *Fennomania*, included many
wealthy peasants in the local branches, but above all, the active members
were ministers and elementary school teachers (ibid.).

The letters reveal the enlightenment project so popular at the time among
this group of people. In fact, the teachers and ministers were sometimes
referred to as the 'people's candles'. Their enlightenment project was more
concerned with the development of the folk than with building a bureaucratic nation state. The central values of the enlightenment project were to

improve yourself and to provide for yourself, while at the same time helping your community. Emphasis was put on the idea of *sivistys* – to be cultured, to have manners, to behave properly.

The role of the teachers and clergy was to improve the local population by instilling proper values, for example through school programmes, church school and voluntary associations. Until the end of the Second World War, the educated class was 'a listener and formulator of the nation's voice, an intermediary between nation and state' (Alapuro 1989: 147). There are echoes of these values in Arvi's diary entries for two days in October 1941, while he was serving with the army during a time of heavy losses. In the first entry there is sympathy and admiration for the tough soldiers and in the second, the difference between the clergy and the soldiers regarding alcohol and notions of shame and proper behaviour.

> Our casualties, until now being announced as two dead and six wounded, have been transferred through us. One of the wounded was quite impossible [badly wounded]. 'Damn Russians' the man mumbled every now and then despite [his] bullet-smashed mouth and broken skull.   (AP, diary, 27.10.1941)

> Under-Sergeant Rähkö came from his home leave and brought liquor for the boys of his own parish. Lt. Eskola came to taste it here and seemed to be in a very happy mood already around 3:00. In the same way soldier Tuominen and Rähkö were already quite soft boys. The men don't have enough shame to go somewhere farther away to drink and not to come to the minister [to drink]. The war rips the men of civilisation [*sivistys*] and shame and when liquor is added they become pigs. I thought to give an evening prayer for the battalion but I got into such a bad mood because of the drinking that I will not. It's not worth throwing pearls to pigs. One should be tough about that kind of shamelessness but there one tends to leave it [that's that].   (AP, diary, 30.10.1941)

During the war Arvi had the chance to sit around with the boys (*pojat*) on the few occasions when they could rest. One evening, after sauna and their first chance to change clothes in one-and-a-half months, he recorded this joke, along with his own comments which reveal that he does not think the joke is all that funny.

> The boys can be heard joking about a soldier who, getting home finally after the last war, spent two weeks naked with his wife. That's how love is. Then, after two weeks, the man asked his wife who should first put the pants on. The wife replied that you put them on first because you are used to wearing pants even before [meaning she was not wearing pants while the man was away]. No wonder. Humour is alive, although at times in a rather thick [vulgar] form.   (AP, diary, 18.10.1941)

A similar sense of improvement and proper behaviour can be seen when Sylvi relates what should be done as part of the Lotta programme or when she is critical of the distribution of aid after the war. A more subtle way of teaching involved politeness and etiquette. During the trip to Inkilä in 1997, her son Kari told this anecdote about his mother, which captures the style of the teacher and minister's wife and her insistence on polite behaviour. Typically it is both truthful and humorous and involves a play on language in the use of *hyvä* (good).

> Sylvi offered a *pulla* to a six-year-old village boy and he took it.
> '*Ole hyvä*' (Thank you), Sylvi said. [He should have said it.]
> The boy said nothing and took a bite. '*Ole hyvä*' she repeated.
> Nothing from the boy.
> '*OLE HYVÄ*' (THANK YOU), she said rather sternly.
> Finally the boy, still chewing, said, '*On hyvää*' (It is good).

In the stories the 'we' favours a particular moral position, although it begins to recognise alternative possibilities as the classes came into contact in the war. These writers had opinions about proper social and political behaviour, which they did not hesitate to express in their diaries, letters, and sometimes in public speeches. In Sweden the bourgeoisie of the 1930s was creating patterns of domestic space and ideas of healthful living (Frykman and Löfgren 1987). Some of these ideas were found in Finland as well but the wartime experience, not shared by Sweden, forced the Finnish bourgeoisie to reconsider the class relations of the national community.

Women and Sacrifice in War

This family was fortunate because, although some members were injured, no one was killed. But many Finnish soldiers were killed and these writers heard stories about the tragedies. There are several accounts in the letters and diaries of other women, the mothers and widows, who suffered during the war. The widows with small children had the hardest time and two cases here, the Metsäpirtti widow and the widow of Tauno Hiltunen, are stories that are exemplars of hardship and sacrifice for the nation. In the stories about widows, the references easily slide from family to nation to God, all centring on the idea of sacrifice.

There has been a gender division in the history of women and war, and that is reflected in the letters. After the First World War there were no monuments to the efforts of women in the war. Instead, their contributions were represented as the sacrifices made by widows and mothers (Gillis 1994: 12) or in Australia by the three women who shared the burden of male sacrifice, the mother, the sister/daughter and the wife (Rowlands 1993: 145). After the Second World War, women's efforts came to be recognised in their own right, not just because of their men. It took several decades in Finland, as with the Lottas, for the work of women volunteers to achieve public recognition.[6] But that came later and these stories reflect an era when women exemplify the sacrifice of their men for the country.

At the end of the Winter War the Karelian border was moved, the Soviet army moved west, and the first evacuation of Karelians from the region, including Inkilä, took place. On 5 and 6 March 1940, the Soviet army broke through the Finnish defence line at Viipuri. On 6 March 1940 the Finnish government began to negotiate peace and a new boundary with the Russians. The government feared that the small Finnish army and population could not hold out much longer and, as Sweden and Norway refused to allow the transit of Allied supplies, the Finnish leadership hoped to preserve what they could of their territory and their sovereignty. Prime Minister Risto Ryti (who became president in December 1940) travelled first to Stockholm, then to Moscow; Sylvi heard the news on the policeman's radio while she and the children were living as evacuees in central Finland. She wrote about it in her diary, where the 'shameful peace' is followed by the comfort of sauna.

> The Ruskies [*Ryssät*] have taken over some islands south of Viipuri. Might they get into the city? Ryti is in Moscow. Why? Not a shameful peace, never!
>
> It is 21.30. I just came from sauna. The charming little sauna gave better heat than the big sauna in the Tuupovaara parsonage. It is difficult to be bathing with four small ones, but it was done in the end. I brought the children in and cooked coffee on the embers of the oven in the *kamari* [room], just like the Tuitu grandmother from Uusikirkko[7] in her refugee place in Muurame. (This grandmother was nice even in that respect that she used to read the newspapers aloud from the beginning to the end so that we could listen to it behind the wall.) Coffee refreshed, and when the children calmed down in their beds, I left again to sauna. (Sylvi's diary, 9.3.1940)

The treaty and loss of territory was a defeat for the Karelians. Sylvi's diary entries for 13 March 1940 reveal her sadness and sense of defeat. After she hears the news on the radio, she asks, 'Did the government deceive our people?'[8] She records how she felt when she got home and the language moves from 'I' to 'we'. The quoted speech also includes a national 'we'; the excerpt ends with a 'we' that includes 'every Finn'.

> I could not feel sorrow or happiness, as if I were drugged, but back at home I loosened and cried. We don't know what the new border means, but one thing is sure – we have lost the war.
>
> Later in the day Mrs. Hämäläinen [the Metsäpirtti widow] came to me, eyes full of tears. Think! Viipuri to the Russians, all of Karelia once again! The Parliament cannot accept the peace. They say Svinhufvud [ex-president] is in Germany and Italy.[9] Still there might be hope. Good God cannot allow us this burden. Why were we told to fight?
>
> [And Sylvi adds her own similar thoughts] Her grief is deep and sincere. Certainly every Finn loving the fatherland cries in the heart about this dismem-

bered country. Do we end up on the other side of the border? (Sylvi's diary, 13.3.1940)

Sylvi felt sympathy for the Metsäpirtti widow. Metsäpirtti was a village near Lake Ladoga, not far from Käkisalmi, and a region known well to Sylvi. The widow's husband had been buried at Pyhäjärvi cemetery; Arvi's birthplace was in Pyhäjärvi. With a new border agreement, this young woman was faced with the loss of her home. She is mentioned in two diary entries from March 1940:

> Across from us lives a young war widow from Metsäpirtti, whose husband was killed in action on the first day of war near their home and is now buried at Pyhäjärvi war heroes' cemetery. She has two small children. Her great sorrow [load] crushes her.   (Sylvi's diary, 8.3.1940)

> Before noon, a Metsäpirtti widow, Emma Hämäläinen, was sitting with me [at her house]. She told that she had acted as head of [war] supplies for the village when war was threatening and her home was one kilometre from the border. Thus she saw the first flames of the war on the border, moved farther north until, with her two small ones, [they] ended up in Karttula. She is 22.   (Sylvi's diary, 15.3.1940)

The story of this young widow's life is reported because her circumstance is out of the ordinary, beyond daily experience. The story provokes existential questions: how can one survive tragedy and how does one have the character to sustain loss? Benedict Anderson realised that the survival of Buddhism, Christianity and Islam over thousands of years and in different social formations was linked to 'their imaginative response to the overwhelming burden of human suffering' (1983: 18). The theme of tragedy and survival, an obvious theme during war but also a theme raised constantly in mythologies, narratives, literature, films and artistic works, comes out in other stories in the memoirs. These themes are powerful loci for discourse because people are interested in them. Stories about other people reiterate the theme of sacrifice. The following story of Tauno Hiltunen, which was told in several letters, is another that emphasises the 'heavy burden that God has given us'.

Because Arvi was a Lutheran minister, Sylvi and Arvi often knew who was wounded and who died from Tuupovaara and from neighbouring parishes, or how to find information about missing people. Letters to Sylvi, and from her to the family, contain news of these people, such as this letter about the death of Tauno Hiltunen, who was killed by another Finn.

> Yesterday some Finnish spy (a deserter from the front at Ilomantsi) shot two men on the Kinnasniemi road about six kilometres from here. One, Tauno Hiltunen, died immediately, the other, the young military police-soldier Pekka Huovinen, later. Tauno Hiltunen left six small children. I will leave to visit and help them.

The man will be buried in the military cemetery [section of the churchyard]. (Sylvi to Helena, 9.12.1939)

The life of a widow with six children was especially difficult because people were being evacuated from the eastern front. A few weeks later, in January, Sylvi received a letter from Elisa Hiltunen, the widow of Tauno, who had been evacuated to Karttula with the children. She expresses her despair in religious terms to Sylvi.

> We are here in Karttula's Ahvenisenpää in Lauri Airaksi's house. A month has passed although I did not believe it would pass in any way [she did not think she would get through]. This time has been as long as a year for me. God's hand is harsh toward me, a sinful human being. But whom God loves [is] the one He also punishes. If only I could thank and praise the heavenly father for all this, because He loves me so that [He] gives in this earthly time many kinds of sorrows and pains and does not give me a bigger cross than what I am able to carry. When I left that parsonage our journey was long and troubled. All the children fell ill and have been sick for several weeks. Now they begin to recover a little. My own health is also very weak. I would have visited a doctor but there is none here. Our living quarters are bad. One small old room that does not even have an oven. There is, however, a stove with which the room is warmed up. It is so cold that every corner is frozen [covered with ice] and the children cannot be on the floor much. There are fifteen of us [people] in the same room; besides us, Heikki Hiltunen's family and grandfather and grandmother. If God would allow that we still would get to our own earthly home but let His Will be done [from the prayer, 'Our Father Who Art in Heaven'].

Elisa reports that her husband's body will be exhumed because there had not been an official autopsy as required by law for every death. She ends again with a reference to God.

> Red Cross relief supplies were given out here during Christmas, even to us. I received clothes and some shoes for the children. I prepare food myself and we take supplies from the house and the shop. I do not know anything about my relatives. I saw one of my sisters at Karttula church. I have received no information about conditions at home because there is nobody who would write from there. I only received that sad information that my husband's body has been exhumed. Why were the officials so careless that they did not inspect the deceased before being buried so that he would have had peace in his eternal home. If God would give him that heavenly peace, because the world does not give that peace to his body. If only the soul would be able to be in eternal peace. (Elisa Hiltunen to Sylvi, 17.1.1940)

Five days later the story ends in Sylvi's accounts with a letter from Elisa's daughter.

> Mrs Pärssinen,
>
> I greet you under my heavy burden of sorrow [something she carries] because little Maija didn't like to be here for long. With her lovely curls she moved to

Heaven on New Year's Eve and was buried in Tervo cemetery, and even [her] father could not take part in it [the burial]. I feel that I have earned everything that my Lord has given me as my burden.

I ask that if information about Heikki Hiltunen's or Mikko Tuupanen's death on the front arrives there in the parish office, could you have the courage to inform me without hesitation because even they are allowed to suffer a lot [because she knows they are suffering].

Yesterday nine men who had fallen at the front were buried here. One of them was a small farmer who left six children. The same burden will wait me but everything is well. Now, thousands of greetings from me to you and hopes for well-being.

Natalia Hiltunen (22.1.1940)

In these Lutheran communities, the sacrifice of the son of God, Jesus, was a key metaphor through which people expressed their sorrow and justified their personal sacrifice for the benefit of the nation.[10] The idea of sacrifice was a concept which made it possible for the writers to naturally understand their personal connection to the national effort. The sacrifice for Karelians was not just the loss of people, but the loss of territory. There is a deeply Christian component to the politics of Karelia; Paasi has described how religious rhetoric has had a long history and a crucial role in the representation of the Finnish-Russian border (1996: 195–99). Christian metaphors were used easily by these writers in the 1940s - and even now, when some Karelians talk about being pilgrims to the 'Holy Land'.[11]

Extraordinary Noted

An important aspect of circulating discourse is replication, how certain stories are reproduced. When Sylvi edited the memoirs into a notebook, she was more concerned to edit out private affairs than to add clarification. However, when her son Rauno edited the family papers, he occasionally put together pieces of the story into his own reconstruction. Through paraphrase, Rauno contributes to the circulating discourse about wartime.

At one point Rauno paraphrases the story of Toini's dream about her husband Jaakko from the letters and other accounts. The dream, because it reveals an extraordinary situation, makes for good narrative; it captures people's imaginations. It is about an extraordinary incident that is real; the pharmacist's friend in the story had experienced the event, in 'reality'. The dream has already travelled from one generation to the next and, due to Rauno's summary and clarification, the story can continue to circulate within the family. It is an example of how one family story can be linked to similar stories of the war years. These stories of the extraordinary during wartime become a form of collective memory into which each family can put their versions. Whereas a type story or motif in folklore is often made local, the reverse happens when narratives link local people to historical events.

There was a letter from Toini to Helena (9.2.1940) about how she was in Pori at the hospital because her husband, Jaakko Linjama, had been injured during the Winter War in an explosion on Independence Day (6 December 1939).[12] While Toini was with Jaakko, Sylvi was in Muurame with Toini's children and her own. There is a second letter from Sylvi to Helena (21.2.1940) explaining how she has been caring for the children in Muurame for three weeks. Between these letters, Rauno inserted the story of Jaakko's injury and Toini's dream. Rauno explained that Jaakko was in a grenade attack on 6 December 1939 at Metsäpirtti, on the eastern front in Karelia. The grenade was thrown into the centre of he and his comrades and Jaakko's mate was killed. Jaakko escaped without any external injuries but he suffered from shell shock for several months. This is what Rauno wrote after he explained the basic incident.

> There is an unexplainable, or at least difficult to explain according to the mind [logic], vision that has to do with Jaakko Linjama's injury. At the same time when Jaakko had experienced that terrible thing, Toini Linjama had a peculiar dream in Muurame. She dreamed that she saw Jaakko coming along a road, yelling a hard-to-understand call for help, his helmet hanging from his neck and gripping his rifle with both hands against his chest. In the dream landscape there was a border bridge and other buildings. In the back she could hear the sound of church bells.
>
> The thing that makes this dream peculiar is what happened at Muurame sometime after the Winter War had ended. Into the Muurame pharmacy came the pharmacist's friend, who saw Jaakko Linjama first after the above-described horrible incident and took him to the field hospital. He would have wanted to talk to Jaakko about the incident but Jaakko was not ready at that point to bring the horrible memories of the war back into his mind. So instead, Toini Linjama went to see this friend of the pharmacist. Before the friend could tell anything about the incident, Toini wanted to tell her dream and the details herself. The pharmacist's friend is good at interpreting dreams and he could translate the dream into reality.[13] So apparently Jaakko Linjama had come from the front line with his helmet hanging from his neck and holding his rifle with both hands so strongly that it was hard to get it away from him. The sounds he was making in distress were unclear. A little farther away was a bridge that had been broken by the Russians. The buildings in Toini Linjama's dream were the same as in reality and the landscape that she had described was the exact same as the landscape at the incident. Toini Linjama had never been to Metsäpirtti, not before the war or after it either.
>
> The night before the incident, Jaakko Linjama had been the organist in the church service. This could explain the church bells in the dream. (Rauno Pärssinen, 1993: 64–65)

Wars are often remembered as a common experience, and commemorated as such. There are markers all over Finland to commemorate the people who died during the Winter War and the Continuation War. Such commemorative markers create a national memory of war that is shared by people who have never met one another but who regard themselves as sharing a common history. In the European historical experience monuments are an important site of the religious force of nationalism (Rowlands 1993: 145). Monuments are a form of memory that Gillis (1994: 6) calls elite memory, that form of memory which helps to construct the boundaries of national territories. By contrast, popular memory is 'more local as well as episodic' (ibid.), relying more on living memory than permanent sites or monuments. Using this definition, the dream story above is a form of popular memory, one that passes along stories of people from one generation to the next. Both are forms of collective memory. But the concept of 'elite memory' used by Gillis puts too much emphasis on the nation state. Monuments to wars can be for the generals or the common men, depending on the observer. Different classes and men from different political orientations (for example, Reds and Whites) joined to fight these wars. As evidenced in the novels of Väinö Linna, they were fighting for their homes and land, not necessarily for a shared version of the national entity. Although the state may view the monuments as state markers, the men saw the wars and their efforts through their own eyes, to the point where some were uneasy about crossing the border into the Soviet Union with the army. Likewise, popular memory credits the common soldiers with winning the war, not the generals. The more popular, personal stories, in this case with a touch of mystification, can be joined to similar stories, which might be labelled the folklore of wartime. Both join personal experience to a communal event, to a defining moment in national history. People come to memory and to memorials by linking their personal experience to the collective one. It does not hold that a national memorial determines the personal response.

These local stories about known personalities link the individual to a national project much more than speeches and programmes emanating from distant Helsinki. Individuals are patriotic or loyal to a community which is sensible, known to them. These stories about their own and others' experiences serve to make known the community and at the same time, in telling, create and recreate a national community.

Narratives and National Events

Memories unshared will fade away, as Halbwachs (1992) recognised. They have to be socially placed and shared in order to have meaning. This is done by telling others in order to make a 'we' group of shared experiences and meanings (Carr 1986). The history of the war years offers a metanarrative for stories of personal experience and stories about other known individuals. It channels local discourse and it is built through local stories. How this happens is demonstrated in two stories of soldiers encountered by the family.

The first is the story of Turunen, whom Sylvi met and talked to. She passed his story along to Helena and it was of interest to them because it is about the famous battle at Kollaa, well known to Finns through the news and a book written about it, and known to Sylvi and Helena also through the experience of family members. Later Rauno picked up Turunen's story because it has an extraordinary ending and thus makes for good story-telling, at least in Tuupovaara where the story takes place and where Rauno lived as a child in the parsonage. Rauno's replication moves it beyond the family towards the 'mythological' end of circulating discourse although the local nature of this story means that it probably will drop away, not reach the level of mythology. It serves, however, to put local people into national experiences and, in that way, the discourse about national history connects – becomes sensible – to local life-worlds.

Kollaa: Turunen's story

In the fall of 1940 both Sylvi and Helena read the book, *Kollaa kestää*, by Erkki Palolampi. It was about the important battle at Kollaa, where the Finnish army suffered great losses but managed to hold their position at the end of the Winter War. The women talked about the book in their letters because each had cried while reading it; each knew some of the people in the book and Sylvi's brother ('our Itti') had been there as well. Sylvi wrote to Helena:

> Do you have the book *Kollaa kestää*? I cried while reading it. Our Itti was in JR 35 [regiment]. I was proud that it says such good things about the Kirvu men. Tuupainen, who is also talked about, is a Tuupovaara man, a boy from a near-by cabin. His younger brother was our iv-boy in the parsonage for the whole war and another brother was killed at Kuhmo and is buried in our heroes' cemetery. (Sylvi to Helena, 20.10.1940)

In 1941 Sylvi meets Turunen, who was also at Kollaa. Although he is reluctant to tell his story, he answers her questions and piece by piece the story comes out, as she tells Helena in the following letter.

> I visited Eimisjärvi with Helena the Sunday before last, along with Arvi. It was a beautiful day and we got a ride with Eero Vatanen's good horse [in the carriage].
>
> On the trip home we started to talk about the wartime with Vatanen's farm worker [who was driving the horse]. It came to be asked where he was during the war. From the short answers to our many questions a story emerged in such detail that the truth was not in doubt.

91

The man, named Turunen, 44 years old, lived as a bachelor working man in Soanlahti [now the USSR]. When he was not immediately invited to military training because of his young age, he volunteered and ended up at the border in Kollaa in JR: 2 [infantry regiment 2]. During the retreat there was a stop at Kollaa River. In December he and his whole company were ambushed by Russians while they were skiing in the forest. The lieutenant fell right away. The troops were dispersed, one part escaped, a large part fell, and Turunen, along with many others, was wounded. When they could not escape, they dug them-selves into the snow to hide. Surrounded, and realising that escape was impossi-ble, two seriously wounded men shot themselves after first begging in vain for the others to shoot them. Then they had to surrender. They were about ten men, among them one healthy man called Löppö, and he then bandaged the wounds of the others and helped them as best he could. Again and again, Turunen said, 'The first night was horrible.'

They were taken immediately behind the border to central Russia. The Russians had done a lot of research but the men did not tell them anything. They were taken to a hospital where Turunen started to get better. The thing that both-ered them the most was that they didn't know how the war was going.

In March they were returned to Finland through Matkaselkä. Turunen had not told his *isäntä*, Eero Vatanen, about his fate even though he had lived in his house for a long time. Only at Easter sauna Eero had asked what those scars on Turunen's back were. Then the man had answered: 'What do you think they are? Look more carefully.' And then he told his story.   (Sylvi to Helena, 18.4.1941)

Rauno Pärssinen added a footnote to update the story of Turunen. Turunen disappeared from Tuupovaara after the peace agreement and there was local speculation that he had been murdered. Three Tuupovaara peo-ple were named as suspects. One of them, a gravedigger, was said to have done it but he committed suicide shortly after. Then when they dug up two Russian bodies in the cemetery (two Russian pilots who had been shot down over Tuupovaara during the war) in order to return them to Russia, there was a third body of an unknown person on the top, rumoured to be Turunen. Rauno concludes: 'It is true that Turunen disappeared. Maybe there's something true in the rumour; there's no smoke without fire' (1993: 104).

Toivo Kempas: a Finnish man

After October 1940, the letters between Sylvi and Helena often mention Toivo Kempas. Toivo met Sylvi during the Winter War when he was sick and stationed in Tuupovaara. Through Sylvi, he came to know Helena. Toivo had been in the Kollaa battle, in the same unit with Itti. In addition, he had been orphaned as a child and his home village of Soanlahti was now on the other side of the border. For all these reasons, and the fact that Sylvi said he was a clean and industrious boy (*'hän kuuluu olevan siisti ja ahkera poika*'), he had the sympathy of these women. In her letter to Sylvi on 27 October 1940, Helena wanted to be sure that Toivo had a chance to read *Kollaa kestää* and she offered to send fifty marks for him to buy the book if he did not have money.

Rauno Pärssinen found all these letters and reconstructed the story of Toivo Kempas. Because individuals are so well documented by the Finnish church and state, Rauno was able to learn the date and place of Toivo's birth and the parish where Toivo was buried in 1987 at the age of 72. Here is Toivo's story as told by Rauno.

> Toivo Kempas was born 12.6.1916 in Soanlahti. His mother died during birth, her first, and his father had to care for little Toivo. Soon however the father also became sick, for which nothing could be done. So Toivo became an orphan at a young age, without brothers or sisters.
>
> Toivo's father's brother, Heikki Kempas, took the young orphan into his family, which already had children. Toivo never said anything about his uncle's care, but about how it is essential for a young man to develop and grow up, he did say: I had the love of a mother and a father, tender and selfless care. At an early age Toivo taught himself not to rely on others to care for him but to take care of himself.
>
> Toivo became a good youth and began to apprentice. Forestry was his special field. During the growth of speciality services in the 1930s, a short time before the Winter War, he became independent and started to do his own forestry work. He was a specialist with an axe and frame saw. His business fit into his backpack.
>
> Toivo Kempas grew into an ordinary man. He went dancing and sweet-talked the girls just like everyone else. He had learned at an early age not to look to another for safety but to do one's own business. Toivo knew from experience that the interests of the well-to-do in the community would not provide for regular people's care without problems. The poor had to help themselves. Masters do not help. Therefore Toivo broke away from the church [stopped attending], which was a brave deed in the 1930s.
>
> As the Winter War threatened, Toivo joined the YH [army unit] with the others. Toivo left his few possessions, his axes, frame saws and good suit, at his uncle Heikki's house and put on the Finnish Greys. His regiment was JR: 34, where axes were traded for rifles and pointy ears. Because his home parish was threatened, Toivo was disciplined and tough in battle. No one has counted how many of the enemy Toivo cut down before this small, depleted JR: 34 got some new recruits. Toivo refused a rest, staying alive as the new recruits were killed, but finally he was tired and disappointed, because after all the struggle to preserve his home parish, Soanlahti, it went to the enemy since it had not been won on the battlefield by the Kollaa heroes. The axes and frame saws were gone. All Toivo had were his army clothes and that which he carried in his pockets. Kollaa had left him tired and weaker against the opposition and now Toivo became sick. Uncle Heikki, who had moved to the Tuupovaara military hospital, offered a small bed to the sick Kollaa hero.

Toivo Kempas was not alone however. When they heard about him at the church, when it was said that he needed shelter, Toivo got a place to sleep and good care for depression. Even those who had split from the church could get shelter and help. Possibly that was it. Toivo was not alone.

The story continues about how Sylvi and Helena worried about Toivo. Rauno then concludes the story, and the book he published of these family materials, with these two paragraphs:

Toivo Kempas is one of the country's quiet ones, one of the fighters without mercy, who preserved the country's independence, its survival. Toivo Kempas is one of ten thousand unknown heroes who rose against the threat, the degree and dimension of which is not properly appreciated now.

Toivo Kempas is an example of the harvest, the thousands of Finnish foot sol-diers in the army, a Finnish war example, strong and peaceful, probably slightly simple, but with a warm heart, who make the ultimate sacrifices. He did not speak foreign languages, he did not understand high culture, he lived here and now, loved this country where he was born, found foreigners strange, avoided the strange, was Finnish, a patriot, and nothing more. That was Toivo Kempas; a Finnish man.   (Rauno Pärssinen, 1992: 105–106, 116)

The story of one man becomes the story of 'a Finnish man'. His experi-ences in war, as a patriot, can speak for the community, can be used to con-struct a 'we' that is not threatening, not divided by class. What circulates easily and becomes replicated by others is community-building discourse. But community-building discourse has to be lifted above the actual com-munity because no one person can speak for the community (Urban 1996). Toivo Kempas is dead; he is no longer a contender in the community. Through his actions in the war years, Toivo can represent the healing of social wounds. Toivo was a simple working-man who was willing to sacri-fice his life for the nation. He was 'Finnish, a patriot, and nothing more'. He brings together a community previously divided by class interests. Toivo's story is not one of aggressive nationalism (as in Finnish versus oth-ers), as much as it is a story about community building. As the novelist Väinö Linna (1960) did in his famous trilogy, *Here under the Northern Star*, so Rauno narrates a story of unity.

This story could be interpreted to be about not liking the strange, about Finnish nationalism in the face of new immigrants. However, in its histori-cal context, it is a story of healing, reflecting accurately what many people had learnt in 1918, namely that the unified community of the nationalist movement was not so unified. The 'we' was, and is, a disputed one and such stories address this problem. The story of Toivo Kempas can be linked to the metanarrative of Finnish history quite easily, and for this reason it can be joined to a circulating discourse. His story becomes part of the national myth about 'the Finnish men' who saved the nation when it was severely threatened. This national myth is grounded in empirical fact; the nation's independence was severely threatened and Finland was the only nation along the Soviet border that did not end up behind the Iron Curtain of post-war Europe. The communal 'we' often depends on such crisis points for defining itself (Carr 1986), allowing a perfect opportunity for one personal story to become part of mythohistory.

Patriotism

Michael Billig (1995) coined the term 'banal nationalism' to talk about the daily experience of living in a modern nation state. Billig finds that nationalism is often described as a negative attribute that other people have, whereas the same behaviour in one's own group is more positively described as patriotic. Banal nationalism, he counters, is found in all nation states and it is 'flagged' by the obvious symbols of the nation (a flag, coins, a national anthem, and so on), by the assumed 'we' in newspaper and media reports, by sports teams and stars, and in numerous other daily occurrences (Billig 1995: 8). The small words of nationalism – 'we', 'they', 'here', and 'there' – are used by politicians to build an idea of community (ibid.: 70). In a similar way, there are points in this narrative when the 'I' joins the 'we', but the level is different. The writers take a political position and talk about Finland, its borders and the need to defend it. But all the talk is about local or personally known people who find themselves involved in national events. Patriotism, as Samuel and others (1989) have determined, is concerned with the local and known world; this talk is patriotic but not particularly national. And yet, as Anderson recognised, there is a force to patriotism so that people will die for a community they identify with.

The wartime is still a period that engages popular attention and a topic that circulates. One need only look each year at the books displayed for sale at Christmas in the bookstores; there are always special tables of books about the wartime and Finnish history. The fate of Inkilä is linked to the war's outcome in 1944, so Inkilä can be an integral part of national memory through war stories. This is especially true for those family members who never actually lived in Inkilä and for other people who have little direct connection to Karelia. With the wartime as the common denominator, Karelia, and the memory world of Inkilä, can be an intimate part of national history. Perhaps for that reason, the movie, *Abandoned Houses and Empty Courtyards*, about the evacuation of Karelia in 1944, was rated as one of the ten most popular films in Finland for the year 2000 in *Helsingin Sanomat*. The family joins the communal 'we' of the nation through the shared experience of a national event that continues to be part of circulating discourse. It is in this sense that Anderson's imagined community exists and perpetuates itself.

What about Anderson's question: why would men die and women make their sacrifices for the nation? Anderson finds a model for patriotism in the family; the family is 'the domain of disinterested love and solidarity' (1983: 131), meaning something perceived as natural, not chosen. As people relate to the family so they relate to the nation. But this idea of 'disinterest' is misleading. The Finnish soldiers were fighting for their farms and villages; they had a deep interest in the war. However, Anderson echoes Schneider and Wagner when he talks about the family as a model of solidarity. The communal 'we' often becomes apparent in the face of danger, when the community is threatened from outside (Carr 1986). With the threat from the Soviet Union, one model for creating a communal 'we' was kinship; as 'solicitude' or 'diffuse enduring solidarity' characterises kinship, so a national 'we' could be constructed on the basis of solidarity in the face of danger during these historical events.

In the replicated stories about war a shared history is the basis for creating a national 'we'. Anderson's conclusion about the power of a mother-tongue for patriotism is only part of what happens and relies too much on language, without acknowledging discourse. A national 'we' in Finland emerges through the common experience of war and a circulating discourse about this experience. The wartime experience reconstituted the national 'we' that was fragmented by the civil war. Paraphrased stories and circulating discourse today continue the work of building a national 'we', a generalised-essential 'we' constructed from the referential 'we' of the known community.

7

MAMMA HYVÄ: MEANING AND VALUE IN LETTERS

The letters in the previous chapter are about the family's position in national events. The following letters are different; they are concerned with the more common, almost mundane, events of everyday life. And yet, these topics are a major part of the body of letters, saved as equally important documents. Pierre Clastres argues that language changes from sign to value in the singing of Guayaki hunters because the words of the song are no longer intended for any listener; instead they are values for the one who sings them (1987: 125). In much the same way, the language in the letters was once a system of signs intended for particular readers. But now there are no particular readers and there has been a conversion of meaning to value; today the letters have a value that is different from the original communication.

The women's letters are an important part of the reciprocity between family members (cf. Besnier 1995). They enable the flow of food, children, and help with projects between members as the family takes care of itself. Certain axioms, or self-evident truths, are often at the heart of their understanding and their phrasing. An axiomatic idea facilitates circulation because it is good to think with (Urban 1996: 160). The self-evident truths which can be found in the text of these letters are that the family is an important group; one should work hard and take personal responsibility for the survival of the family; one should live a Christian life; one should help others in need; one loves one's home and region (Karelia); and one must occasionally make sacrifices for the greater good.

Apples and Sugar

Reciprocity through work and marriage alliances was at the heart of social activities in these rural communities. David Sabean (1998) has noted women's central role in kinship activities and in making family economic and social arrangements in Germany. Much of the historical evidence for his conclusion is based on letters written between middle-class women. In the Finnish letters a similar process was going on; women were commonly responsible for the daily arrangements within the family and between different family members. They were the driving force of kinship relations; as noted, Helena informed her daughters about property and inheritance matters. The letters of this chapter are somewhat exceptional because the war looms behind daily experience. But here too the letters between women reveal the daily reciprocal and social arrangements of the family.

In addition to reciprocity, the letters about domestic concerns – apples, boots, children and money – reveal that individuals live first and foremost, as Martin Heidegger proposed, in humanly resolved worlds. It is the things in our environment, towards which we direct our projects, towards which we direct our care and concern, which ground our consciousness (Heidegger 1971). The world only becomes ontological when humans turn their attention to it and establish a relationship with it. It is the direct involvement in one's surroundings that positions the person and produces knowledge and understanding. The letters reveal the exchanges, the work, the care and concern for their world, as performed by the women writers. These sections of the letters are not part of a national story; they reveal the deeper structures of being in place, at home, through one's work and the security that knowledge of one's place gives one. These seemingly mundane events are the basis of the analogy between Inkilä and home. A typical example of family reciprocity can be read in a letter from Helena to her daughter.

> As usual this summer we grew many apples. I gave some to every house here, to Eino, to Wäinö, and to home. I have saved some at home, but just in case I will send some to you [plural]. I will send some to Sylvi also, if their apple trees have not produced. It is really good that you have your own potatoes – what about carrots and turnips?
>
> We have sugar; they managed to buy ten kilograms for home, to Wäinö, and to Eino, 5 kilograms each. Now we have bought as little as we can. Aili went one day to the shop and got one kilogram each of cube sugar and granulated sugar; they had only given half a kilo to other people. So on the next day I sent Aili again to the shop in Inkilä and told her to tell Mikko that he should again give a kilo of each, because this sugar I could send to Toini, because they do not seem to be getting any sugar over there. Well, Mikko gave her the sugar; they [the sugars] are on their way there with the apples. Tomorrow, on Tuesday, Wäinö will take them to the station and send them.   (Helena to Toini, 25.9.1939)

The work of provisioning for the household was an important element of daily existence in these rural villages and it remains important in the photos and memoirs about village life. Work was largely gendered, with women and men working in same-sex groups and occasionally in mixed groups. It is not surprising therefore that much in the letters between women was about the demands of women's work. The rhythm of women's daily lives was marked by children to care for; clothes to sew, repair, wash, buy and exchange; food to grow, raise (pigs, cows, chickens), gather (mushrooms, berries), store, bake, cook and serve; all in addition to cleaning the house, keeping the fire going, decorating and caring for appearances. Any Finnish woman should be able to serve a proper coffee (coffee, tea and baked cakes) but Sylvi had to do so more often than a normal household because the minister's family received many visitors. There were many demands on her and the letters, more to Toini, but also to Helena, discuss the work of the household. Some of the most confidential material is written to Toini, two years her junior, who, as a teacher and mother of five children at this time,[1] shared many of Sylvi's daily experiences and concerns. The discussion of women's work was central to the letters because they assumed that they would help and rely on one another. Nor do they ever question that the work has to be done. At the same time, however, Sylvi could step away and write about new washing power, reflect on women's work and offer her own critique, in which she prefers to spend her time on child development rather than household chores. Here is a sample letter with her opinions to Toini.

Toini *hyvä!*
It is snowing rather heavily – just perfect Good Friday weather. There is a lot of measles – our children have been spared this.
I went last Sunday to Korpiselkä. Greetings from Paul Kosusela! (Did you know that he is also a Laestadian?)[2]
I crocheted your old sweater into a dress for Helena. It is, however, still too large, so I sent it to Pirkko [Toini's daughter]. Helena has also some small pants, which I sent for your baby. Helena walks every day, pushes a sled, and skis. Her speech lately is quite comical because she 'makes' the sentences herself. (Note. Helena is now 1 year, 10 months.)
Last week Hilja [servant] and I washed the month's clothes [and linens] for the family in two days. We did not scrub [on a washboard] like for really dirty clothes, but cooked the 'whites'. We used the advertised washing powder, we saved 53 marks, the soap then washes but I wonder about this strange washing which took all of two days; I have my doubts if it is any easier.
You have enough work to do as a teacher and watching children. Do as little bodily work as possible – because there are two servants – be of a peaceful mind that you do enough – that you make the most of your 'talents' – do not be worried even though every place is not perfect – if now, when you are recovering from life-threatening danger, if you care for everything and do this and that – your home will soon do without you.

I have tried myself to worry less about mundane things and worry more about the 'heavenly'. Of course, the children's welfare and health are things that cannot be ignored, but vacuuming, coffee cakes, social life with visitors, whether or not the children have beautiful clothes, these are secondary issues. Arvi says I am lazy, but I know myself that my laziness and negligence in some things is actually self-preservation and self-protection so that I am capable of more important tasks. I am doing better work rocking and singing with Rauno in the rocking chair than fighting in the kitchen about using too much butter or dirty handles on the cups. Rauno enjoys so much sitting in mother's arms. Rauno is five years old. Aarno too needs mother's company. In the evening I had to explain how an aluminium mug is made and why it weighs less than an enamel one.

The washing that I mentioned before went well even though I did not want to do it. Arvi watched the children and made coffee while I did it. 'What you can do tomorrow, don't do today', in Tuupovaara slang: 'don't do at all', when you do not have enough time to do something. When I was in Helsinki I realised that Jesus loves me and will forgive me of my sins. I decided to give him more [of my] time.   (Sylvi to Toini, 7.4.1939).

Clothes were exchanged as much as services. Sylvi commonly asked her mother for help with some of the household's necessities. For her part, Helena helped both her daughters with food, with clothes for themselves, with childcare, and with clothes and presents for the children. In September 1939, anticipating a long, cold winter and possibly war, Sylvi wrote to Helena asking for help in the purchase of a winter jacket.

We need to get some fall and winter clothes but it is inconvenient. I planned a trip to Viipuri but many of the purchases are still in question. My winter jacket looks its four years and I think I could use a new one but Arvi said that 'it can still go a little more'. Aarno should buy a jacket and skiing suit, all boys need hats and sweaters, and a shirt for Arvi. I don't want to trouble you, but could I ask a large question: 'Could I hope to get some money from home?' I need these clothes for the war time and probably much longer.   (Sylvi to Helena, 9.9.1939)

Because of the way the letters are organised, Helena's answer is unclear; there is no return letter or thank you letter back from Sylvi. However, this was not an unusual request and it was likely granted. There was a similar request the following spring, although this time money was sent along and the request itself contained a side comment about village social status.

I am sending now 400 marks extra money and ask, if you go with Toini to Jyväskylä, if you could buy me a summer jacket. I have had the existing one for four summers – it was bought when we were in Korpiselkä. And now the pharmacist's servant has bought herself the same jacket! (Sylvi to Helena, 11.6.1940)

At the end of the Winter War Sylvi was pregnant again and the money situation was difficult. She writes to Toini to borrow a nursing bra and baby clothes.

I spoke to you about the nursing bra which I need. We eat well but the money is gone by the end of the month. It would be a big help if you could send me some baby clothes. (Sylvi to Toini, 11.1.1941)

As in Helena's household in Inkilä, it was not uncommon for the larger houses to have one or two servant girls and a few hired men. This began to change with the war. A mother's problem, which continued over the months, back and forth in letters to Toini, was how to get household help. As the war began, and certainly at the height of the fighting, women increasingly worked on the home front. As a result, it became very difficult for women like Sylvi and Toini, who worked as teachers and relied on the help of servants, to find someone to help with housework and childcare. This report begins like news, telling of the situation, but it changes to become a comment about human nature.

I now begin to have servant problems because Hilja leaves for Pyhäjärvi at the end of this month. She is going to apprentice for Osuuskauppa shops. I paid her part today, which comes out of tomorrow's teaching [money] of 150 marks a month. As you know, she likes to go with men, drinking, she's sloppy and lazy. Lovely! But we are all the same and we all make mistakes. And there aren't maids sitting on every branch. (Sylvi to Toini, 3.5.1939)

The next day she continues the letter to Toini, talking about the children, with a comment about the new servant:

Aarno improves and is playing outside. Hilja and the new servant [se '*uusi*'] lay out the washing. Of the new one I have noticed little but that every five minutes she sniffs her nose appealingly.

From the kitchen I can hear the sniffer. Better not to leave the wash outside to dry and to bring it in because it is beginning to snow. (Sylvi to Toini, 4.5.1939)

Spring was a time for women to clean the house, wash the clothes and hang them outside, mend clothes and sew new ones. It was also a time to start the planting and clean up outside after the snow had melted. In a letter to Toini, Sylvi tells about her cleaning plans, expecting to have help from Arvi's sister, Mari Pärssinen. The final sentence is probably self-reflexive and not directed at Toini since Toini would already know this. Perhaps Sylvi has been reading about cleaning techniques in the magazines that had begun to focus on domestic chores during the 1930s.

I have a lot of spring work and I am without another servant. Now that Mari is coming here, I hope that she will help me repair clothes and sew new ones. You should clean every corner from the ceiling to the floor and even the basement. (Sylvi to Toini, 7.4.1939)

In November 1939, because of the war, Sylvi made plans to send her children to Toini in central Finland where it would be safer. She wrote to Toini about their common problem of finding female help.

101

If you don't have a proper servant, don't hesitate to send back, for example, Aarno or Kari [her two oldest sons]. I understand that you have enough trouble with five small ones and your school teaching [work], and if you only have a 'silly' girl, that doesn't help much.

There are no girls here who I could send to Muurame. Would it be possible for you to find a good servant there and also a child-minder? I would participate in paying by paying for the girl myself and therefore contributing equally. (Sylvi to Toini, 13.11.1939)

Two weeks later, Toini writes to Helena that the problem with help continues.

I don't want to talk about servants. Last Saturday a new one came and on Sunday she left. She said she did not want to care for so many children.   (Toini to Helena, 27.11.1939)

On 30 November 1939 the children were evacuated to Muurame. The Pärssinen children were joined by their Kuisma cousins from Inkilä and later by their grandmother and grandfather from Inkilä. Sylvi was able to arrange for another Tuupovaara woman, Toini Lauronen, to watch the children so that Sylvi could return to Tuupovaara and continue to work in the war effort. Toini Lauronen agreed to care for the children until the end of January, at which point she wanted to do her Lotta work at the front. Sylvi sent supplies and money for the children and confided in her sister that she hoped Toini Lauronen would not leave.

It gave me great pleasure to hear that the children are well and healthy. The church has given money to the parish and paid Arvi's January salary. From that, I am sending 1,500 marks to the children. Pay Toini Lauronen her salary now and save what is left over to buy necessary things. Toini is of the opinion that the food should be saved, but there should not be unnecessary saving. I hope that you and the children have enough butter, sugar and milk so that you stay healthy. If only Miss Lauronen doesn't get bored and leave.   (Sylvi to Toini, 15.12.1939)

The letters establish how one lives properly through these descriptions. Family members are polite and formal in their letter salutations (Dear Mama/*Mamma hyvä*). A child is advised to study, to go to Sunday school, and to save some of his birthday money and not spend it all on sweets, as we see in this letter from Sylvi to her oldest son Aarno during the time when the children were evacuated from the war zone.

Mother wishes happy birthday to her own little Aarno![3] You will be eight on the 13th. Wow, what a big boy I have! It makes me feel a little bit old because you have grown so much. Grow up to be a man and remember that Dad wants you to be a decent man.

Here there is good weather. Have you been skiing? Please ask uncle to kindly carve holes in the soles of your ski boots. I have not been skiing. There is plenty of snow. Dad sent you 10 marks as a birthday present. Use the money to buy yourself something nice, a notebook, crayons, a book of fairy tales, or other fun things, but not caramels. You don't get too much if you just buy sweets. Be a happy and good boy and don't forget to do your catechism homework. (Sylvi to Aarno, 9.1.1940)

By the middle of January, Toini Lauronen is looking forward to Sylvi's arrival so she can leave and join the war effort. However, she writes that she will keep to her agreement. The letter gives a clear sense of how the personal 'I' gives way to the communal 'we'. The war was a time of sacrifice by everyone, one could not, and should not, 'seek or want easy days'.

Dear Mrs Pärssinen,
It has been very cold; the children do not even want to go out to sled. The kitchen has been uncommonly cold so that we stay mostly in 'our room', even eating in the living room. You wrote in your letter that you will come to care for the children yourself. Of course it is much better for the children if their own mother cares for them. But don't worry, I won't leave the children. Now we need the cooperation of everyone. While some are on guard in the cold dark nights it's wrong for others to seek or want easy days. (Toini Lauronen to Sylvi, 17.1.1940)

In October 1939 Sylvi's workload increased as Arvi became involved in the war. She notes in her diary that he is away for three weeks for army reserve manoeuvres. The call for him to leave came suddenly, leaving her to pick up the extra work of household and parish.

One night there is a phone call and in the morning the man [Arvi] leaves. I tried to keep the confirmation class going but because the local reserve leader, cantor Aapo Sinervo, was in a hurry, we ended it and sent the children to shelter. (Sylvi's diary, October 1939)

Later, in a letter to a friend from Inkilä she tells of the changes in the village and how she tries to keep the church work organised.

There are many evacuees from Suojärvi and from here they are relocated. Everything here is peaceful. Women are doing men's work. The doctor and nurse have gone – where, I don't know. I am keeping the marriage and funeral lists, but I am not giving the blessing.[4] (Sylvi to Sanni P., 17.10.1939)

It is a great help to me that Arvi came home last Tuesday. The office has accumulated a lot of undone work, even though I have tried to do it in his absence. Assistance for soldiers' families creates much additional work. (Sylvi to Helena, 2.11.1939)

In addition to doing the parish and household work, Sylvi continued her voluntary association work, listing five different meetings or events for the week in her letter to Toini.

Yesterday I went to the final meeting of the Martta cooking course with Helena [daughter]. Today is the Lotta leaders' meeting, the women's work meeting, tonight is the Children's Protection League meeting, on Wednesday a meeting of the Free Services, and then a meeting of the Red Cross, and so forth.   (Sylvi to Toini, 13.11.1939)

In an earlier letter to Toini her regional preferences came out regarding the Lotta celebrations and the dresses they wore.

The Lotta's summer party is at the end of July. I did not take any schedule [agree to do anything] but I belong to the choir and I'm painting [designing] the schedule. This summer getting the national dress was off the bills [not financially possible]. I am tired of that western Finnish dress and I thought I'd get either a Kirvu or a Pyhäjärvi dress. Now I can't.   (Sylvi to Toini, 23.6.1939)

The women in the Scottish village I studied joked that they were busier than city women, with all the voluntary association meetings they attended and the business of running the village (Armstrong 1978). The same seems to be true for Sylvi in Tuupovaara. But Sylvi does not complain of being tired because of too much work. She states that she has a lot of work, that she is very busy, but it is positive. The only time that she complains of being tired is at the end of the Winter War, and it reflects a psychological more than a physiological condition. This echoes Eeva Jokinen's (1996) findings for the metaphor of 'tired' (*väsynyt*) in her analysis of more recent Finnish women's diaries. Jokinen found that women wrote of feeling tired when they found themselves isolated in the house with young children, repetitive household chores, problematic husbands and financial difficulties. Sylvi is of an earlier generation, and rural, not urban, as were most of Jokinen's writers. She describes herself as tired, and the word is used with repetition, when she feels that Finland has been defeated and at the same time she faces the work of reestablishing her home and taking care of evacuees and their problems. In June 1940 there is no coffee, only coffee substitute, two of her children are sick, a local boy dies and another is mourned. Sylvi expresses her feelings in one word, 'tired'.

4.6. Tuesday. *Väsyttää.* [I am feeling tired.] Vihtori Ratinen's boy was buried today. I was at the funeral. I went from there to Kauravaara, to Vatanen's, where Aune cried and read Toivo's letters. I stayed there some time, and then Aune and I went together to the church to put flowers on Toivo's grave.   (Sylvi's diary, 4.6.1940)

Food, as a central element in the household and in exchanges, was an important element in women's lives. It is also part of the material world that is transferred into sensual, emotional memory by succeeding generations. Although Sylvi and Arvi were educated and middle class, and therefore exceptional within the village, they did not have a large income. She tells Toini in a letter in March 1941 that Arvi's annual salary was 41,000 marks.

The large parsonage was provided for them and perhaps an occasional extra amount of money for coffees and entertaining, but otherwise they had to live a thrifty life. Providing their own food was an important part of this and frequent references reveal that Sylvi had a cow and a few pigs, and that she grew a garden of potatoes, cabbages, carrots, turnips and other vegetables, and herbs such as dill, relying on berry bushes and apple trees to add fruit to the diet. These foods, with fish, rye flour for baking bread, wheat flour for baking coffee cakes, along with sugar, tea, coffee, butter and milk, were the staples of their diet. Acquiring, storing, preparing and serving food consumed a major part of women's daily time and it is talked about frequently in the letters, especially as food shortages and rationing became part of the wartime experience. Here is an excerpt from Sylvi's prewar letter to Toini in March 1939, which describes some of the work they were doing without the strain of war.

> I have only done a little handwork. Reading is not a priority except for the newspapers. Yes otherwise the job of providing meals is nasty this spring. No matter what I cook, hunger seems to come back. We very seldom have pork: we become disgusted by pork over the winter; from Christmas on we ate about 80 kilos of it. Now we will slaughter a second pig but [I] really dread thinking about the meat. They do not even buy it for the shops. Part of it will be smoked.
>
> I have invented a lovely meal: herring casserole prepared with eggs and grated, sugared carrots. The top of the casserole should be prepared with fat.   (Sylvi to Toini, 29.3.1939)

What made this an 'invented lovely' meal? A fish or any other kind of casserole is quite common in Finland so in a family discussion with Sylvi's children and grandchildren, the first suggestion was that it was the herring; perhaps it was a bit exotic in Tuupovaara. But Sylvi's son said, no, herring was not unusual. The next guess was sugared carrots; perhaps carrots in March are tasteless so the sugar would make them more attractive to the children. Again Rauno said no; they ate sugared carrots. Rauno's wife, Anja, suggested it was the eggs. She lived on a farm in a nearby village and remembers that they had chickens but only used the eggs for baking and only ate the chickens when they were too old to lay eggs. In the 1930s the social welfare state was beginning to plan the health and welfare of Finnish citizens and this might be an example of how local patterns changed as a result. Anja remembered that a woman came to the village and taught them that they could use eggs in other ways in their diet, for example in making pancakes. These suggestions by state employees were made to add nutrition to the country people's diet. Sylvi implies that she invented this herself but she also notes (8.1.1939 letter to Toini) that she received two magazine subscriptions for Christmas: *Kotiliesi*, a magazine for housewives, and *Suomen Kuvalehti*, a magazine which reports news from all realms of Finnish life. The social planners of the 1930s focused attention on the domestic economy and women's work, especially on such things as nutrition and the design of the housewife's work area (Ollila 1993),[5] so it is likely that Sylvi had read an article or heard a lecture which inspired her to try something new in her own kitchen. The central planning of the emerging welfare state was beginning to reach the countryside through medical staff, social workers, magazines and women's associations.

The taste of food from one's childhood is a memory that carries into the next generation with strong emotional connotations. Its appeal links the sensory to the intelligible although the sensory is lost on those who have not eaten the remembered food. Rauno, in his editing, fondly remembers the foods of his childhood and inserts this comment.

> At the parsonage we grew a lot of potatoes and root vegetables. Dad-Arvi fished regularly and often the whole family made the trip to Loitimo Lake. I remember especially that the first *lahna* [bream] in the summer of 1941 was outstanding. The smoking oven was hot the whole time and many were selling fish. Many were the times when someone would phone and ask for the minister and when we said that he was not at home they would ask: 'Is he fishing?' ['*Kalassako se on?*']. Usually the answer was 'Yes he is' ['*Niin on*']. (Rauno Pärssinen, 1992: 2)

Certain material aspects of life, like food, have public and personal meaning that can travel easily within a Finnish discourse. Food is often connected to sauna. Both food and sauna connote an emotional state of well-being, being home, being relaxed. Sauna is remarked upon in the letters from the men at war, by the women when they are evacuees, it marks returning home at the end of the war, and it is a sign of May Day fun. The sauna was a practical and central part of daily life but it is, importantly, part of the material world that carries meaning. During a time when many houses had no running water, or if they did they did not have hot water, the sauna was an efficient and practical way to bathe and wash clothes. There was customarily, and certainly so in the Inkilä house and at the Tuupovaara parsonage, a small separate sauna building which contained a sauna chamber with stove and benches, a washroom and perhaps a small room with a fireplace for changing clothes and cooking sausages. Sauna provided a way to bathe without heating enormous amounts of water; the sauna stove had a container (*pata*) where water was heated. It was a relatively easy way for people to have a weekly bath, it was a place to wash clothes and linens, and a hygienic place for women to give birth.[6] Sauna was, and is, a central feature of Finnish life, so much so that one of the first things the soldiers did during wartime was build a sauna whenever they moved camp.

In a letter from Sylvi's brother Eino Kuisma to his wife Jenny, written from the front, he tells of his 'gang of boys' in the army and how they made themselves *pulla* and took sauna.

Life here is great; coffee, pulla, good soup. We went to the shop and bought two kilos of wheat flour, eggs, yeast, cardamom, ginger and all that it takes to make pulla dough. Pulla cannot really be done without women's hands. We warmed the dough three times in a warm oven, but the baked pulla came out with watery sugar, however that happened. Then we warmed the sauna and, after bathing, had coffee and pulla. The two kilos of dough were not enough because the pulla ran out half way through the coffee.

This gang of ours is extremely talkative to a man, which is not really funny because of the serious business.   (Eino to Jenny, 14.10.1939)

Few families live on wage income alone anywhere in the world (Wallerstein and Smith 1992). In this case, the flow of goods and services was constant. It was understood that the extended family would share food and services, much as work had always been shared, to ensure that the family could provide for its own. Letters like the following are concrete reminders of the solicitude created through reciprocity.

Mamma hyvä,
The two letters that I wrote to you in Inkilä came back yesterday. Now it is full summer and a notable day because you can get bread with the card. Is the Bible's word true that those who have should give and those who don't have much are taken away a little? You had only some saved grain and now they would buy it away too. But I guess this grain deal was also thought through carefully before it was put on the card. I am going to hold my tongue according to your advice.

I have not been able to send you potatoes because the cars will not take the sacks, but tomorrow I hope again to find a car that can take the sacks.

On Monday, 20 May, our house was emptied of the stranger generals. – Thank you very much for the money, but I am going to send it back to you and ask you to buy 4 metres of black men's suit cloth, which will cost 100 marks/metre and would be good for me as a winter coat or for the children's coats. Just in case for next winter. Then too if you can get 3-4 packages of candles. Father wrote to me a while ago. Tell him that his legal mind wants to resolve things with different people to the penny. But in this life it's very hard to divide things to the penny. Because he refuses to take payment then I thank him on behalf of Arvi's father. It was very nicely done that you took him with you away from the war in Inkilä.

When Mari comes, then she should bring some of our jam but let her leave you half of all the jams. Arvi wrote about this to her but the card came back. If you want to, then you can also give some to Toini. The Free Services brought a large amount of marmalade here – sympathy from foreign countries. Now you should not send letters here by the *kenttäposti* [army post]. Helena [her daughter] was three years old on the 25th. (Sylvi to Helena, 26.5.1940)

Living Properly

A political position includes values about how life should be lived. The letters occasionally spell out these positions, often by using contrast, to give a sense of how one should live properly. These values were not limited to Karelia; evidence from life story interviews indicates that members of this generation of 'war and shortage' (born 1900–1912) throughout Finland shared a common work ethic and nationalist sentiments which set them apart from later generations (Roos 1987). So in some ways they share the values of their class and generation, and yet to this must be added that they were Karelians. As David Carr (1986) accurately pointed out, an individual can choose many communities with which to identify and one choice does not necessarily eliminate another.

Some letters reveal the attitudes of the times and the expectations of the writers. They are important to the family's construction of its moral and political position. During 1939, before the war broke out, Sylvi wrote about two local events that were inversions of the way things should be. One involved cleanliness and the other fidelity within the family.

> I'll continue my letter now here in Sonkajanranta, 20 kilometres from home in the small house of Meronen. I left home in the morning around nine with Arvi by car all the way to Kovero. From there with a horse to Sorronsuu, where Arvi baptised a child, and I visited a certain Karhapää family that had 13 children. We came by car towards Ilomantsi to Onkimäki and from there on skis 5 kilometres here to Sonkajanranta. We visited one miserable cottage as representatives of the godparent association of the *Kotiliesi* journal.[7] We took clothes, soap and cockroach poison there. Oh if you could also be able to visit here and get to know these friends of mine. I wonder how they have the strength to live in this misery. In one cottage was the less than one-year-old Kalle, smiling sweetly, in his cradle hanging from the ceiling so the bedbugs and cockroaches could not bite him. Despite this, the [boy's] head was covered in grey scabs, scabies completely covered the body, and the feet were abscessed, dripping puss. In another cottage the beds of the small children had worms.   (Sylvi to Toini, 21.3.1939)

> In this village just now there is a young wife who has been married for two years. She has a beautiful husband and a lovely small girl, but on her shoulders there is a burden which is greater than one could believe. She has confided in me. One young girl from the neighbouring village will give birth to her husband's baby just in these days. In addition, this man, after everything has come into the open, has tried to violate a young servant girl of his who has now left the house. Despite this, the man says he likes his wife who has decided not to divorce though all the relatives recommend it. All the village gossips ('gossiping ladies') are amazed that the couple does not divorce. According to my mind, it is real heroism on the side of the wife when she tries to mend her broken life. I feel we can learn from a distance what good we have been given. (Sylvi to Toini, 30.7.1939)

The attempts do not work for the young couple, and Sylvi writes about the court proceedings to Toini in November 1939. Sylvi had privileged information about court proceedings, both in Tuupovaara and about other places, because the court was held in the parish hall and the travelling judges stayed in the parsonage when they visited for the court sessions.

> Right now the district court is in session in Tuupovaara. The county governor, Pulkkinen, is staying with us. The other judges are not available; they are in the [army] reserves. The children's maintenance decision is on Thursday. I am in the parish hall today providing for [feeding] the court men. The young couple left 'on vacation' from the court proceedings to have their discussions in the neighbouring parish. That allows the woman some humility so that she is not here to hear the people's mockery. (Sylvi to Toini, 28.11.1939, two days before the village is evacuated)

The letters often contain ideas about living a Christian life. Occasionally, it is spelt out in one or two phrases, such as in the following letter. This letter contains references to two issues in the metanarrative, the civil war political split and ideas about living a proper Christian life. Sylvi begins with a description of her work in the Lotta organisation. The first paragraph refers to the civil war; she apparently agitated a man who was sympathetic to either the Red or White side. She then continues with the idea of being 'full Christian beings'.

> May 16 was a Lotta celebration. I went with the regional head Sainio and put a wreath on a hero's grave. First Sainio spoke, and then I spoke skilfully (although Arvi was of two minds about this) for ten minutes about the well known, remembering the first free spring [1918]. I agitated some man with prejudices from the Karelian Isthmus.
>
> I saw in the Lotta-Svärd paper that Mrs Pyhälä has another year [as head]. She is an energetic woman, but it's a bit of a pity that she does not use her energy in a Christian way. I am trying to teach [my Lotta groups] that people should be full Christian beings. Now the other day I went with the speaker and the vice-speaker to the Luutalahti village group. There we said that neither light entertainment nor dance evenings should be planned. We don't dance. (Sylvi to Toini, 24.5.1939)

The June 1940 letters are full of reports about the redistribution of food and goods to the people affected by the war. The parsonage and the parish hall were at the centre of the redistribution. It was time-consuming work and work that Sylvi came to dislike. Her entries increasingly complain that people argue too much about getting their supplies and, in the end, she refused to do the job, turning it over to others. Sometimes she heard stories that made her sympathetic to the situation of the evacuees, as in the first letter below. She was sympathetic because the people had lost their home and household goods behind the new border. She was not always sympathetic towards the people of her own district, however. In the end she became critical of her neighbours for expecting too much help and not helping themselves, as the second two letters reveal.

Today the *emäntä* of the Saarivaara guesthouse, Solehmainen, came to ask for clothes. The Ruskies had already lived in her home but had had to move away after the border was drawn. At departure they had broken everything they could, they had even thrown the cooking utensils into the well. The border now goes through Solehmainen's field. The *emäntä* told that they are allowed to cut rye as close as five metres from the border. The Russians cut [the fields with a scythe] a few tens of metres on the 'wrong' side of the border. They had a secret hiding place, where they buried the clothes [and sheets] from three houses, but now they can't get them away. There is, amongst others, 35 sheets. They go always to look if the Ruskies have found the hiding place but until now it is untouched. The busy Ruskie guard road passes it close by. It's been heard that during the fall darkness they will try to get their things out. The Ruskies plough their fields with rifles on their backs.   (Sylvi to Helena, 14.9.1940)

We now have many root crops, potatoes, sugar beets and chicory [growing]. Tapani [Arvi's brother] has taken a shovel and planted potatoes wherever he can.
   Here 3,000-4,000 kilos of goods for evacuees and the poor have been distributed. The area around our storage sheds is bare of grass because of the traffic of large trucks. I think there you do not have this. Here everyone is begging, both the gypsies and the rich. Over the last few weeks we have received about 500 kilos of Danish butter, also cod, tins of marmalade, and so on. Today a large truck from Joensuu has brought fat, margarine, butter and clothes. Everyone gets a little. Everyone quarrels and wants more.
   Certainly here in the backwoods some people are starving, there the fall grains were taken away and the cattle were sent to Savo, and little of this has been returned. Residents had to leave their homes and soldiers have been stealing and evacuating whatever they can get. Miserable conditions are the fate of many families, although I think it would help the dissatisfaction if they would go back home and get to work [on their homesteads]. Now they don't remember how they missed their homes last winter. They should forget about [getting] washboards and milk cans now, and not rely on the local government, which is a mess anyway.
   I received a letter about giving household goods, clothes, etc., to ministers' families who are homeless. But I decided not to do anything because all my relatives are homeless [also].   (Sylvi to Helena, 11.6.1940)

Finnish Aid has provided a hospital here for the refugees. They are also building a pre-natal clinic. In the Tynkä–Korpiselkä region [those villages on the Finnish side of Korpiselkä] they will pay for a church social worker. There have been many things sent here as gifts: 125 bicycles, skis, fishing rods and nets, canvases, and so on. These things are worth several tens of thousands of marks. No one admits to getting too much.   (Sylvi to Helena, 23.11.1940)

Helena wrote back that she was sending cabbages and some felt boots manufactured in Inkilä, if there were any left in the shops, and she encouraged her daughter to keep going with one of the traditional sayings that she collected.

> Now here is an ancient woman's saying, that 'I'm in such a hurry, I'm in such a hurry, so much that I don't have time to do anything' [*Nyt saapi sanoa muinosen naisen lailla, että 'Nii o kiire, nii o kiire, jot ei kerkiä tekemää mittää!'*]. (Helena to Sylvi, 27.11.1940)

Sylvi's diary entry in December 1940 looked back over the year since the last Christmas. Helena sent them presents but there were no candles for the tree or the church service. Because December is the darkest time of the year, they had to move the church service to a later time in the morning so people could see. National events have affected their lives.

> A few final words in this messy diary. Sad times, sad memories. It is winter. A lot warmer than before, the war winter of 1939–40.
> Now that the population has been moved, they should organise their lives. The Free Aid [society] has tried to help people in adverse circumstances and has caused envy among neighbours. Still some of these people are sincerely grateful for the help. Arvi puts his back to the work [distributing aid] and approves of it. I have taken myself out of it. I don't like it.
> These days almost all groceries are by card. In a month per person we get 750 grams of sugar, 1.5 kg of wheat, rye and other kinds of flour, 1/8 kg of coffee and 1/2 kg of coffee substitute, 250 grams of butter every ten days or 500 grams of cheese. Meat and milk are controlled and rationed. Butter costs 37 marks/kilogram and milk 2.50 marks/litre.   (Sylvi's diary, December 1940)

There were 25,000 dead and 55,000 wounded at the end of the Winter War (Engle and Paananen 1992 [1973]: 142); this was a heavy toll for a nation with a population of about four million. Christian metaphors were a way to understand the loss and the Lutheran Church was a central institution in distributing social services. Nevertheless, people were expected, by the moral code of these writers, to work and to make life better for themselves. Personal responsibility was an important component in Sylvi's attitude towards those she met, and not even war could excuse a person's behaviour. This value on personal responsibility, since the nationalist movement of the nineteenth century, linked the individual to the national project of building a democratic society.

Rhubarb and Cultural Transmission

The extended family has a history of personalities and views about how one should live. Roles and attitudes learnt in childhood, within the domestic unit, are deeply ingrained. 'We live our childhood as our future. ... We shall think with these original deviations, we shall act *with* these gestures which we have learned and which we want to reject' (Sartre 1968: 101). Values and roles are discussed in the letters and passed along to future generations in the small printed books that they have published themselves. By reading the saved materials and repeating stories, the extended family knows itself through contrast and comparison. In the act of circulating these stories they continue to reproduce the family: this is who we are, this is what we have done. From opinions, stories, folklore, gossip and eyewitness accounts, the family portrays itself, implicitly and sometimes explicitly, in comparison to others. This is a continuous process, repeated in the letters, and replicated in the stories of following generations.

When the language remains in the first person, the 'I' of the narrator, it is often about the local, the personal and the family. There are stories of trying new laundry techniques, advice about babies, requests for clothing, and opinions about others. But there is seldom evidence of completely individualised writing, the kind of psychological self-searching that Jokinen (1996) finds in more recent Finnish women's diary writing. A psychological meta-narrative is for later generations. These writers are busy, they are active in maintaining their households and they observe life around them and report on poverty, love and infidelity, bickering and gossip, superstition, sadness, empathy and humour. The memoirs – both in the letters and in the life history – aim at an emotional truth rather than the truly true (Crapanzano 1980).

At times, especially in regard to the events of war, they use the 'we' of the national community. And yet, these writers do not assume that they speak for the whole community. Rather, their words reveal some of the possible positions, how local systems of thought were being employed to interpret and organise experience. These writers, people with strong opinions, articulated their positions and joined them to common themes being discussed at the time in Finland. This is how they used 'available notions' and the 'cultural equipment ready to hand' to make sense of their world (Geertz 1995: 3).

The dividing line between a political and a moral position is thin or nonexistent. The memoirs position the family not only in a home community and homeland; they position the family within political ideologies across generations. The fundamental split of the civil war was so persistent because of its link to political and class values which were passed along in community narratives (e.g., Knuuttila 1989) and family stories. The repetition of stories links certain themes to present experience. Stories about Karelia continue to circulate, reminding people that there was once a lively Finnish society there. They can be woven into a recent novel set in Karelia,[8] they can be linked to collections of folklore research collected in different regions of Karelia,[9] they provide a position when reading newspaper letters and editorials,[10] or they can be joined to the lectures and activities of the

112

Karelian Association in Helsinki.[11] Public discussion of Karelia is possible, if one wants to join in. It is part of the collective experience of Finland, part of the metanarrative of Finnish history.

In the spring of 2000 I went to an outdoor market to buy rhubarb. There were two types to choose from: on the left in the front of the stand was normal-sized rhubarb, while at the back, on the right side, there were some very large rhubarb stalks. I had decided on the normal, but when I asked for this, the farmer suggested that I buy the large rhubarb because it was very good, it was 'from Karelia'. In the story that followed, he explained that he lives about forty kilometres from Helsinki and he got the rhubarb from his neighbour. His neighbour had been a ten-year-old boy in Karelia, in Antrea (the neighbouring parish to Kirvu), at the time of the evacuation. As they were leaving the house, the boy took along some of 'mother's rhubarb' and it is this rhubarb that he still grows in his garden. As Mr Peltonen told me this story, he waved his arms to indicate the smoke from the house in flames and pretended to shoot a machine gun as he told how the Russians were moving in while the small boy dug up the rhubarb. Mr Peltonen would have been a small boy himself in 1944 and he said that he is from the region of Häme. He has no direct link to the events; therefore his story stresses the war – a national story he knows from books, television and films – rather than life in Karelia. When he replicates the story, he can only do so in the frame of national history, in the metanarrative about Karelians and the war. This replication approaches nationalist discourse more than the stories do when told by the family, who in fact experienced Karelia.

I was intrigued by Peltonen's story so I phoned my friend (on our mobile phones) and told it to her. She was eating in the lunchroom with academic colleagues and told them about the rhubarb from Karelia. One man at the table then said that he buys Karelian potatoes in Riihimäki from a man who brought the potatoes from Karelia. Another man said that his wife got some tomato seeds, from which she grew plants, from a man who had brought them from Karelia. In the current social context, Karelian vegetables are valued as being more natural (organic) because they are still the old-fashioned plants and not the new hybrid varieties.

Pierre Clastres described a characteristic type of speech given by chiefs among the South American Indian group that he studied. The chief will typically give a speech every morning or evening about the ancestors while other members of the group go about their business, apparently without listening to what he says. Clastres calls this a 'steady flow of empty speech' which serves to keep the social body intact and ensures that no displacement of forces will upset the social order (1987: 154–55). The chief's speech, seemingly without content, guarantees that 'all things will remain in their place'. In much the same way, the letters are a steady flow of everyday commentary that outsiders have little interest in reading. They are not empty of meaning although they seem to be empty because they are now out of context. But the actual content is not the issue today. They now have a different value: they tell about the lives of the ancestors, the relation of the family to national events, and that there is continuity from previous generations to the present. And those messages ensure that things remain in place, that the community of the extended family continues.

Stories about Karelia circulate in Finnish society. The war, for some, recalls Karelia. For the family, the letters about domestic life, by analogy, recall home and their Karelian homeland; in particular, they are a paradigmatic message about family values and how one should live. Even the seemingly insignificant, like sharing clothes or sending apples from one house to another, has significance once home has been lost. The emotive power of the letters is in the analogical relationship of Inkilä to home and the paradigmatic messages about who 'we' are, not so much in the actual content of the letters. When the stories are replicated, the emphasis is on the family and its history; when outsiders repeat the stories, the stories are tied to national events and take on a slightly different meaning. The small turn in meaning, from 'our' rhubarb to Karelian rhubarb rescued from the front-line of war, is an example of the distilling process that takes place as part of creating a national political culture.

8
TOWARDS MYTHOLOGY

The memoirs symbolically reconstitute Inkilä and all of Karelia as a memory world. Part of the process of creating a memory world requires a detachment from the current spatial and temporal world. This happens through a crucial turn in writing about the evacuations. Helena wrote two descriptions of leaving, one about the evacuation of 1941 and the other about the second evacuation of 1944. These specific narratives reveal the way in which Karelia is 'walled off' and moved towards mythic time. The narrative move towards mythology is a way to continue to inhabit and hold the space. The process of walling off protects the restricted-empirical 'we', and Karelia is protected and preserved within the generalised-essential 'we' of the Finnish nation state. What happens with Karelia in this process is a model for how some elements become distilled to form a national political culture. Karelia, as a memory world, now almost mythical, can be recalled by the mention of even a tiny part: rhubarb or tomato seeds.

Greg Urban (2001) has noted that sometimes the 'we' is not national, as in the 'Hell no we won't go' of the Vietnam War protesters in the United States. The situation of Karelia is not as combative, but the Karelian 'we' continues to mark a time and place that is 'Finnish', albeit outside the boundaries of the present nation state. Because of this status, the story of this family's experiences can be joined to stories of evacuation experienced by many others. What is perceived is the meaning of the event more than the details, and the meaning of evacuation can be linked to the 'we' of people in northern Finland who were moved to camps in Sweden, to the 'we' of the Finnish children who were evacuated to Sweden during the war years, and to contemporary refugees from the Balkans, Somalia and other areas who have recently arrived to be residents in Finland.[1] Evacuees and refugees are, by definition, a group 'we' in a special relation to nation states.

Although not a transnational diasporic group, the Karelian experience differentiates Karelians from other Finns. Ilmari Kuisma, Helena's son, read a Finnish translation of my article and commented on it in February, 2001. His comments followed the text and added details about Inkilä related to issues that I had raised: house names in Karelia, the contributions of male and female members of the family, class relations in Inkilä, and his mother's writing. At the end of the letter he wrote, 'there is still more work for the axe', a Finnish saying that means much more could be written about, 'as they would say, going for training in Siberia'. This reference to Siberia underlines the serious consequences of war for the losing side; in neighbouring Estonia and Latvia for example, the Soviet Union took over the state and exiled many non-Russians to Siberia. Ilmari did not want me to casually overlook this; the options of war were harsh. He continues with an anecdote about the feelings of his brother Israel (Ismo), followed by a description of his own last visit to the 'home village', giving the passage a title and a seal by typing his name, date and place at the end. The first 'we' is 'we people' (*meikäläiset*) and the second is 'we Karelians' (*meille Karjalaisille*).

> Brother Ismo was evacuated to Muurame and he said to others in that place: I would like to see *keskisuomalaisten* [people from central Finland, where Muurame is located] with backpacks march across the Torniö bridge [into Sweden], and then we would be in the same position.
>
> The Inkilä Trip, Briefly [*Inkilän matka lyhyesti*]
> I received, on 4.9.1944 in Tienharra near Viipuri in the office of the 1st Artillery Company, a phone call from Headquarters at 4:00 that informed [us] that the cease fire begins at 7:00. The order was to be delivered. We people [*meikäläiset*] stopped shooting but the Russians shot all their ammunition fiercely before 8:00. Then began the silence and the soldiers climbed up out of the trenches.
> We Karelians [*meille Karjalaisille*] were given a leave to evacuate. I travelled during the night, walking 40 km home with one Kirvu soldier. The home village [*kotikylä*] was disserted, only in *Puumala* [house name] some Lottas were living and station master Pekurinen was dispatching the last trains [waving the flag to send the last trains]. The home trip took six days without food. I returned via Elisenvaara by train to Lapeenranta and from there onwards to the Bay of Viipuri to my unit. There were puddles of blood in Elisenvaara because the Russians had bombed an evacuation train [evacuating civilians]. A lot of evacuees were killed in the bombing. That is my first experience of the cease fire. What else can one add to this.
> Nikkilä, 20.2.2001   Ilmari Kuisma

Ilmari's comments were triggered by reading my article about letters as a type of history, not about the evacuation. The topic of Inkilä or Karelia brings to mind the evacuation. Ilmari concludes with a story about leaving home, introduced by another story about leaving home. Leaving Inkilä is analogous to leaving Finland for Sweden; analogous to leaving one nation state for another. It was not experienced by a national 'we'. However, the wars that lead to the evacuation were experienced by most of those living at the time. When Ilmari's story circulates, the similar experiences of one group, the 'we people' (the Finnish soldiers) and that of 'we Karelians', can be recognised, just as 'we Karelians' can be recognised in 'we refugees'. The story has meaning for each group because the group 'finds there its own image' (Sartre 1968: 150). Whenever this collapsing occurs, a group 'we' emerges. When it happens, as in the first case, the group is a national 'we'.

The First Evacuation

Some of the events written in the letters were presented as news at the time. Retold later as a written narrative, the writing merges with the stories of other Kirvu and Karelian residents who later put their memories together in books, museum displays and so on.[2]

Karelia was evacuated twice. The first evacuation, under conditions of warfare, was disquieting but there was the expectation that people would be able to move back, that an alliance with Germany would help the Finns reclaim their territory. This in fact happened in 1941 when the Finnish army, with the support of the German army, reclaimed Karelia and other territory and the residents moved back. But by the time of the second evacuation in 1944, supplies were low, the German army was in retreat and burning the north of Finland, and there was an understanding, perhaps not always spoken, that this was it; they would not be returning easily or soon. The last years in Karelia are significant in memories of the village.[3] The evacuation, as an event in Finnish history, carries strong emotional and political meaning both for the participants and for outside observers.[4] The plight of the evacuees continues to circulate. It is reprinted over and over in pictures of the roads crowded with people in carts or walking with their few belongings into Finland.[5]

Much of what is reported is about how the ordinary is suddenly transformed by the extraordinary nature of war. The extraordinary events in turn implicitly refer to the known, to that which is obvious to both the writers and the readers, by virtue of the difference. The war was fought in Karelia. It was known directly through personal experience in Inkilä and Helena's account is full of local people's names and fates. The referential-empirical group is Karelia, although she is also a patriotic Finn. This is evident in her note about the news of the war and in the songs which the men sing as they leave on the train for the army:

117

9.10.1939 Paasikivi is in Moscow to talk about politics and economics between Finland and the USSR. (Karelia)   (HK, p. 73, the parentheses are hers)

10.10.1939 Matikkala's [a part of Inkilä] men and boys are leaving tonight for 'somewhere'. As the train leaves they sing on the train *Kuullos pyhä vala, kallis Suomenmaa* [Listen to our Holy vow, precious Finland, violence must not touch you...] and *Kaunis Karjala* [Beautiful Karelia] – they are going to protect the border, [going] to an unknown fate.   (HK, p.73)

At the end of February 1940, during the Winter War, Helena wrote that Inkilä had been bombed seven times. The Jantunen house nearby had been hit during a raid; nine soldiers died and the *emäntä* and *isäntä* were injured badly and died later. As a result, Päivölä was not safe and they moved their cows to Arvi's father's farm outside the village centre. By the beginning of March, the Finnish state wanted all civilians out of the area although the train was not running and the roads were crowded with refugees. Helena, Israel and Simo Pärssinen (Arvi's father) finally had to leave.

Father and I left on 9 March in the morning. Eino [their son] took us and also Ukko-Pärssinen [grandfather-Pärssinen] to Kallislahti station where we took the train to Jyväskylä and the bus to Muurame.   (HK, p.76)

After this brief description, written as part of her life story, Helena returns to the subject, which she titles 'Our First Evacuation'. The complete version of this narrative gives the context for their leaving. It appropriately links the personal experience of Helena and her cows to the war experience; both the woman and her cows suffer the disruptions of war. At the same time – 'summer 1939 was a favourable summer' – the story begins at home where the summer was bright and productive. A road or journey is often the narrative setting for encounters with others and events governed by chance. Here the 'spatial and temporal paths of the most varied people ... intersect' (Bakhtin 1981: 243).

The evacuation narratives appreciate the chance encounters of the road but Helena's 'journey through the woods' differs from the road of the adventurer or wanderer. The evacuation is a journey of pain, captured by one Christian reference – *ristintie* [the road of the cross] – which describes Christ's walk with the cross.[6] The lives of the cows in the story parallel that of the people; both are taken from their familiar surroundings and both are homeless. Two stories of encounters are inserted into the story. At Kallislahti, with its images of the white coffins at the train station,[7] the narrative juxtaposes the seriousness of war with the giddiness of young girls, reminding them ('you') and the reader about proper behaviour and the ordinary people caught in the events of war. Comments about the war are patriotic comments; they are about people – dead soldiers, Karelian refugees and Russian prisoners – not nation states. The second insert is about the problem of finding a shelter for the cows and the household goods. The 'we' of the opening paragraphs is a Karelian 'we', linking the family to other Karelians by the work that had to be done (e.g., grain harvesting). It turns to an exclusively family we' with the paragraph beginning, 'We too'.

Our First Evacuation

Summer 1939 was a favourable summer in terms of vegetation and weather but in the autumn when it was time for grain harvesting we were wondering why the radio and the newspapers rushed farmers to reap and winnow the grain into sacks. I guess we started even laughing that country folks can't reap their grain without the advice of the masters in Helsinki. Later on, however, every Karelian found that advice to be good.

So the war between Finland and the Soviet Union broke out during the same autumn. Men in arms all across Finland stepped under the same flags[8] and marched to the border to defend their country; so too did the Karelians, as the first ones, because they were close to the border. Three boys from our house went to the front, Eino, Wäinö and Ismo, and a fourth one, Ilmari, went to military service on 4.1.1940 and stayed for five years less two months, that is until the end of the Winter and Continuation Wars.

We passed the winter in the turmoil of fighting. Places including Kollaa, Tolvajärvi, Taipale, Muolaanjärvi, Summa and Viipuri, only to mention a few, gave unforgettable honour to the meagre troops of Finland.[9]

The forced peace agreement was signed in March 1940 when Finland had to cede all of Karelia to the Russians. That marked the beginning of the Karelian people's journey through the woods, the evacuation; [this was] not out of force, everyone left of their free will because no one wanted to stay as a subject of foreign rule. They would rather leave their homes and land inherited from their fathers and move to other areas of Finland, everywhere in the country.[10]

We too left our home in Inkilä village in Kirvu on 9.3.1940 and headed to Muurame parish close to Jyväskylä where our son-in-law and daughter are elementary school teachers. At that time we could no longer leave Inkilä by rail straight to Jyväskylä because of heavy bombing by the Russians. Russian fighter planes were always stalking and bombing such junctions like Hiitola and Elisenvaara.

So we left our home, Päivölä, early in the morning on the ninth of March and started by car to the Kallislahti station through Ruokolahti and Sulkava. At one house at the Ruokolahti church we made coffee because we were cold. After we had warmed up there we continued our journey to the Kallislahti station. At the station we gave the goods that we had brought, mostly foodstuffs, flour and such, to the warehouse to be forwarded to Jyväskylä. At this warehouse four soldiers rested in their white coffins brought from the front. At the station stood a fully packed long cargo train filled full with refugees from Karelia, old people, women and children. At the same time another train came from Karelia and three cars were filled with Russian prisoners of war. A large crowd of girls from around the station had gathered at the station and what do they do but go and talk to the prisoners. One of them could speak a little bit of Russian. After the train had left she said that she had asked the prisoners if they had wives at their homes. They had answered that even if they had, they were going to get new ones in Finland. There they were, laughing and giggling at the prisoner train car, so that in the cold evening weather they had to jump on one foot to keep warm. After the train started moving these wretched girls were waving their hands at the train. At the same time the refugee train also started moving but not a single hand was raised as a sign of compassion. A great shame to the Kallislahti girls. Oh how I wanted to say to these girls that you would have made a much more human impression if you had waved to those refugees even as a sign of compassion. Because some of these refugees had had to leave their homes partly because of those prisoners. Or you could have gone to the station warehouse to those four coffins brought from the front and sung some hymns from the hymnbook or a patriotic song.

Later in the evening we were able to continue our journey in a fully packed train to Jyväskylä. From there at about 10 o'clock we continued our journey to Muurame. Our daughter had already earlier rented a dwelling from *isäntä*-farmer Otto Salmela in the parish. We lived in that dwelling in a self-sufficient household economy until about midsummer. We were fine because our hosts were polite and favourable to us. After the servant left the house I milked the cows of the house with the *emäntä* who paid me one mark per day for it. Our own four cows had been evacuated to the Teuva community close to the shoreline of the Gulf of Bothnia. During the week before midsummer we went to fetch our cows from Teuva but out of the four cows we only retrieved two. They had killed one because they suspected hoof and mouth disease. The second one they had given to some house to be taken care of but the takers could not be found in any books.[11] Those two cows were lost. We brought the other two with us on a train to Jyväskylä and by truck to Muurame.

After we had arrived to the house where we kept our quarter,[12] to Otto Salmela's yard, and had taken our cows off the truck, the *isäntä* of the house came and said that the cows had to be immediately taken away from the yard altogether. We had bought bales of hay as feed[13] and the *isäntä* ordered us to take even those away as soon as possible. I went to the *isäntä* and asked where we could take the cows. He answered take them wherever you want. The cows of the house were in their new cowshed and the old one was completely empty but as we could not take our cows to the old one either, so that was that. We took our cows and the hay and took them to the roadside 200 metres away and tied them to a birch tree. The cows were there for three days. Then we obtained a small corral 1.2 kilometres away in which the cows could stay till the autumn with the help of extra feed given to them. All sorts of our household goods were kept on the house's premises and the *isäntä* told us to take them out immediately. Since we had no idea where we could take them at such short notice, we had to pile them on the roadside under the open sky. There they were in a big mess, tables, chairs, cupboards, linens, etc. Even such a sad thing happened that before we could get these things under any kind of cover there was a heavy rain and, although we tried to protect them from getting wet, all the clothes, bed sheets, pillows, and so on became soaking wet. After this the boys began to look for a new place to live and managed to get one from the headman of the municipality, a dwelling of three rooms and a kitchen in which we lived till the following autumn, October 1941, when we were able to return to our home in Karelia.

No one can quite understand that joy and happiness who has not first experienced the heartfelt agony of leaving one's home and birthplace. Now after one and a half years we were able to return to our Karelian home.   (HK, pp. 76–78)

This is a narrative of moving through places, but it is a forced journey. As it begins, the place names are Karelian and form a path through a known landscape. When they are in central Finland only a few very general names are given, Muurame and Jyväskylä. It is a story of disruption with a positive end; all returns to normal when they return to 'our Karelian home' and the story comes full circle. However, the end is in the past tense ('we were able to return'). The one present tense addresses a general 'humanity' who have never experienced this ('No one can quite understand'). The narrative does not project a future.

Experiencing Otherness

The population of eastern Finland was evacuated to safer, more central or western towns. Evacuation was difficult and it upset the normal cycles of farm management. The evacuees often felt out of place in the makeshift arrangements and experienced a kind of otherness unknown in their normal village life.

The Pärssinen children were evacuated from Tuupovaara to Muurame (in central Finland) and were then joined by their mother. Sylvi wrote of her problems in Muurame to Helena three weeks after arriving there. She writes that they are in a small place and often in the dark because there is no oil and the house does not have electricity. She explains that the lack of friendship makes life difficult for a Karelian woman refugee with her children. In the following letter segment, the immediate 'we' of the events experienced are 'Jenny and I' but the emphasis then turns to a Karelian 'we'. The Karelian 'we' highlights regional distinctions that were still typical of Finland at the time the letter was written:

Yes, I am of the opinion that the Karelians, who must depend upon the central Finns and the Häme people [two regions in Finland], are in a difficult place. Here it is of course cold and raw, but one could really freeze from the lack of friendliness.

Let me give you a small example of the central Finnish behaviour that Jenny [her sister-in-law from Inkilä] and I encountered. We were in the parsonage's sauna. Everyone else had finished their sauna; it was only the two of us. We laughed, talked and chattered, as we did our sauna. Then a woman stuck her head in the door and told us that the children could not sleep the whole night because we were making so much noise, and other ugly words. We were upset at first, but then we continued as before and began to smile as we thought about it. Finally Jenny said – the woman had already disappeared from the doorway – that, 'these Häme people should come to us, to Karelia, where you can make noise and stay up all night' (using Karelian dialect: *Lopuksi Jenny sanoi - akka oli jo kadonnut oven raosta - että 'tulkaaha työ hämäläiset meill' Karjalaa, ni saatta roiskaa vaikk' kaiket yöt'*). And the next day when we saw the minister we said that, 'No one lives in our saunas. How could we know that Häme people live in the parsonage's sauna?' (also in Karelian dialect: *'eihä meiä pappiloihe saunois' asu kettää, mist myö tiijettii, jot hämmee pappila saunois o asukkaat'*).

[To make her point, she adds] 'It's no wonder that Toini doesn't like it here.' (Sylvi to Helena, 21.2.1940)

There is some irony here as she realises that Häme people think that Karelians are loud and boisterous while at the same time, the stereotype of Häme people is that they are quiet, shy and serious. And, while Sylvi, Toini, and probably the above Jenny, had travelled and were familiar with various regions of Finland, there were still many people who knew only their own region and little of other styles and customs. In this sense, Finland was still a map imposed on local worlds and these worlds could quite often seem strange to fellow countrymen. In a similar vein, one of Helena's sons wrote that the men in the army with him from other regions 'do not understand our soil' and ask him questions about how Karelians grow their crops.[14]

The distance was not only regional, however. It could also be about manners and proper behaviour. During the war especially, the expected behaviour for a minister's wife was to help people in need and Sylvi was very busy helping refugees in Tuupovaara. In a diary entry, Sylvi writes about a minister and his wife whom she visited while looking for a place to live with her children. The minister's house is large, the minister is well-known and his wife is young and pretty. They do not have children and everything is finely planned and organised when they serve the coffee. But the young wife is cool to Sylvi and makes it clear that she cannot have them there. Sylvi summarised their positions in the image of her dress: 'The woman quite lovely and me – in my shabby Lotta dress!'[15] On the trip home, I didn't know whether to cry or laugh, thinking about how many were housed at the Tuupovaara parsonage – soldiers, evacuees, known and unknown – all were accepted by us' (March 1940).

Sylvi's son Rauno edited the memoirs and made a few comments that are carefully separated from the original text. Much of his editing explains who certain people are and their relation to the writers; at other times he adds to the story by quoting published books about the war years. At one point he adds his own memories about evacuation. In this short passage he gives an interpretation based on personal experience and brings these materials into the present. The written text, therefore, allows Rauno to conjoin a new discourse to the discourse of the text (Ricoeur 1991: 118). And when Rauno does this, it is a resaying that reactivates what is said by the text (ibid.: 124). First-hand accounts by children evacuated during the war years, many to Sweden for safety, have been popular in Finland in the 1990s. Rauno's personal story thus joins a collective recollection about the experiences of Finnish children in wartime.

> The beginning of the Winter War and the evacuation are certainly one of my first childhood memories. Of course there is a lot I do not remember. I remember however the dark November evening, when the clothes were packed into large boxes in a great hurry in the parsonage's kitchen. They were certainly large and so deep that it was hard to peep over the boxes' sides to see what was inside. Then I remember the train trip; the cars were cold, the train was frightening and the engine steamed oddly in the freezing cold night. Everything was dark. The outside toilet, which we had to use, smelled bad and was really cold. Much I do not remember, except that everything was threatening and scary, because these pieces of events eat indelibly into the mind of a boy just a few weeks over 5 years old; it was certainly powerful, so that now, over 50 years later, it is still a strong life memory.   (Rauno Pärssinen, 1993: 41)

Such stories place family members into national events, into collective memory, and into a circulating discourse about the threat to the national community. It is a patriotic discourse that circulates in local stories and links the experience of the restricted-empirical 'we' to the experience of the generalised-essential 'we' of Finland. A transfer happens in the interaction between the national historical discourse (as with general motifs in folklore) and the individual narrator or reader who conjoins his/her experiences to these stories to make the more general 'mine', and conversely to make 'mine' more general.

Back Home in Inkilä

Helena was fifty-nine years old in 1941 when she returned to Inkilä after the first evacuation. Even though she faced a mess, she took time to write about the return in her letters. She describes the work of returning the house to normal and ends with a Christian reference.

> At home again. We arrived here, father on Sunday and me and Mari together in the middle of the night on Monday. I went to the mill's *tupa* that is habitable because Ilmari had made a kitchen there. – We made coffee and it was at least four in the morning before we went to sleep. –[16]
> Certainly it was nice to get the foreigners out of the house. I do not know the feel of warm country dirt under the feet because I came straight home from the station. Mari wants to go home but not before cleaning. In the next few days we

will work also at Päivölä. They say that cows are stupid but they are not so stupid.[17]

I'll tell you how it is here. Every place is full of junk, from where these quarrelsome people [Russian soldiers] were in every house. Here on the side of the porch there are goods, hats, buckets, sacks and whatever. I threw it all away.

Päivölä is taking all our time for repairs. Now it is in a really pitiable condition: the cellar is totally empty, the windows broken, locks and handles torn off every door, dented doors and walls full of cracks, and dirty as if people had never lived here before. The food storage room is now clean, although the walls were full of chicken droppings and the smell is there, there is a pile of rubbish between the kitchen window and the porch, a small one near the *tupa* and another near the bell. That's how it is at Päivölä. But thanks to God that He preserved our home and it was not burned. (Helena to Toini, 5.10.1941)

Other people return to Inkilä and this too makes it normal, as home includes the social relations of the community.

I now have Päivölä warmed every day, today I will edge the double windows. Now at home things are getting more like before, the small cabins are again warm.[18] At this time the old Reimis and Antti Reimi are here, also Puumala's women and children and Korte's Eemeli. The old Leppälä grandmother is still alive and here at home. (Helena to Sylvi, 18.11.1941)

Early 1942 was a difficult time for the Karelians, who had been living through several years of war. Usually there is little mention of money; this letter is an exception as Helena explains how the family is managing their household economy and taking care of her and Israel.

I say little about our money affairs. Now that the evacuation is over and we are at home, we, with father, are getting some help as Itti [son Israel] sends 100 marks per month. It is good that we put this money in the office. During his fall vacation Wäinö gave me 700 marks and now in January he sent 1,000 marks from the front. Itti sends all his pay [money] from the front because there money means nothing. Ilmari also has sent some, but not all, as he buys supplies (food). So in that way you can see how the boys care for us. (Helena to Sylvi, 25.2.1942)

There were Russian prisoners living in Karelia during the Continuation War and they were forced to work on the Finnish farms. Helena was prepared to fight the Russians 'to the last man', but all the same she could distinguish people from nation states and appreciate that most of the prisoners were just ordinary people.[19]

Here there are now three hundred prisoners living in the Worker's Hall. They are used to clear land between Inkilä and the village of Laalo but they stay in this house. We had ten Russians on the weekdays to help with sawing; now for three days they will work on this 'estate' ['*kotikartano*'],[20] planting turnips, some drive the horses and others work the fields. Today they were here under the window turning the garden soil. You would not believe how bad looking they are. I feel sorry for them. Two of them said to me 'niet ruski, mortva'.[21] One is a *Tsekkiläinen* [a Czech]. One is an agronomist. He seemed clever but he was too embarrassed to do a lot of work; [he] was there more to swell the numbers. During the day I cooked them a good potato soup,[22] the guard told them to sit on the grass and I gave pieces of bread and two plates of soup to everyone, or all of what was cooked. They were grateful – even the guard approved. The Russians do get bread, 500 grams per day, but not much else.

The guard said his home had been in Sotkamo parish and to look at he seemed like a reserved [type of] man. I invited him into the *tupa* for coffee-substitute and he talked about the evacuation time. They had been moved to Oululanni Pyhäjärvi. I have never seen a man cry like this man. Twice he tried to talk about his son but on both times stopped short [couldn't continue]. I believe that it was too sad for this man and I believe also that everyone there on the front is sad. They predict that the war will be over in the fall but I don't believe it.   (Helena to Sylvi, 26.5.1942)

The war intensified in the Karelian Isthmus during February and March of 1944. On 3 February, Helena wrote to Sylvi that she would prefer to fight to the last man rather than sign a peace accord and lose their land. But one week later they were aware that the Russian attack on Finland was relentless.

Last night father came down to the cellar and said he rose because of the noise of the bombing. It sounded like it was coming from Enso and Wuoksi and lasted about one and a half hours – reminding us of the Winter War. Aira said she couldn't sleep, same for Jenny. Now in the day we have heard that the Russians were bombing Kotka and its area. It was really bad to raise people here from their sleep.[23]   (Helena to Sylvi, 11.2.1944)

The Second Evacuation

On 19 May 1944 Helena wrote to her grandsons. She described the beautiful spring and how 'the Finnish men' have been fighting for three years 'to keep our beautiful country from the Ruskies'. She writes that it is peaceful, that they do not see many Russian planes and only occasionally hear the noise of war from Viipuri. She does not seem to realise that the war was coming to a close. Perhaps it was a possibility that was talked about, but it was not written.

The experience of the end, written first as a letter, was rewritten into 'Our Second Evacuation' as part of Helena's life story. However, the structured narrative, written in the early 1950s, is oddly devoid of details compared to her writing style in other parts of the memoirs and in the story of the first evacuation. The story focuses on the last hours in Inkilä, and then the journey begins. It ends in the present, with Inkilä firmly in the past. The story of Esko is included here but devoid of the details of his weak condition and there is no mention of the confusion about Kari, who in fact did leave Inkilä with his grandfather Pärssinen. It seems as if the story can only be told in factual, unemotional terms. And yet, this account is at the heart of the family story. Did Helena want to keep it as close to history as possible? The 'we' is the family, there are no cows, and the inserted stories are about helpful people they encountered on the journey. When she describes the encounter with the local authorities the language is almost quotation; otherwise it is descriptive. I have kept the translation close to Helena's original phrasing, with my own comments in footnotes.

Our Second Evacuation

The repossession of Inkilä in Kirvu happened in August 1941. My husband Israel Kuisma and myself were given permission to come back home as early as September. We were the first residents of our home village to come back to their homes and start the clean-up work. Even before us, clean-up troops [from the Finnish army] had been ordered to the communities but there was still enough work for everyone as it was so messy everywhere in the rooms and in the yards. Our own four boys were on the front. The three eldest, Eino, Wäinö and Ismo [Israel], were on the eastern front (east Karelia), the youngest, Ilmari, was in Walkeasaari on the [Karelian] Isthmus.

The great attack by the Russians started in the summer of 1944. Ilmari happened to be on leave at the time. The radio and newspapers were reporting continuously that everybody on leave had to return to their unit, so our boy returned to the front in the middle of his leave and found his troops already retreating in Wammeljoki. Our other two sons had already been ordered from eastern Karelia to the Isthmus. Wäinö by truck to the Isthmus front, Ismo had also been ordered from eastern Karelia to the Isthmus. All of a sudden Ismo came home on a semi self-authorised leave.[24] He said he had come to pack things for departure for a new evacuation.

When we left on our first evacuation journey on 9.3.1940 most of our goods stayed at home because we could only take a fraction with us and part of that also disappeared during the journey. They had been taken to Jalasjärvi where they had been spoiled and some of them lost, having been under the open sky for a couple of months.

We managed to pack our things and Ismo went back to the front but already from the Sairala station he telephoned home saying to start quickly towards the border even if it's by foot and Jenny and Aira can push the kids[25] in carriages so that you make it across the border to the Finnish side as the Russians were already at Wuoksi (30 kilometres from Inkilä). As we were thinking [about this] and making preparations for the departure, we realised that Wäinö drove a truck to the manor's yards used for transporting ferryboats to Wuoksi. He stopped on his way on a self-authorised leave to fetch the home troops and things to take across the border. Then after we had drunk our chicory-coffee[26] and loaded our things on the truck we got on board the truck and left for our new evacuation journey.

Our journey took us to the Punkasalmi station, where we arrived at night. We rested on the floor of a small hut during the early morning hours, where there were already travellers sleeping. The next day we moved to a nearby community hall in which almost all evacuees were from Inkilä.

The local Lottas distributed soup and bread to the large group of people once a day. Even now after many years I remember the Punkasalmi Lottas with gratitude.[27] After a couple of days the people from Inkilä started their journey, now to Jalasjärvi, which had been assigned as the placement community for the people from Kirvu.

The journey was free of charge and the fully packed train started taking Karelians to other parts of Finland. Esko, the son of my eldest son Eino, stayed in the Kirvu sanatorium to be taken care of. At that time the sanatorium was a field hospital and they had promised to let him out after one week. We stayed where we were to wait for him. However the local authorities came several times to order us out explaining that we were in such a dangerous zone that no one could say when there might be a bombing, so that we can't guarantee your lives and now you would have been given a free journey. We explained to them that we are waiting for our sick son from hospital who is supposed to meet us here and if we would now leave, where would he then go when he comes. We are also not afraid of an air raid because we already saw some of that at home and we can continue our journey with our own money. Then the local authorities left us alone and they even gave us one room to live in.

After one week Eino and the station chief Pekurinen[28] brought Esko to us from the hospital. The next day we could continue our journey, not to Jalasjärvi, but to Muurame parish where my son-in-law and daughter are elementary school teachers. The families of my two sons both obtained a small room to live in but my husband and I were not given a dwelling, but they said that let them live at the school. It was difficult for my sick husband[29] to be in the raucous noise of the children so we decided to move away.

Now they had again switched the community placement for the Kirvu people to the Hyvinkää rural commune. My eldest son went there to look for a dwelling for me and father and he obtained a small attic room for us to live in close to the Nuppulinna station. We moved into it on the seventh of February 1945.

We lived in it for a little over two years. While we lived in it my husband died at the Helsinki Surgical Hospital, after having been ill exactly eight years, in March 1946, and he was buried in the old cemetery of Suonenjoki because my eldest son Eino lived at Suonenjoki at the time.[30]

After I was left alone, I moved to my two sons in Riihimäki who were employed at the Orava factory. After they moved away from Riihimäki, I also moved and went to live with my eldest son in Joroinen in the summer of 1949, where my son had founded a wheat mill.   (HK, pp. 98–99)

If the first evacuation narrative is compared with the second – both were written after 1944 – the flatness of the second denotes the end of an era (in Inkilä) and the beginning of another (in Finland proper). This second narrative is distinguished also because it is about an ongoing experience; it continues into the present of the writer (the early 1950s). The first narrative, richer in details, approaches myth because it is about the epic past or the absolute past. It lacks any temporal progression with the present and is 'walled off absolutely from all subsequent times', forming a boundary between then and now (Bakhtin 1981: 15). 'By its very nature the epic world of the absolute past is inaccessible to personal experience' (ibid.: 16). In this way, across the boundary of time and the very real boundary of the Soviet Union, Inkilä had become impossible to experience except through memory and stories passed down. The epic world, like Inkilä, is 'beyond the realm of human activity' and 'impossible to change, to rethink' (ibid.: 17). The first narrative is about leaving Inkilä and returning there, a difficult journey with a favourable end. It begins with the pleasant summer of 1939 and ends with the joy of returning, where the woman and her cows are back in place. But the second narrative notes a temporal turn; the journey is out of Inkilä forever and at the end the narrator is in the present, the known world of Finland proper, with no prospect of returning to Inkilä in the future. The woman's husband has died, the cows are gone; she is fortunate to have her sons to care for her. The second narrative ends in the developing and incomplete present, so different from 'past times, that now seem so bright compared to this time that we now live' (Helena to Sylvi letter, 24.2.1946).

Whereas much of the writing in the memoirs emphasises the continuity of the community (of customs, of genealogy, of morality), the second evacuation narrative does not; even family members are now separated. At the heart of continuity is not a shared history so much as the ability to make the analogy that the present is like the past. In the continuity model, the basis of social cohesion is likeness, which extends across time and space. It is, by extension, a model for what society ought to be (Urban 1991: 81). By contrast, in 'hot' types of discourse – those at the mythical end of the continuum – the present is distinct from that which has come before (ibid.: 102). The evacuation narratives, and the stories of Inkilä, are not simply nostalgic memories. They are concrete examples of how discourse creates a relationship between past, present and future. The present is not like the past for those Karelians who lived there. The present cannot easily call on the Karelian past to justify political action, except around themes that summarise what happened, such as evacuation.

End of War, 1944

The war with the Soviet Union ended in September 1944. Her son Ismo wrote to Helena from the army.

> The peace with the Russians was agreed 4.9.1944 at 5:40. In this place many were relieved to hear of peace – only the Karelians were of mixed emotions. (Ismo to Helena, 6.9.1944)

On the same day another son, Wäinö, wrote about his visit to Inkilä with the Finnish army, which was still in Karelia. The letter is an example of how 'diffuse, enduring solidarity' symbolically includes family and nation. The letter begins with a general 'we' that includes the nation and the family ('We don't know anything about the borders'). It turns to the family and Karelians ('Now we are homeless'), but this is quickly followed by nine mentions of a national-and-family 'we' of the present. At the end he turns the family towards the future in three mentions of what 'should' be done (or not), ending with a national-family 'we' dependent on 'the smarter ones'. The final greeting is to a referential-empirical group of family and friends. The fate of 'we' Karelians is in the hands of a national 'we' ('the smarter ones'), while the fate of 'the Finnish people' is in the hands of God.[31] This collapsing of categories is so complete that it is not always clear which 'we' Wäinö is referring to.

> Dear Mamma,
>
> Greetings from home. I came last night again from Inkilä. Esko and Jenny had dug up three sacks of potatoes and I brought them here to Puumala, but it is not sure if they will be sent on from there.
>
> Now the long awaited peace is here. We don't know anything about the borders yet but it is still fairly sure that Karelia is gone. I don't think this is anything new or strange because ever since early spring I have been sure about this kind of peace. I told about it when I was [home] on leave.
>
> The house at this time is fully evacuated, but the biggest problem was that the wheat did not get cut before leaving. The potatoes were partly dug up, if not all the way.
>
> Now we are homeless again but I believe all hope is not lost. Because of the world peace the last shots are being fired on Russia's battlefields – then we will talk about Karelia again. I believe this will happen for sure. Now we have this negotiation time before us and I think that our destiny depends on whether we can wait and agree on things. But I believe that God has not given up on the Finnish people yet.
>
> We will get along together again when we at some point get away from here. Now we have experience but the last time we left home we didn't.[32]
>
> Many thanks for the package. There were all kinds of delicious things in it. But you shouldn't send anything here anymore because we can make it [don't need it]. Next winter is probably going to be so tough that all edibles have to be saved if possible. We shouldn't even give the cows and pigs anything edible. I am afraid that next winter during mealtime in many places the hunger belt has to be tightened. But we will see what happens, and there is nothing to do but calmly wait and see what the smarter ones decide.
>
> A good fall to all of you and greetings to all our friends.
>
> (Wäinö to Helena, 6.9.1944)

Wäinö's letter, despite the defeat, tries to look to the future. The close future is one of possible hunger 'in many places'. The more distant future is in the negotiation time 'before us' and in the hope that 'God has not given up on the Finnish people'. The war was over, they had left Karelia, and the family turned its efforts to everyday affairs. The letters that follow are mostly about where people are, the availability and price of food, and the growth and development of the children. Occasionally Helena meets other Karelians,[33] or other people from Inkilä, who speak of the day when they might go back. The 'we' is now the Karelian evacuees and the future is in the hands of fortune-tellers and trance preachers:

> Last week I went into Hyvinkää and saw Alma Lintunen, Eemeli Korte and Mattila's Matti and Vilho. Almost all the evacuees believe that we will go home again. But I am beginning to feel that at this rate we won't be getting there soon. Even Eemeli Korte said to me there in Hyvankää that, 'Believe Helena, that we will not be here for long before we go Karelia' ['*Usko Helena, ettei täällä oikein kauvan olla, kun mennään Karjalaan*']. He believes in fortune tellers and in some trance preacher who is from Jaakkima. (Helena to Sylvi, 17.6.1945)

Boundaries

The Winter War is often remembered as a heroic event. The small country of Finland was attacked by the Soviet Union, 'the eastern superpower', and although they lost many lives, the community survived intact and life continued after the war more or less as it had been. The Continuation War was longer and the end of this war was a period of difficult adjustment for many people, not a time of heroism. The difference means that the Winter War circulates more in popular versions of history, as found in novels, films and television shows.

About eight years after these events, Helena wrote the evacuation narratives that create a boundary between then and now. The absolute past was established and walled off from the ongoing present. A similar process happens in a book by Kaarina Uusihakala (1989). In her rendition of the events of 1939–44, Kaarina (born 1923) writes 159 pages about the outbreak of the Winter War, the Winter War evacuation, and about life during the war years in the village of Tiitua, in the parish of Pyhäjärvi, Karelia (the same parish where Arvi Pärssinen was born). The book is written as a novel, that is, in dialogue form. But the events and personalities are real and the characters speak Tiitua dialect. A description of how the Russians shot her father's cousin, Heikki Kukko (d. 4.9.1941), and later her father Tuomas (d. 5.10.1941), forms the climax of the book. Both men were buried in the heroes' section of the Pyhäjärvi cemetery, which is now in Russia. Only in the last four pages does she describe the final evacuation of the women, children and cows, as they made their way, walking, into 'Western Finland'.

Kaarina's story, written in a different genre, is structured much like Helena's; the focus is on life in Karelia, not on the leaving. But her story contains a double death: the actual death of members of her family and the loss of Tammela house and the social relations of the community. All had to be left behind and the abrupt ending of this book also serves to 'wall off' the absolute past. Karelia becomes for both women a mythical place, a place that lacks temporal progression, a place that remains alive only through memory. As poetry brings the far near (Heidegger 1971), so these narratives bring Karelia near through details which everyone who is not there, and even those who have never been there, can recognise as their own. The memory world is not a perfect place – there is gossip, even death – but it is bounded as 'theirs', as Karelian, by the people who once lived there. By holding the image of Karelia as it was before the evacuation, and by freezing time and space, Karelians continue to belong to a common community.

The details in these narratives create a virtual social structure, an Inkilä (Karelia) that the reader can enter. This is important for the writers and the readers. The writers want to remember that which is lost from their personal experience and draw the reader into that world. The details about real characters, work and events ground the memories in experiences that can be recognised by the readers, in particular by those who have never lived there. Without this, the memory world would be too fantastic or too remote for others to enter. The details of personal stories create a template for memory. By analogy, the world described can be identified as 'mine'. But it also carries paradigmatic messages: this is the world as it ought to be.

A person with Karelian family ties will be interested in books about Karelia, others might be interested merely in the past. For example, in a book in the library about Finnish Karelia, someone had written in, next to a picture of a school, 'my father was a student there', along with other comments about father in Käkisalmi. This is located memory, evidence of the restricted-empirical 'we' of those who lived there. As noted, the past is often known through personalities and when the personalities fade away, the memories become more general, they merge with more general descriptions of history. Tarja Raninen-Siiskonen (1999: 366) has found similar changes towards the general in her study of how Karelia is remembered by evacuated Karelians in Finland. She argues that Karelia has become 'an abstract imaginary province, a province of memories, ... where members perceive themselves and fellow-members as belonging to a common entity' (ibid.: 378). The common entity is the Karelian 'we', found also in these memoirs. The written memoirs, however, serve to capture what fades from oral memory and they are more open. The writing provides for all readers with an interest to take part, although it does not determine their interpretation.

The memory world is distinct from collective memory and from imagined communities in its symbolic possibilities. It cannot be so easily dismissed as nostalgia for the past. It is a world. This world can be called up by a few details (the loci); it is material (in the Kirvu bell in Orimattila, the hymn book, the wedding scarf, the property deed) and virtual (in the photos, stories of others), made 'official' by genealogical lists. Some material objects serve to anchor the memory of Inkilä, while at the same time the virtual world of Inkilä can be moved wherever people go, it cannot be bounded. The memory world remains open because 'a boundary is not that at which something stops but, as the Greeks recognized, the boundary is that from which something *begins its presencing*' (Heidegger 1971: 154). I have focused on one small village, but similar stories, photos and objects are saved and replicated in memory books and personal writings for many other villages in Karelia.[34] It is a nonlimited space, a mythic place. Karelia was the imagined homeland of all Finns in the nineteenth-century nationalist imagination, now it is the mythic homeland of very real Finns with Karelian roots.

The walling off protects Karelia. Although the Russians burnt the land, destroyed churches and cemeteries, and settled people from other parts of the Soviet Union in Karelian houses, the narratives that construct the memory world cherish it and protect it from the Russians. The events of 1944 put talk about Karelia into a special position relative to the circulating discourse about community in Finland. Made into a world, and joined to events experienced nationally, Karelia is a potent reference. At the moment, the generalised-essential 'we' of political rhetoric still has to take Karelia into account, even though there are many efforts to normalise everyday interaction between Finland and the former Finnish territory of Karelia.

9
CONCLUSION: NATIONAL POLITICAL CULTURE

The nation state is a bureaucratic political system of relatively recent development that has become global during the twentieth century. It is characterised by fixed boundaries while at the same time it encompasses different communities. The consistent problem has been how to unify these different communities into an imagined whole, as Benedict Anderson realised. Beginning with the idea of interest or commitment, I have looked at written memoirs to see how and when loyalty to a national (or other) community is expressed. While the fate of the state has dire consequences for its citizens, the language of ordinary people – talking amongst themselves – reveals how they place themselves in national events that affect their lives deeply. The meaning and logic found in the memoirs reveals how culture plays a role in political events.

The evacuation of Karelia was a serious disruption in the lives of those who experienced it. Leaving home broke the social relations, practices and established routines that were the basis for continuity with the past. This happens in all situations of diaspora and it is not surprising that people in such situations write down their memories to recollect and *re*collect the fragments of that life through new narratives. However, the Karelian diaspora was different from other situations of diaspora and not a particularly typical case. In recent cases of diaspora, refugees are often unwanted populations, caught in a global no man's land, as it were, searching for a country to take them in.[1] The Karelians were evacuees, not refugees. They were Finnish nationals who were welcomed within the new borders, moved, resettled and compensated for their losses at the expense of the state. And while there were problems – sometimes conflicts and misunderstandings in the new communities – there was never a question about the relationship of Karelia or Karelians to the Finnish nation state. After all, Karelia had been, and still is for some, a sacred site in the national mytho-historical landscape.[2]

The connection between the modern nation state and a mythical territory positions people passionately, pro or con (some people also work to downplay Karelia as a special place). Whatever the position, nationalism and certain political issues generate a kind of religious fervour, as recognised by Benedict Anderson and developed further by Bruce Kapferer. Evidence that this fervour (for or against) continues around the topic of Karelia can be found in the constant references to Karelia in the circulating discourse in Finland.

Do the present-day visits, the so-called pilgrimages, contribute to the fervour? Victor Turner was basically correct: pilgrimages may link politics and religion, but pilgrimages in the long run actually serve to maintain the structure. This is the case for most visitors to Karelia; they are there to establish a link with their personal past, not for political reasons. However, in situations of political evacuation or diaspora, maintaining the structure is politically significant in ways that Turner did not anticipate. Maintaining Karelia, walling off Karelia, protects and holds Karelia as a Finnish territory despite historical developments.

Situations of diaspora, whether forced or voluntary, twist the interpretative lens regarding places, structures, and the relation of people to national (state) communities. Anthropologists have always recognised that people are mobile, but they have been less cognisant of what this means for theories of social structure. Structure, as meant by habitus, does not depend on place, or state boundaries. That is why, in situations where various groups suddenly find themselves living in the same area, all differences cannot be reduced to vague notions of culture, which can be 'fixed' by courses on how to assimilate. The misunderstandings that result are evident daily in Europe; contemporary news reports are full of stories of conflict generated by mobility, habitus, and state boundaries.

In the Finnish situation, the historical events mean that Karelia is a topic of memory, and memory accentuates the symbolic aspect of behaviour. The memoirs reveal that people live in communities personally known to them, places they are concerned about and have an interest in. Everything in these memoirs indicates the primary importance of the known referential 'we' and the interest a subject has in a named, experienced, lived-in world. Messages about the significance of this known world are analogical (this is like something we know) and paradigmatic (this is how it should be). These messages are taught in childhood, usually in a family context. They are not a rigid structure that determines all behaviour. They are a set of logical possibilities, albeit deeply ingrained, which the subject can apply to various situations that arise. This is important in situations of diaspora (forced or voluntary) because, away from the significant environment and detached from previous social relations, the subject relies on the messages learned at home and applies that analogical and paradigmatic logic to new situations.

The political implications of this process are twofold. Political loyalty, or identification with, a national community is grounded in systems of cultural meaning and logic. There has to be some basis for commonness in order for a group 'we' to emerge. The unity between national goals and the local/family community is most apparent around the events of war in these materials. Certain events, like war, have the ability to draw in membership because of a common threat and a common experience. Because most people living in Finland at the time experienced the war years, war served to crystallise a national 'we'. Stories about the war years continue to replicate a story of the national 'we'. People from different local communities, such as the small Finnish Jewish population, are drawn into this 'we' because in such stories 'we' see 'ourselves'.[3]

Culture operates in a second way that affects national political culture, and this is apparent in the way in which certain material items or local practices signify an entire community. This can be seen in the structure of the writing about Karelia, and in material form in the consistent focus on church hill in Kirvu as a significant and contested site in the landscape. While practices change, the significance of the site remains, and draws in even the contemporary Russian residents. This site and a few material items – a wedding scarf, a Bible, a bell – can immediately recollect, reassemble, a social structure and social relations from a previous era. A few objects, along with some old letters, begin to have new meaning as a once lived-in place becomes a memory world. And it takes only a piece of the configuration to recall the whole world. These are the processes that occur as cultural elements become distilled into a type story about an event.

The territory of Finnish Karelia is just across the eastern border of the Finnish nation state. Walled off and protected as it is in the memoirs, it is symbolically outside the realm of both nation states concerned. Similar attitudes towards disputed territories are found in other situations of forced diaspora. Disputed territories are symbolically meaningful exactly because of the very real communities, not state borders, that once existed there. Any study of the nation state has to recognise the long-term structures that form communities and the process of adding to and subtracting from that constitutes the symbolic dimension of social organisation everywhere. People may live anywhere on the globe, and they may move frequently and voluntarily, but only a few places are significant. The significance of a place is not always obvious in spoken or written accounts. It is so deeply understood that it often lies in what is not said directly, but referred to. With all the recent sensitivity as to how data is collected in anthropology, it is still easy to overlook this and assume the hegemony of the state. Studies of diasporic groups challenge assumptions about state hegemony. And self-generated texts serve to remind researchers that, in studies of the state, one has to recognise simply who is talking to whom, about what, because that is an aspect of political positioning.

Situations of diaspora are of interest in the social sciences because they are prevalent in the contemporary world and because they challenge some common scientific categories. I claimed earlier that Benedict Anderson did not appreciate that patriotism and nationalism refer to communities of a different order. In diaspora, especially, patriotism does not necessarily equal nationalism. One small situation, on a global scale, reveals how patriotism is based in a referential 'we' community, based in places, people and situations known personally or through local stories by the subject. And the referential group 'we' may be beyond the borders of the state.

Through the experience of common historical events, the referential 'we' joins other community 'we's' to become the generalised-essential 'we' of the national community. Elements of the experiential world are 'distilled', as Bruce Kapferer says, into stories and by certain material symbols, to form a national political culture, with the possibility for talking about a national 'we'. The elements are lifted from personal experience into a circulating discourse about community. The ongoing relation of memory to the present, and the replication of stories that happens with Karelia and the events of 1939–44 in Finland, happens in a similar way in other places although the context is different. One event in history becomes a unifying moment that can be employed to sign many communities who shared the experience. From real situations, a metadiscourse develops to describe the community, and in turn, it conditions or forms the community in every replication. Certain metadiscursive 'we's' are quite powerful – the genealogical 'we', the aggrieved 'we' – and they circulate beyond the immediate reality they first described. As a result, a particular 'we' may come to structure other discourse in an imbalanced way. All together, the various levels constitute a discourse about the various 'we' groups, and about the nation. It circulates and describes the nation, sometimes it challenges the nation, and at the same time it creates the nation.

NOTES

1 Event and Meaning

1 I use notes frequently to show this refraction as seen in public discourse in newspapers, films, etc., or to explain the context of what is being said.
2 Of this number, Karelian Finns are estimated to number about 407,000; the total number of people moved in 1944 because of war was 430,300 (Raninen-Siiskonen 1999: 15).
3 An editorial in *Helsingin Sanomat* warns that the plans of a Finnish forestry conglomerate to rent and manage forest lands in northern (Russian) Karelia is a bad plan. The editorial refers to the complicated history of Finland and Russia in this region, especially because the land in question is called Kalevala National Park (30.7.2002, A4).
4 The Karelian Association was established 20 April 1940, at the end of the Winter War. Their web page is: http://www.karjalanliitto.fi
5 Greg Urban (2001: 72) notes that Anderson is only partially correct about language. Urban's argument centres on the fact that the extraction of culture from printed materials requires literacy, and that influences processes of circulation (ibid.: 255).
6 Greg Urban summarises the cultural and social aspects of language acquisition (2001: 44). The relation of language to social groups is the subject of an earlier book (Urban 1996).
7 In a study of transnational Chinese, Andrea Louie finds a similar distinction between what she calls 'popular nationalisms', based on local identity, and 'official nationalisms' (2000: 662). I am arguing that these are collectivities of a different order.
8 John Kelly and Martha Kaplan (2001: chapters 1 and 2) offer an extensive critique of Anderson's dialectical model and its shortcomings regarding the nation state and modernity, especially in postcolonial situations.
9 Greg Urban (2001: 252–55) distinguishes the nation from traditional social groupings and links the origin of the nation to the spread of a metaculture of newness. While I think Urban's analysis of the American Declaration of Independence (2001:

chapter 3) is excellent, there are problems with generalisations about the voluntary nation state. For example, Kapferer (1988), following the work of Louis Dumont on hierarchy (1972 [1966]) and individualism (1986), distinguishes Sri Lankan and Australian nationalisms. The relation of the 'I' to the 'we' is very different in these two cases, producing two different conceptions of a national community, and this is not recognised by Urban.

10   Heidegger is cited because he defines 'care and concern' and 'knowing one's world' as central to practical habitus. In this sense Heidegger outlines elements of a habitus appropriate to Karelians of these generations. However, Heidegger does not recognise the significance of social structure or other 'I's' (the latter point is argued in all the work of Hannah Arendt). Bourdieu (1998: 8–9) expands the concept of habitus to include 'classificatory schemes', and Kapferer (1988) talks about 'embodiment'. Urban (2001: 23), expanding Bourdieu's ideas, argues that there is 'habitual inertia' in culture, that is, 'the flow of new expressions follows pathways laid down by old elements'. For Urban, there are ways to get around this inertia; acceleration happens through metaculture, culture that is about culture (ibid.: 3).

11   See also Readings's (1996) criticism of Bourdieu's limited habitus.

12   In a comparative project on diaspora, called 'Departures', in the Department of Anthropology at the University of Helsinki, various ethnographic examples have been examined to analyse how cultural identity does not necessarily correspond to a single territory, citizenship, government or language (Siikala 2001). Jorge Duany (2000) makes exactly the same point for Puerto Rican identity. In a more radical way Deleuze and Guattari (1987: 382) talk about the deterritorialised nomad who lives outside the boundaries of state control. The Karelian diaspora is different from contemporary transnational diasporas, although Karelians might be called nomads. All of this research points to the persistence of collectivities, the permeability of state boundaries, and problems with the accepted notion of citizen.

13   The codes are related metaphorically as part of a symbolic system so that the basic assumption of kinship is 'we are the same', which then has to be differentiated (Wagner 1977). John Borneman (1998: chapter 9) reviews the elements of Schneider's semiotic system and demonstrates how the diacritical marks of American kinship are used in the political-sexual (national) classification of Cuban refugees to the United States.

14   Heidegger (1971: 219) says much the same thing more poetically: 'The same gathers what is distinct into an original being-at-one. The equal, on the contrary, disperses them into the dull unity of mere uniformity.' The emphasis on equality in the nation state easily becomes an emphasis on uniformity, whereas a community is constructed with the recognition of difference.

15   For example, in 2002 a new border crossing opened at Imatra, Finland, in order to allow easier crossings. There are many bus excursions organised to Russia. One is a three-day trip to visit the battle sites of the 1940s on the Karelian Isthmus (*Helsingin Sanomat*, 21.7.2002, B4).

16   Päivölä is a name from the epic poem, the *Kalevala*. The epic was recorded by Elias Lönnröt in Karelia in the early nineteenth century.

17   I have kept all the translations as close to the original as possible because of the focus on language in my analysis. The letters are especially unpolished at times, but that is the nature of letter writing.

18   *Risti* is 'cross' and this refers to the road that Christ walked when he carried the cross, the road of pain and suffering.

19   This Toini was not Sylvi's sister; she was probably the daughter of Helena's sister Katri.

20 *Ryssa*, which I have translated as 'Ruskies', is a pejorative term for the Russians.

21 The *tupa* is the main working and living room in a Finnish farmhouse; tupa can also mean house.

22 People commented that the bright blue was a Russian colour, not a Finnish house colour.

23 The original Kirvu church cemetery was likely divided into village sections, which was common. At the beginning of the nineteenth century the practice changed to graves in rows and that is why Helena makes this distinction. At the same time, churches began to employ gravediggers; before this, close relatives of the deceased dug the grave (Talve 1997: 204).

24 This is a literal translation of the words on the monument. In an American Bible, King James Version, Psalm 90: 1 has been translated, 'Lord, thou hast been our refuge [dwelling place] in all generations.'

25 For example, as we passed a burnt-out house, she told us whose house it had been when Finnish and that more recently it had been a small shop.

26 By 2002, this project had gained international support, for example from the Museum of Modern Art in New York City, and part of the restoration has been completed, often by Finnish workers who know how to do the woodwork details specified by Aalto.

27 In the largest national newspaper, the *Helsingin Sanomat*, under the title 'Return to Karelia', a 'former Finnish house' was for sale for US $9,000.00 by a seller in St Petersburg (16.8.1997). After this there was advice in the same paper that Finns could buy back their houses and farm buildings - but not the land, which they are not allowed to own.

28 In 1999, in the business pages of *Helsingin Sanomat*, there was an article about the chief executive of a successful Finnish enterprise. When interviewed, the man said that he had bought back and restored his family's farm in Karelia and that he spends his summers there (9.7.1999, A7).

29 This 'as an evacuee' (*evakkona*) underlines that she died away from home, but Helena is also buried alone, without other family members, in the cemetery at Elimäki in southern Finland.

30 Making the same point, Lewis Coser talks about his experiences as an immigrant to the United States; at first he did not share the same collective memories and that blocked full communication (1992: 21).

31 She won a prize in May 1939 for an essay submitted to a national folklore-collecting project.

32 It is the first letter after their first return to Inkilä. At the end of the Winter War (1940), Inkilä (and Karelia) were in Russian territory. After the Continuation War started, in June 1941, Karelia was retaken by the Finnish army and the Karelians moved back home.

33 He uses the patronymic, *Arvinpoika* (Arvi's son), which was the traditional form of naming. He can be classified, therefore, as one of the Pärssinens, Arvi's son, Rauno.

34 I owe these insights to Urban's analysis of the American Declaration of Independence, a text he describes as 'the concrete representation of that intangible social entity that perdures over time called "The United States of America"' (2001: 115). Significantly, there is no analogous text for Finland, no one text that establishes the 'we'.

35 Urban (2001: 103–104) argues that 'the microflows of discourse in textual time parallel or model the microflow of historical time', for example in the way that the Declaration of Independence expresses and creates the collective.

36 Risto Alapuro (1988) has written an analysis of Finnish state formation in English.

2 Subjective Meaning

1 Pierre Bourdieu (1998: chapter 4) asks the rhetorical question: Is a disinterested act possible? His answer is that disinterest is possible only when disinterest is defined as important, such as in bureaucratic positions where one should not have a personal interest. I use the same definition of interest and disinterest.

2 Maurice Godelier makes an analogical argument about the sacred (1999: 176), where something is mentally subtracted from or added to, making imaginary relations which then become social reality.

3 In a few cases log houses were dismantled, loaded on a train, and moved to Finland. Log house construction had always allowed the possibility to take the house apart, for example to split it between brothers. In Orimattila today there is a former felt factory from Kirvu which was dismantled and removed during the war and reconstructed in Orimattila in the 1950s.

4 Finnish folklore and ethnological studies offer ample evidence of regional diversity although, ironically, they are often labelled as 'nationalistic' disciplines because of their traditional focus on folk customs.

5 *Pulla* is a type of coffee cake, commonly served with coffee or tea, usually baked at home. 'Coffee' almost always includes such cakes or sandwiches. Roberts (1989) has written a description of the importance of the coffee ritual in Finnish social events.

6 According to the Karelian Association (1996: 21), Karelian food was almost unknown in western Finland until after the Second World War. Helena's writing implicitly compares Karelian food with what is known in the time of her writing, the 1950s. Karelian stew is a well-known food in Finland today.

7 She implies that raisin soup, usually eaten as a sweet topping on rice pudding at Christmas, was new to Inkilä at the time. Rice pudding is still a Christmas food.

8 The stars and cones (*kekoja*) were common Christmas decorations before the appearance of Christmas trees. 'The population at large adopted the Christmas tree in the 1870s–1880s, first in the southwest and later in other provinces in the 1890s and around the turn of the century' (Talve 1997: 219).

9 This holiday is on 6 January; it commemorates the three wise men bringing gifts to Bethlehem in recognition of Christ's birth.

10 This was the Thursday before Easter. The Finnish *kiirastorstai* comes from ancient Nordic *skirathorsdagr*, 'Cleaning Thursday', and the day was set aside for cleaning (Talve 1997: 209).

11 Good Friday was the most important day in Holy Week (in Finnish, Quiet Week). No visits were allowed on that day, it was forbidden to light a fire, and only cold food was eaten. 'Evil forces were abroad between the death and resurrection of Christ, performing all sorts of witchcraft' (Talve 1997: 210).

12 Sarmela's Atlas of Folk Tradition (1994) has a map (Map 26), for Festival Swinging, which shows that in Karelia it was the custom to have a rope swing for young people at Easter. This was different from southeastern Finland, for example, where there was a cloth swing or jump board in the cow shed at Easter. Helena is talking about the Karelian tradition even if she does not openly make the comparison with other regions.

13 *Mummot* (plural of *mummo*), meaning grandmothers or old women, is used for women much as *ukko* is used for grandfather or old man. Talve (1997: 210) reports that it was a common folk belief that on Easter morning the sun danced for joy at the resurrection of Christ.

14 Perhaps Helena is referring to an annual ritual noted by Vilkuna (1994 [1950]:

202–203) for buildings with chimneyless fireplaces. He relates that in southern Finland the smoke was cleaned from the walls and the floor twice a year, at Christmas and Midsummer, with branches and leaves. After the Midsummer cleaning, they cleaned up the leaves on *Jaakon päivä* (25 July). Vilkuna's picture, taken in 1929, shows the children sitting in the leaves while the women clean.

15 Meaning Miss Helvi was there; she gave the coffee spoons.

16 The long veil was worn by brides throughout the country at this time. The white bridal gown, introduced by the upper classes in the nineteenth century, had become widely popular in the early twentieth century (Talve 1997: 146-47).

17 The boy's mother noted that 'the menu was never discussed', meaning that it was just known or assumed.

18 '*Ylös sinä joka makaat ja nouse kuolleista, niin Kristus sinua valaisee.*'

19 Pirkko Sallinen-Gimpl (1989) looks at how these practices changed as the evacuees from Kirvu's Tietävälä village became more integrated into Finland proper.

20 The *isäntä* was the male head of household. The term is still used; for example, the man who has the daily responsibility for the courtyard and buildings of the university is called an *isäntä*.

21 Rauno's edited text explains that the Old Testament was revised in 1933 and the New Testament in 1938.

22 Psalm 137, about Israel spending 16,000 nights away, and Exodus 3:5 are often cited as Karelian favourites (Lehto and Timonen 1993). Paasi (1996) mentions Verse 459 in the 1981 Hymnal as being a current favourite.

23 The second hymn listed (*Oi Herra*) is sung mostly at funerals, even today.

24 The poem/song in Finnish:

> *Jo Karjalan kunnailla lehtii puu,*
> *jo Karjalan koivikot tuuhettuu,*
> *käki kukkuu siellä ja kevät on,*
> *vie sinne mun kaihoni pohjaton.*

When I asked my friend if she knew the song, she immediately sang it in Karelian dialect.

25 This is the Sunday after Ascension Day (*helatorstai* in Finnish), which occurs forty days after Easter Sunday. According to Vilkuna, these days were fixed by the Christian Church at Arles in 1260 (1994 [1950]: 151).

26 His wording implies that there were visits from one parish to the other's festival, with a counter-visit.

27 Meaning, as part of the cycle the people of Kirvu, Jääske, Joutsen and Rautajärvi would make return visits to Ruokolahti on successive Sundays.

28 Matti Sarmela (1969) has described how, for Finland as a whole, there was a long and determined attempt by church personnel and local authorities to 'civilise' country people. They persistently tried to domesticate local celebrations within the church and national institutions. The markets near the church were often the site of disputes about civilised behaviour.

29 *Kihut* is from *kihuta*, to become engaged.

30 A form of this identifying can still be heard, for example, in the dentist's reception area. The nurse calls the next patient by the possessive surname (earlier, house name): e.g., Lutz's Annika.

31 There are parallels here with Sahlins's discussion of Hone Heke's war with the British over a certain flagpole (1995: chapter 2). Sahlins distinguishes structure inscribed in habitus from structure objectified in mythopoetics, which was the structure for the Maori uprising (ibid.: 53). The later is characterised as the 'heroic I' or, Sahlins's earlier term, the 'kinship I' (ibid.: 47). In Karelia the significance of church

hill continues because of a structure inscribed in habitus (not because of the 'heroic I'), just as the Maori poles continued to be significant in 1982–83 according to their own logic (ibid.: 72).

32 In 2001, the ashes of Reijo Virolainen, who was born in Kirvu parish in 1936, were buried in what remains of the new Kirvu cemetery (near the commemorative memorial and the military camp). This was the first burial of a Finnish-born Karelian in Karelia since 1944 (*Kotimaa*, 7.12.2001, p. 5).

3 Significant Worlds

1 This was the woman head of the household. I will use the Finnish *emäntä* because it is still used today for the woman who takes charge of the household, the work project, and many other situations. Her counterpart, the male role, is the *isäntä* (see *Helsingin Sanomat*, 14.3.2000, for the updated importance of these terms and roles).

2 In the original dialect: *Noustiin mäelle ja huhuiltiin näin: 'Huuu, huu'. Toinen paimen vastasi: 'Huu huu.' 'Oot sie kuult Eskola lehmit?' 'En oleee' tai 'Ne on Linnamäen puole'.*

3 The phrase means: it seems as if something is sitting on the back, as a cowboy rides a horse. I had trouble translating this and asked Rauno Pärssinen what he thought. He felt that it implies that the cow is bewitched, with something holding it down, and that Olli is saying this to indicate that it is not an easy job that Olli is doing. Sarmela (1994) notes that it was commonly said that the cow was bewitched in the *metsänpeitto*; obviously, Rauno understood this reference.

4 Helena switches pronouns as if this were spoken but she does not use quotes. She often switches like this in her text and I have left it as she wrote it.

5 For Heidegger dwelling is not only practical, it also includes the 'poetic taking of measure', that is, 'man is creative and thinks about who he is, about life and death, and about his relation to the divine' (1971: 227).

6 *Vuori* means mountain, but in fact this was a small hill or knoll.

7 This is another example of a motif story; my father (b. 1920) told the same story about a meat-slicing machine in a village in Pennsylvania.

8 In Finnish it rhymes: '*Hei-juu, junttanpoo, pikkuinen tyttö se kahvia tuo.*'

9 The right to vote was granted in 1906, before the nation state was created in 1917.

10 This was a form of ostracism; they were not accepted by some local people.

11 In Karelian, *Kopossilla kahe puole*. It is written in local dialect and it refers to the way in which Inkilä spread out on both sides of the bridge.

12 One can find similar maps in other Karelian memory books and they all include photographs and firsthand accounts. There are memory books for every Finnish Karelian parish.

13 Ilmari Kuisma (b.1919) died in April 2001.

14 The book's title is *Yksi Tie, Monta Polkua* (published privately, 1989).

15 The same logic was used by Finnish engineers working on environmental problems in Russia in the area around St Petersburg, where they are working on forestry, water and waste projects. 'We know how to do it, it's our nature,' they told a journalist (personal communication with Johanna Lemola, 1999).

16 The Karelian Association held a one-day seminar in May 1999 on how to travel to Karelia and how to search for one's roots, with maps and tips about what to take along (notice on bulletin board, *Karjalantalo*, Helsinki).

4   Genealogical Narratives

1   See Wilson (1976) and Paasi (1996) for reviews of this political history in English.
2   For example, Vuorela's (1975) detailed research of Finnish folk culture describes these regional distinctions.
3   Ilmari wrote that his mother had contributed about 1,200 sayings, proverbs and old traditions to the national ethnological collection.
4   Another parish in Karelia.
5   The same family attended Wäino's wedding (described in Chapter 2), showing how people were related through distant kinship ties and through social activities. Note that the new husband joined the wife's house and took the name of the house.
6   The sound of *synagoka* is close to *synnit koossa*.
7   The variations in spelling are common in the records. Helena most consistently uses Aadam, and spells the house name Poja-Aatam.
8   It was renamed for Aadam when he became the *isäntä*.
9   Meaning that the birch tree branches were made into sauna whisks in early summer (June).
10 *Suku* means family in the sense of descent, line or ancestry.
11 In a later passage Helena mentions that her mother's birthplace was *Aatila* in Worniola village and that her mother also lived at *Weikkola* house there.
12 The master of *koivuniemi* – from the place of the birches – is a euphemism for a birch whip.
13 In Finnish, '*hyvä on tyttökii tyhjää kättee*', meaning if you do not have anything, a girl is better than nothing.
14 Helena uses the word 'lustig', borrowed from Swedish (and also German), so she has put it in quotation marks.
15 This is how she was called later in life, when she lived at *Ylioja* as an old woman (*mummo*).
16 The *porstua* was a large centre hallway, unheated, where tools could be stored, etc. Helena has written *porstupa*, although I think she is referring to a similar space.
17 This implies the dishes, utensils, pans and milk pails – all the things that clatter and rattle.
18 People stood to sing these songs, including one man who insisted that he be lifted out of his wheelchair.
19 Ilmari listed several examples for Inkilä, giving first the house name following the first-name logic, and then the family name associated with it. These are his examples: Laurila [Lauri] = Inkinen, Simola [Simo] = Kuisma, Pien Mattila [small Matti] = Kuisma, Poja- Aatamila [son Aadam] = Kuisma, and so on.
20 The house name, place, owner and year first appeared in the land records like this: Eskola (Kuismala) Eskill Nilsson Kuisma 1818 (Lehikoinen 1988: 174).

5   Kinship and Nation

1   For example, Sabean finds that the early death of a wife, and subsequent remarriage, allowed a husband to accrue property through inheritance.
2   He went close to the river called Alajoki, where there was open water, and fell in. The dinner every day was important in the economy of a poor widow's household.
3   Michaelmas Day is 29 September, in honour of the archangel Michael. Helena always calls it 'Michaelmas Sunday' (*Mikkeli suununtai*). In Finnish the original is:

Isäni haudattiin Mikkelin sunnuntaina.

4   They were not blood relatives because Helena's father was *kotivävy* to the house, but Helena was living in the Kuisma house of Israel's grandfather's brothers, where the two old ladies were his aunts through marriage into the house.

5   These are Christian symbols for belief, love and hope.

6   Brides in the eighteenth and early nineteenth centuries were married in their local costume but a change took place in the nineteenth century, with black, grey, green or brown dresses being fashionable. She may have worn one of the silk scarves on her head for the journey to the groom's home, which was the practice at that time (Talve 1997: 146–47).

7   Rauno Pärssinen has inserted an update to the text in 1990: 'Sylvi Pärssinen gave the scarf to this book editor's daughter, Maarit, who wore it as her *feresi* scarf in her own wedding in 1981. So the scarf was a wedding scarf again after 82 years.' The scarf is still with Maarit; occasionally one of her sons takes it to school when the children are told to bring something 'historical' to show the class.

8   In the memoirs, the Finnish name for St Petersburg, *Pietari*, is always used, although the city had been renamed Leningrad.

9   He bought access to the whole forest and had the wood chopped by his own employees.

10 A *halko* was a one-metre-long piece of wood, which was in turn cut into firewood pieces.

11 She means a teacher's training college. I do not know what place she had in mind but the Seminar at Sortavala in Karelia was an important teacher's training college.

12 The phrase in Finnish is *tulipa minkälainen miehenvätys tahansa jostain alavirroilta päin*, which means a lazy, good-for-nothing man (not doing what he could or should do) from a place you do not know, and therefore cannot trust.

13 Israel did not lend the man money, but had to pay the amount if the person could not pay his debts.

14 This wording was noted by a family member because the 'previously' would be marked in the Finnish construction of the sentence.

15 Ray Abrahams (1991) has a complete description of the Finnish marriage laws in English.

16 Helena's two daughters also received a dowry when they married in the 1930s. Sylvi writes that she received money to buy a cow (not the cow itself) because she was living in another village.

17 The Finnish government sold the gold to finance the war and gave the donors rings made of iron as replacements.

18 She uses the common naming practice with the house name first: Laurila's Tuoma.

19 The state of Finland compensated Karelians for their lost property and she is referring to that decision.

20 Perhaps she is worried about a potential conflict over money, but it is more likely that she wanted to pay the 'outside' debts first. She recommends giving them a bit more than their share to close the matter. Arvi was her son-in-law, Sylvi's husband, and Pekurinen was son Wäinö's father-in-law and probably a business partner.

21 The same could be argued for modern Finland. Likewise, for Bourdieu (1998), the state regulates all other fields. I don't deny that the state is important, but it should be clear by now that my claim is that the situation of diasporic people raises questions about the symbolic field of the state and the ontological worlds that people live in. It seems to me that the emphasis on family values so prevalent at the moment is to some degree generated by the Finnish welfare state, in the way that ethnic discourse is generated by the Australian state bureaucracy (Kapferer 1995a; 1995b).

See also a related discussion about family values in the capitalist nation state by Schneider and Schneider (1996: 279–84).

22 Edwards and Strathern (2000) claim that Schneider does not recognise the self-limiting aspect, that he overemphasises the expansive. Their main contribution, and the focus of the edited volume, is the exploration of Euro-American indigenous kinship models, the need to distinguish categories of nature/culture more clearly, and the impact of this for the anthropological study of kinship (Carsten 2000). Their analysis is based on contemporary expressions of kinship; as I have indicated, the emphasis is different – the meaning changes – in the study of memory and memoirs.

23 In fact, Ilmari complained mildly that his mother's writings were for the family, not for the public. He advised me that there was a lot of public information about Karelia at the Karelian Association library or in the National Folklore Archives.

24 On the practical level, one can read in the *New York Times* about the Indian caste-family group of Patals, who own and operate almost all the rural motels on the east coast of the United States. Or, on the conceptual level, it is commonly stated in conversations about Scotland that there are more Scots living outside Scotland than in Scotland itself. This is a conceptual scheme which includes people who were not born in Scotland, may reside elsewhere for several generations, and may never visit Scotland, although they can make a genealogical claim to place.

25 Wagner's argument is that the flow is different in non-Western societies and he goes on to elaborate this point for the Daribi of New Guinea.

26 For example, a work situation can be analogous to a family organisation, with a patriarch in charge. This emphasises the hierarchy aspect of family structure over that of solicitude, although both are features of the category 'family'.

27 War is the organising story in Finland; it can be colonialism or other perceived unfair treatment. Benedict Anderson (1983: 19, n4) has a footnote about how President Sukarno constructed a 'we' who endured the colonial experience, even though there was no 'Indonesia' during the 350 years that he was referring to. And Greg Urban (2001) demonstrates how an 'aggrieved we' creates a persuasive national 'we', as long as it remains general. When the 'aggrieved we' is used by feminists, for example, it does not include all.

6   Wartime: A National Event

1 Lotta is short for the Lotta-Svärd voluntary association. Many of these women were very young and inexperienced. Most had not lived far from home before the war and many came directly from school to war service. Certainly they had not experienced war and death as they did when they were Lotta volunteers.

2 For example, Paavo Rintala wrote a novel after the war in which the Lotta women were frivolous characters.

3 In Karelian dialect: *Joka mies, joka mies, joka Karjalan mies, jos on jäljellä rehtiys, kunto, sua kutsuvi maa ja kutsuvi kansa, sydän, järki ja omatunto. Kaikk' eestä nyt yhden, yks' kaikkien eest', veli toiselle on joka miesi, siis synnyinmaatasi puolustamaan, ylös taaskin joka miesi.* She uses *maa*, land, country (as in *kuolla maansa puolesta* = to die for your country, or *luvattu maa* = Promised Land, as Karelia is sometimes called today) and *kansa*, the people, the nation. She does not use *valtakunta*, nation state.

4 In the current middle-school social sciences textbook, the Swedish speakers are listed as one of Finland's minority groups. However, Swedish speakers were once the

colonial elite of Sweden–Finland and differ significantly from other minority groups, such as the Gypsies.

5 Ilmari Kuisma (20.2.2001) explained that, 'There were almost two classes in Inkilä: the Reds and social democrats had their events in the Worker's Hall, and the home guard, the Lottas and the sports people had their events in the Youth Hall. The Worker's Hall people marched though the village with flags on May Day, whereas the other side gathered on church hill.' Ilmari concluded with a third possibility: 'Most of the village stood by and watched these events with amusement.'

6 A popular movie in 1999, *Rukajärventie*, depicts the Lotta women sharing the hardships of war with the men.

7 Uusikirkko was a town and region in the very southern part of the Karelian Isthmus.

8 The Winter War peace agreement gave valuable Finnish territory to the Soviet Union, including the nation's second largest city of Viipuri, the Arctic port of Petsamo, the strategic peninsula of Hanko, the entire Karelian Isthmus and the Saimaa Canal (Engle and Paananen 1992: 143).

9 She is reflecting on media reports about foreign policy. There was hope that one of the larger states, for example Sweden, would help to defend Finland. From 1941 to 1944, Finland was allied with Germany and Italy. This meant that Finland paid reparations to the Allied side after the war (from 1944 to 1952) and it strengthened the Soviet claim to Finnish territory.

10 In an American Lutheran communion service, the minister says: 'Take eat, this is the body of Christ. Take drink, Christ died for your sins.' In Finnish the last line is: 'Take drink, because of you Christ's blood was running.'

11 Victor Turner (1974: 29, 290) also uses the concept of the multivocal symbol, often religious, which can represent an ensemble of ideas, images, sentiments, values and stereotypes. Greg Urban argues that ideas about God circulate as a metadiscourse; metadiscourse seems to make sense of all other discourses (1996: 255). It operates as Urban claims, for the reasons given by Turner.

12 We do not know much about Jaakko from these memoirs. He was a composer, a teacher and a musician; he both played and wrote music, much of it well known in Finland. For example, he composed the song for the 1952 Olympic Games in Helsinki (*Sulasol* No.2-3/2002). His son, Jouko, wrote the music for 'Inkilä's Song' (in the *Muistojen Inkilä* book). Jouko helped to organise the family reunion in 1999, although he did not come because of a musical engagement in Paris.

13 Meaning, because he had been there and had seen the incident.

7 · *Mamma hyvä*: Meaning and Value in Letters

1 Toini (1911–95) had twelve children during her lifetime.

2 The Laestadians are a sect of the Lutheran Church in Finland.

3 The firstborn son, Aarno, died in May 2000.

4 She would not have been allowed to do this. Women's theological studies were approved first in Finland in 1953. In March 1988, ninety-four women were ordained as ministers in the Finnish Lutheran Church. In May 1990, it became possible for women to become bishops.

5 Here too there are echoes of the Red/White clash, as it was thought that working-class women could not properly take care of their families and that they needed special counselling in the home (Ollila 1993: 342).

6 At the bottom of the typed letter from Ilmari Kuisma, written in February 2001, his

daughter, Seija, added in her own handwriting, 'Extra information about my father's birthplace: *Kaukola Koverilankylän savusauna* [in Kaukola, the Koverila village smoke sauna] 11.05.1919'.

7   There was a 'godparent society' organised by the journal, *Kotiliesi,* whereby the journal was the godparent for a poor family. She means that they were the representatives of the journal for this family.

8   A novel by Illka Remes, *Karjalan lunnaat* [Karelian Ransom] (1998), is described by the reviewer as an international political thriller set in Karelia (*Helsingin Sanomat,* 15.8.1998).

9   See, for example, *Gender and Folklore: Perspectives on Finnish and Karelian Culture,* edited by Satu Apo, Aili Nenola and Laura Stark-Arola. Helsinki: SKS/FLS (1998).

10 One example was an editorial about whether or not Karelia should be returned (*Helsingin Sanomat,* 23.8.1998), with a reply letter (26.8.1998), as well as an earlier letter in the same newspaper titled, 'Why don't the politicians talk about Karelia?' (29.5.1998)

11 A seminar titled *Karjalaisesta Naisesta: mielikuvia, luuloja, valittuja totuuksia* (Thoughts and some truths about the Karelian woman) was held in the society's building in Helsinki on 25 April 1998.

8   Towards Mythology

1   A dramatic increase in immigration to Finland has occurred since 1990, with immigrants from the former Soviet Union being the most numerous group.

2   For example, someone has made a small display of Kirvu war artefacts in Mäntsälä, there are the small published photo and memory books such as have been used here, and there has been a study of people who moved from Kirvu to Orimattila (Sallinen-Gimpl 1994). There are ongoing lectures, craft demonstrations and displays in the Karelian Association House in Helsinki. Raninen-Siiskonen (1999) has studied the narrated memories of evacuated Karelians.

3   There is a calendar in one of the memory books to document all the important dates.

4   When President Putin of Russia visited Finland in September 2001, one man near Turku stood in protest with signs, in English, 'Give Karelia Back Now' and 'I want to return to Viipuri, my home' (*Ilta-Sanomat,* 3.9.2001). The next day a small group of demonstrators stood in Helsinki with signs, Karelian and Finnish flags, and demanded that the Russians give Karelia back to Finland and that they remove their troops from Chechnya (*Helsingin Sanomat,* 4.9.2001, A6).

5   One of these pictures was on the cover of *Sota Lehdet* (War News), February 2001.

6   It is called ristintie in the letter version, Chapter 1.

7   As one more example of how these themes and images continue to circulate, in a recent documentary about old people's memories – they were all born in 1900 – a woman told of her work in the hospital tent during the war years. As she said, 'we prepared the boys and sent them on their last journey', the camera showed old film footage of men carrying a white coffin out of a hospital tent and putting it next to four other white coffins. In the same show, an old man cried when he told how his friend was killed in the Winter War. A third woman began her talk, 'I am a Karelian'. (YLE/2, 10.1.2001, 'Sadan vuoden muistot'['One Hundred Years of Memories'])

8 This is a direct translation of the Finnish; by 'same flags' I assume she means many blue and white Finnish flags.

9 The names of these battles still carry the history of the war and are simple linguistic references to the war years and the sacrifices that individuals made.

10 Meaning, they would now be scattered everywhere around the country, but the break-up of the community was preferable to remaining as a community under Russian rule.

11 When people were evacuated, the cows were numbered and registered in a book so that they could be reunited with their owners at some point in the future. She is referring to these register books.

12 She means a temporary residence.

13 They had bought bales of hay for the trip with the cows.

14 Local knowledge was only shared with some people. Wäinö wrote during the war, when the soldiers were short of food, that he and the boys had killed an elk and had a delicious feast. German soldiers nearby, with whom they were allied, asked the Finns how they found the elk but the Finns only replied, 'They are out there, you just go and find them.'

15 Sylvi was a Lotta volunteer; this signals that she was doing war service, while the other woman was not.

16 The letters are marked where they were edited (–). I have chosen only a few sections from the whole text.

17 This comment about the cows is oddly out of place. What does she mean? Perhaps it means that the cows, too, are glad to be home. The cows, after all, parallel the lives of their *emäntäs*. A Finnish colleague of mine offered an alternative interpretation: she means that the cows are not as stupid as the Russians.

18 There is special mention of the fires in the houses, the warming of the houses. Lighting a fire was done traditionally as a legal act in connection with possession or occupation (Talve 1997: 229).

19 I have been told by Mrs Viljanen that there were Russian prisoners at a farm in Tuusula (forty kilometres from Helsinki), where her family and the family of Jean Sibelius got their milk during the war years. In Tuusula, the Russian prisoners were free to walk around wherever they wanted.

20 She occasionally calls Päivölä a *kartano*, which means a manor house or estate in western Finland. Päivölä was not a manor in this sense although it was a large house with several other buildings in the yard and extensive land holdings. *Kotikartano* recognises this smaller-than-estate holding.

21 They are saying 'not Russian but Mortva', that they belong to a Finno-Ugric group within the Soviet Union. They are emphasising their similarity to Finns.

22 Potato soup with bread was a meal that was typical everyday fare on a farm (Talve 1997: 133).

23 Meaning, it was an attack of long duration with heavy shelling for them to hear it. Kotka was more than 100 kilometres away, on the southern coast of Finland.

24 He came home without official permission to do so. Later Wäinö does the same thing in order to 'fetch the home troops'.

25 They are her two daughters-in-law and their children.

26 She uses a term that means substitute coffee, usually made from chicory during the war (*Niin sitten korvikkeet juotuamme*).

27 Compare these women to the frivolous girls in the first evacuation story. This appreciation of the Lotta workers is frequently noted in the discussions of the contributions of the Lotta women in the 1990s.

28 He was the stationmaster in Inkilä.

29 Born in 1876, Israel was sixty-eight at this time. Helena was sixty-two.

30 To understand the displacement of these last few moves, remember that Helena wrote, at the beginning of the war, that the cows went as far as Jokinen, 'wherever' that was. The familiar world to her was the Karelian Isthmus; all of this was new territory, made familiar by living with family members and occasionally seeing old friends.

31 Karelian writing often invokes an absent higher authority, much as autobiography makes its case (Fernández 1992: chapter 1).

32 The 'we' seems to refer to the Finnish nation, as it follows from the prior sentence. But the 'we' of the second sentence is vague, and can refer both to the family and its ability to survive, and to the ability of the nation to negotiate a better peace with the Russians.

33 In the narratives collected by Raninen-Siiskonen, meeting other Karelians is compared to meeting 'brothers and sisters' (1999: 375).

34 The same point can be made about the memoirs and memory books of the pre-Holocaust European Jewish communities. Wachtel (1990) gives evidence of this although his analysis fails to appreciate the significance of a virtual world.

9   Conclusion: National Political Culture

1 In Finland, there are periodic stories in *Helsingin Sanomat* about individuals or groups seeking asylum. There were two examples in summer 2002: a picture of a foreign man waiting in a prison in Helsinki until the authorities decide what to do with him, and a picture of a group of Romany being sent back to Central Europe after the decision that they could not stay in Finland. These cases are common news; part of the general discourse about immigrants in Europe.

2 In autumn 2002, a group of students and faculty from the University of Helsinki travelled to see the old regions of Karelia where the epic poem, *Kalevala*, had been recorded.

3 Finnish soldiers who were Jewish fought in the Continuation War when Finland was allied with the Germans. In their stories they stress how they fought for their home community, not as allies of Hitler's Germany (Jill Kotel, 2000, 'Being Jewish in Helsinki, Finland Today', master's thesis in anthropology, University of Helsinki).

REFERENCES

Abrahams, R. 1991. *A Place of Their Own*. Cambridge.

Alapuro, R. 1973. *Akateeminen Karjala-Seura*. Helsinki.

—— 1988. *State and Revolution*. Berkeley.

—— 1989. 'Intelligentsia, the State and the Nation', in *Finland: People, Nation, State*, eds. M. Engman and D. Kirby. London, 147–65.

Anderson, B. 1983. *Imagined Communities*. London.

Armstrong, K. 1978. 'Rural Scottish Women: Politics without Power', *Ethnos* 43(1–2): 51–72.

—— 2000. 'Ambiguity and Remembrance: Individual and Collective Memory in Finland', *American Ethnologist* 27(3): 591–608.

Bachelard, G. 1969 [1958]. *The Poetics of Space*. Boston.

Bakhtin, M. 1981. *The Dialogic Imagination*, ed. M. Holquist, trans. C. Emerson and M. Holquist. Austin.

Balibar, E. 1996. 'Nation Form: History and Ideology', in *Becoming National: A Reader*, eds. G. Eley and R.G. Suny. New York, 132–50.

Besnier, N. 1995. *Literacy, Emotion and Authority*. Cambridge.

Billig, M. 1995. *Banal Nationalism*. London.

Borneman, J. 1992. *Belonging in the Two Berlins: Kin, State, Nation*. Cambridge.

—— 1998. *Subversions of International Order: Studies in the Political Anthropology of Culture*. Albany.

Bourdieu, P. 1977. *Outline of a Theory of Practice*, trans. R. Nice. Cambridge.

—— 1998. *Practical Reason*. Stanford.

Carr, D. 1986. *Time, Narrative, and History*. Bloomington.

—— 1997. 'Narrative and the Real World: An Argument for Continuity', in *Memory, Identity, Community: The Idea of Narrative in the Human Sciences*, eds. L.P. Hinchman and S.K. Hinchman. Albany, 7–25.

Carsten, J. (ed.) 2000. *Cultures of Relatedness*. Cambridge.

Clastres, P. 1987 [1974]. *Society against the State*, trans. R. Hurley in collaboration with A. Stein. New York.

Cohen, A.P. 1996. 'Personal Nationalism: A Scottish View of Some Rites, Rights, and Wrongs', *American Ethnologist* 23(4): 802–15.

Coser, L. (ed.) 1992. 'Introduction: Maurice Halbwachs, 1877–1945', in *Maurice Halbwachs: On Collective Memory*, trans. L. Coser. Chicago, 1–34.

Crapanzano, V. 1980. *Tuhami: Portrait of a Moroccan*. Chicago.

Deleuze, G. and Guattari, F. 1987 [1980]. *A Thousand Plateaus: Capitalism and Schizophrenia*, trans. B. Massumi. Minneapolis.

Duany, J. 2000. 'Nation on the Move: The Construction of Cultural Identities in Puerto Rico and the Diaspora', *American Ethnologist* 27(1): 5–30.

Dumont, L. 1972 [1966]. *Homo Hierarchicus*. London.

—— 1986. *Essays on Individualism*. Chicago.

Durkheim, E. 1969 [1912]. *The Elementary Forms of the Religious Life*, trans. J.W. Swain. New York.

Edwards, J. and Strathern, M. 2000. 'Including Our Own', in *Cultures of Relatedness*, ed. J. Carsten. Cambridge, 149–66.

Engle, E. and Paananen, L. 1992 [1973]. *The Winter War: The Soviet Attack on Finland 1939–1940*. Harrisburg, Pennsylvania.

Fairburn, M. 1995. *Nearly Out of Heart and Hope*. Auckland.

Fernández, J.D. 1992. *Apology to Apostrophe: Autobiography and the Rhetoric of Self-Representation in Spain*. Durham.

Fox, J.J. 1997. 'Place and Landscape in Comparative Austronesian Perspective', in *The Poetic Power of Place*, ed. J.J. Fox. Canberra (Research School of Pacific and Asian Studies), 1–21.

Frykman, J. and Löfgren, O. 1987 [1979]. *Culture Builders: A Historical Anthropology of Middle-Class Life*, trans. A. Crozier, Foreword by J. Gillis. New Brunswick.

Fussell, P. 1975. *The Great War and Modern Memory*. London.

Geertz, C. 1995. *After the Fact*. Cambridge, Massachusetts.

Gillis, J. 1994. 'Memory and Identity: The History of a Relationship', in *Commemorations: The Politics of National Identity*, ed. J. Gillis. Princeton, 3–24.

Godelier, M. 1998. 'Afterword', in *Transformations of Kinship*, ed. M. Godelier. Washington, D.C., 386–413.

—— 1999 [1996]. *The Enigma of the Gift*, trans. N. Scott. Chicago.

Goody, J. 1983. *The Development of the Family and Marriage in Europe*. Cambridge.

Halbwachs, M. 1992. 'On Collective Memory', in *Maurice Halbwachs*, ed. and trans. L. Coser. Chicago.

Hanks, W. 1996. *Language and Communicative Practices*. Boulder.

Heidegger, M. 1971. *Poetry, Language, Thought*, trans. A. Hofstadter. New York.

—— 1996 [1926]. *Being and Time*, trans. J. Stambaugh. Albany.

Herzfeld, M. 1997. *Portrait of a Greek Imagination: An Ethnographic Biography of Andreas Nenedakis*. Chicago.

Hirsch, E. 1995. 'Landscape: Between Place and Space', in *The Anthropology of Landscape*, eds. E. Hirsch and M. O'Hanlon. Oxford, 1–30.

Hobsbawm, E. and Ranger, T. (eds.) 1983. *The Invention of Tradition*. Cambridge.

Ingold, T. 1993. 'The Temporality of the Landscape', in *Conceptions of Time and Ancient Society* (special issue), *World Archaeology* 25(2): 152–74.

Inkilän Nuorisoseura 1982. *Muistojen Inkilä: Kuvakertomus karjalaan jääneestä kotikylästämme*. Varkaus.

—— 1986 *Kopossilla kahe puole: Kirvun Inkiläläiset muistelevat*. Forssa.

Jackson, M. 1995. *At Home in the World*. Durham.

James, P. 1996. *Nation Formation*. London.

Jokinen, E. 1996. *Väsynyt äiti: Äitiyden omaelämäkerrallisia esityksiä*. Tampere.

Kapferer, B. 1988. *Legends of People, Myths of State*. Washington, D.C.

—— 1995a 'Bureaucratic Erasure: Identity, Resistance and Violence – Aborigines and a Discourse of Autonomy in a North Queensland Town', in *Worlds Apart*, ed. D. Miller. London, 69-90.

—— 1995b 'The Performance of Categories: Plays of Identity in Africa and Australia', in *The Urban Context: Ethnicity, Social Networks and Situational Analysis*, eds. A. Rogers and S. Vertovec. Oxford, 55–80.

Karelian Association 1996. *The Karelian Issue*. Helsinki.

Kelly, J.D. and Kaplan, M. 2001. *Represented Communities: Fiji and World Colonization*. Chicago.

Keryell, G. 2000. 'The Kalevala, *Suku, Kansa*, and the Finnish Nation', *Suomen Antropologi* 25(4): 14–36.

Knuuttila, S. 1989. 'What the People of Sivakka Tell about Themselves', in *Studies in Oral Narrative*, ed. Anna-Leena Siikala. Helsinki, 111–26.

Lahti, M. 2001. *Domesticated Violence: the Power of the Ordinary in Everyday Finland*. Research Series in Anthropology, Vol. 2, University of Helsinki.

Lehikoinen, L. 1988. *Kirvun talonnimet: Karjalaisen talonnimisysteemin kuvaus*. Helsinki.

Lehto, L. and Timonen, S. 1993. 'Kertomus matkasta kotiin: karjalaiset vieraina omilla maillaan', *Kalevala seuran vuosikirja* 72, Helsinki, 88–105.

Lévi-Strauss, C. 1966 [1962]. *The Savage Mind*. Chicago.

—— 1999 [1979]. *The Way of the Masks*, trans. S. Modelski. Seattle.

Linna, V. 1960. *Täällä Pohjantähden alla II*. Porvoo.

Louie, A. 2000. 'Re-territorializing Transnationalism: Chinese Americans and the Chinese Motherland', *American Ethnologist* 27(3): 645–69.

Mannila, O. 1969. *Karjalainen suurperhe ja sen hajoaminen Salmin kihlakunnassa*. Department of Sociology Research Report No.124, University of Helsinki.

Mauss, M., and Beuchat, H. 1979 [1950]. *Seasonal Variations of the Eskimo: A Study in Social Morphology*, trans. J.J. Fox, Foreword by J.J. Fox. London.

Munn, N. 1995. 'Essay on the Symbolic Construction of Memory in the Kaluli *Gisalo*', in *Cosmos and Society in Oceania*, eds. D. de Coppet and A. Iteanu. Oxford, 83–104.

Nora, P. 1989. 'Between Memory and History: Les Lieux de Mémoire', in *Memory and Counter-Memory*, Special Issue, eds. N.Z. Davis and R. Starn, *Representations* 26(Spring), 7–25.

Norton, R. 1993. 'Culture and Identity in the South Pacific: A Comparative Analysis', *Man* (N.S.)28: 741–59.

Ollila, A. 1993. *Suomen kotien päivä valkenee: Marttajärjestö suomalaisessa yhteiskunnassa vuoteen 1939*. Finnish Historical Society Research Report No.

173, Helsinki.

Paasi, A. 1996. *Territories, Boundaries and Consciousness: The Changing Geographies of the Finnish–Russian Border*, Foreword by W.R. Mead. Chichester.

Paasivirta, J. 1988. *Finland and Europe: The Early Years of Independence, 1917–1939*, Studia Historica 29, Helsinki.

Radcliffe-Brown, A.R. 1940. 'Preface', in *African Political Systems*, eds. M. Fortes and E.E. Evans-Pritchard. London, xi–xxiii.

Raninen-Siiskonen, T. 1999. *Vieraana omalla maalla: tutkimus karjalaisen siirtoväen muistelukerronnasta*. Helsinki.

Readings, B. 1996. *The University in Ruins*. Cambridge, Massachusetts.

Richards, A. 1960. 'Social Mechanisms for the Transfer of Political Rights in Some African Tribes', Presidential Address, *The Journal of the Royal Anthropological Institute of Great Britain and Ireland* Vol. 90 (Part II): 175–90.

Ricoeur, P. 1991. *From Text to Action: Essays in Hermeneutics, II*, trans. K. Blamey and J.B. Thompson. Chicago.

Roberts, F.M. 1989. 'The Finnish Coffee Ceremony and Notions of Self', *Arctic Anthropology* 26(1).

Roos, J.P. 1987. *Suomalainen elämä: tutkimus tavallisten suomalaisten elämäkerroista*. Helsinki.

Rowlands, M. 1993. 'The Role of Memory in the Transmission of Culture', in Conceptions of Time and Ancient Society (special issue), *World Archaeology* 25(2): 141–51.

Sabean, D.W. 1990. *Property, Production and Family in Neckarhausen, 1700–1870*. Cambridge.

—— 1998. *Kinship in Neckarhausen, 1700–1870*. Cambridge.

Sahlins, M. 1981. *Historical Metaphors and Mythical Realities: Structure in the Early History of the Sandwich Islands Kingdom*. Ann Arbor.

—— 1985. *Islands of History*. Chicago.

Sahlins, M. and Kirch, P.V. 1992. *Historical Ethnography Volume One, Anahulu: The Anthropology of History in the Kingdom of Hawaii*. Chicago.

Sallinen-Gimpl, P. 1989. 'Karjalainen kulttuuri-identiteetti', in *Kansa Kuvastimessa: etnisyys ja identiteetti*, eds. T. Korhonen and M. Räsänen. Helsinki, 209–26.

—— 1994. *Siirtokarjalainen identiteetti ja kulttuurien kohtaaminen*. Kansatieteellinen arkisto 40. Helsinki.

Samuel, R. 1989. 'Preface', in *Patriotism: The Making and Unmaking of British National Identity*, Vol. 1, ed. R. Samuel. London, x–xvii.

Sarmela, M. 1969. *Reciprocity Systems of the Rural Society in the Finnish-Karelian Culture Area, with Special Reference to Social Intercourse of the Youth*. Helsinki.

—— 1987. 'Swidden Cultivation in Finland as a Cultural System', in *Special Issue on Swidden Cultivation*, ed. J. Raumolin, *Suomen Antropologi* 12(4): 242–62.

—— 1994. *Suomen Perinne-Atlas*. Helsinki.

Sartre, J.-P. 1968. *Search for a Method*, trans. H.E. Barnes. New York.

Schneider, D.M. 1970. 'Kinship, Nationality and Religion in American Culture: Toward a Definition of Kinship', in *Forms of Symbolic Action: Proceedings of the 1969 Annual Spring Meeting of the American Ethnological Society*, ed. R.F. Spencer. Seattle, 116–25.

—— 1980. *American Kinship: A Cultural Account*, 2nd edn. Chicago.

—— 1984. *A Critique of the Study of Kinship*. Ann Arbor.

Schneider, J. and Schneider, P. 1996. *Festival of the Poor: Fertility Decline and the Ideology of Class in Sicily, 1860–1980*. Tucson.

Scott, J. 1998. *Seeing Like a State*. New Haven.

Sihvo, H. 1973. *Karjalan kuva*. Helsinki.

Siikala, A.-L. 1990. *Interpreting Oral Narratives*. Helsinki.

Siikala, J. 2001. 'Tilling the Soil', in *Departures: How Societies Distribute Their People*, ed. J. Siikala, The Finnish Anthropological Society Vol. 46, Helsinki, 22–45.

Silverman, M. and Gulliver, P.H. 1997. 'Historical Verities and Verifiable History: Locality-Based Ethnography and the Great Famine in Southeastern Ireland', *Europaea* III(2): 141–70.

Skultans, V. 1996. 'Theorizing Latvian Lives: The Quest for Identity', *Journal of the Royal Anthropological Institute* (N.S.)3: 761–80.

Spens, M. 1994. *Viipuri Library, Alvar Aalto*. London.

Strathern, M. 1982. 'The Place of Kinship: Kin, Class and Village Status in Elmdon, Essex', in *Belonging: Identity and Social Organisation in British Rural Cultures*, ed. A.P. Cohen. Manchester 72–100.

Talve, I. 1997. *Finnish Folk Culture*, trans. S. Sinisalo. Helsinki.

Turner, M. 1987. *Death is the Mother of Beauty: Mind, Metaphor, Criticism*. Chicago.

Turner, V. 1967. *The Forest of Symbols: Aspects of Ndembu Ritual*. Ithaca.

—— 1974. *Dramas, Fields and Metaphors: Symbolic Action in Human Society*. Ithaca.

Ulrich, L.T. 1990. *A Midwife's Tale*. New York.

Urban, G. 1989. 'The "I" of Discourse', in *Semiotics, Self, and Society*, eds. B. Lee and G. Urban. Berlin, 27–51.

—— 1991. *A Discourse-Centered Approach to Culture: Native South American Myths and Rituals*. Austin.

—— 1996. *Metaphysical Community*. Austin.

—— 2001. *Metaculture: How Culture Moves Through the World*. Minneapolis.

Uusihakala, K. 1989. *Yksi tie, monta polkua*. Kurika.

Valeri, V. 1990. 'Constitutive History: Genealogy and Narrative in the Legitimation of Hawaiian Kingship', in *Culture Through Time*, ed. E. Ohnuki-Tierney. Stanford, 154–92.

Vilkuna, K. 1975. 'Kieliraja, etninen raja, kulttuuriraja', Plenary lecture, IV International Fenno-Ugric Congress, Budapest, 15.9.1975, in *Pars I Acta sessionum*, ed. János Gulya. Budapest, 49–58.

—— 1994 [1950]. *Vuotuinen ajantieto: vanhoista merkkipäivistä sekä kansanomaisesta talous- ja sääkalenterista enteineen*. Helsinki.

—— 1964. *Kihlakunta ja häävuode: Tutkielmia suomalaisen yhteiskunnan järjestymisen vaiheilta*. Helsinki.

Voionmaa, V. 1969 [1915]. *Suomen Karjalaisen Heimon Historia*. Porvoo.

Vuorela, T. 1975. *Suomalainen kansan kulttuuri*. Porvoo.

Wachtel, N. 1990. 'Remember and Never Forget', in *Between Memory and History*, eds. M.-N. Bourguet, L. Valensi and N. Wachtel. New York, 101–29.

References

Wagner, R. 1977. 'Analogic Kinship: a Daribi example', *American Ethnologist* 4(4): 623–42.

Wallerstein, I. and Smith, J. 1992. 'Households as an Institution of the World Economy', in *Creating and Transforming Households: the Constraints of the World-economy*, eds. J. Smith and I. Wallerstein. Cambridge, 3-23.

Wilson, W. 1976. *Folklore and Nationalism in Modern Finland*. Bloomington.

Yates, F.A. 1966. *The Art of Memory*. Chicago.

Zonabend, F. 1984 [1980]. *The Enduring Memory: Time and History in a French Village*. Manchester.

INDEX